协作的艺术：
领导者如何影响团体成长

The Art of Facilitation:
Discovery of the Group Growth Process

All the best Andrew.
Keep making a difference
everywhere you go!

Steve

First Printed in the United States of America in 2020

ISBN (print book): 978-1-7348772-0-5

ISBN (digital book): 978-1-7348772-1-2

Steve Haines, President/CEO

Global Education and Cultural Alliance Consultants

P.O. Box 304, Jamison, Pennsylvania 18929, U.S.A.

Web: www.Advantage-USA.org

Email: Advantage-USA@comcast.net

献给每一位曾以无私的工作提高了另一个孩子的人生的人，
我向你致敬。
To anyone who ever worked selflessly to improve the life of another child,
I salute you.

献给每一位经意或不经意教育我的人，我赞美并感谢你。
To anyone who had to teach me, I commend and thank you.

献给唐.马丁代尔，你改变了我一生的方向和目的地。祝福你。
To Don Martindale, you changed the direction and destination of my life.
Bless you.

目录
Table of Contents

引言
Introduction

本人在中学任教超过 25 年（教授体育、健康和美国历史），设计和指导了许多夏令营活动，这些经历都在团队引导方面给了我完美的训练。领导学生、夏令营营员和营地工作人员等多样化的训练让我了解了团队成长的过程，只要人们聚在一起，这一过程就会发生。无论是一个班级的学生、一群营员或是一群同事聚在一起制定课程或设计一套营期日程，在团队运作的过程中，都会有一个过程发生。一位有经验的引导者应该是这样的领导，他能够提高团队的效率，并引导它朝着预期的目标或目的地前进。

Spending more than 25 years as a middle school teacher (Physical Education, Health, and U.S. History) and designing and directing summer camp programs has been a perfect training ground for group facilitation experience. Leading students, campers and camp staff members, the diverse training has taught me about the group growth process that occurs anytime people come together. Whether it involves a class of students, a group of campers, a group of colleagues creating a curriculum or designing a camp schedule, there is a process that occurs within the functioning of a group. An experienced facilitator is a leader who can improve the efficiency of the group as well as steer the direction of the group towards the desired goal or destination.

在过去的十多年里，我多次来到中国，这又为我个人的成长提供了新的契机。我原本是为了招生而去的，结果却变成了教师培训之旅。每次面对 40-50 名中国英语教师，让我有机会利用自己担任教师和团队引导者的经验，去帮助他们在教师和学生之间建立联系的课堂体验。我深知人际关系的价值，所以我的目标是为这些教师提出挑战，使之成为领

6

导者，并因此成为他们自己课堂上的引导者，并引导班级团队的成长过程。我把教师们训练成为领导者，而这将惠及他们的学生。

Taking many trips to China over the past 10+ years has afforded me new opportunities for personal growth. What started out as primarily student recruitment trips have turned into teacher training tours. Finding myself in front of 40-50 Chinese teachers of English has given me the opportunity to assimilate my experience as a teacher and group facilitator in helping them build a more connected classroom experience for teacher and student. Knowing the value of personal connections, my goal is to challenge teachers to be leaders and therefore facilitators of their own group growth process that will take place in their classrooms. My training of teachers to be leaders benefits the students they teach.

本书内容取自我在"趣味研讨会"上向受训教师展示的材料。在研讨会上，我向教师们展示了团队成长的过程。尽管我和每个小组共处的时间只有短短两天，他们却能够在他们与学生长达十个月的关系里看到有力的成果和潜力。我将教师们训练成他们自己的团队成长过程中有意识的构建者。通过培养正确的思维方式、提高引导技能、学习领导力特征以及运用细致的定向设计，老师们得以学会引导的艺术。

The content of this book has been taken from materials I present to teachers in my multi-day "fun-shop" seminars in which I model for them what the group growth process looks like. Although I have only 2 days with each group, they can see the powerful results and potential for their 10-month relationship with their students. I train teachers to be the intentional architects of the growth process that will happen in their group. By developing a proper mindset, sharpening facilitation skills, learning leadership characteristics and utilizing careful directional design, teachers learn the art of facilitation.

领导他人就意味着影响他人。教师之所以能成为领导者，正是因为他们能够对学生的人生产生巨大的影响。教育所涉及的远不止教授考试内容而已。教师应该成为学生的导师，教会他们如何度过难关并为未来的人生做好准备。教师的责任不仅仅是为全班授课，他们也承担着教育每一个孩子的责任。要做到这一点，他们必须接受引导者的角色，并认识到他们对每一个孩子的人生会产生多么大的影响。

To lead is to influence. Teachers are leaders because they have a tremendous opportunity to impact the life of students. Teaching involves far more than just communicating subject content to be given back on an examination. Teachers are mentors who help teach students how to navigate through and prepare for future life. Teachers bear the responsibility to teach not only the whole class but also each individual child. To do so, they must embrace the role of facilitator and recognize the impact they can have on the life of each child.

我希望本书的每一位读者都能在书中找到有助于其个人和职业成长的元素。我感觉教师这一身份让我成为了一位更好的父亲。同时我也感觉父亲这一身份，反过来也让我成为了一位更好的教师。我的个人成长促进了职业成长，反之亦然。我们每个人都应该努力对那些与我们最亲近的人和那些我们所领导的人产生最大的影响。在我作为教师、领导者和个人的几种角色的成长和发展过程中，许多老师都做出了贡献。我的动力来自帮助别人做到同样的事情，来回报我的那些老师在我身上倾注的心血。

I hope each reader finds elements within this book that are helpful to both personal and professional growth. I feel I am a better father because I was a teacher. I also feel I am a better teacher because I am a father. My personal growth fed my professional growth, and vice-versa. Each of us should strive to maximize our impact for those closest to us and to those we lead. Many teachers contributed to my growth and development as a teacher, leader, and person. My motivation is to pay that investment forward by helping others do the same thing.

　　每个人的人生旅途都是独一无二的。拥抱个人成长的过程吧。在这一过程中，我们将承受痛苦，但也享受快乐，因为成功总是建立在另一个成功基础上的。学会庆祝所有时刻吧，因为它们对你的个人旅途有着同等的贡献。

　　Each person's journey is unique. Embrace the process of personal growth. The process has moments of pain, but also moments of pleasure, as one success builds upon another. Learn to celebrate all the moments because they contribute equally to the story that makes up your personal journey.

——史蒂夫 Steve

引导的艺术
The Art of Facilitation

Image credit: Alexy Krivitsky

　　不知你有没有经历过那种无聊的研讨会或者培训呢？我指的是那种让你眼皮发沉，忍不住要睡着的无聊。它们的吸引力确实太低了，低到你一个字也听不进去，更不要说吸收掌握了。问题也许并不在讲授内容本身，而是在授课人身上，或者说问题在于他们没有能力靠任何个人魅力征服一个课堂或一群听众。与这种无聊形成对比的是音乐会歌手们的表现，无论他们的演出是在 300 人的场地还是在 3 万人的体育场，他们都能完全掌控，让在场的每一个人都感觉自己融入了这场表演。在这种情况下，由于你完全沉浸在其中，想睡着压根儿就不可能。伟大的表演家会在"舞台表现"方面下很大的功夫，因为让观众感受到连接能帮助他们传递音乐，给听众带来全面的体验。为什么有些人上台之后能抓住观众，而有些人就——客气点说吧——让人过目即忘呢？要制造难忘的回忆而不是遗憾的回忆，关键是要掌握引导的艺术。虽然引导者无法直接让观众深信他们所讲授的内容或信息，但他们可以在信息呈现的过程中创造或者破坏一种氛围，要么让观众听得入迷，要么弄得他们恨不得立马走人。

　　Have you ever been in a workshop or training that is painfully boring?

Andrew.

To all the fond memories
of OSDC years. Great to follow
your rise & experience helping
schools & students. Delighted to
observe from afar.

Hope you enjoy the read. I
welcome feedback, thoughts &
ideas.

Doing the trainings has been such
a blessing, & I am very fond
of the Chinese people & their food.

Who knows — maybe one day
we'll both be there making
a small difference for students.

Best

Steve

I am talking about the type of boring where your eyes are so heavy you cannot even keep your head up and eyes open. The level of disengagement is such that you cannot listen or absorb a single spoken word. The content itself may not be as much of the problem as the person who is delivering it. Maybe it is their monotone voice, their apparent lack of personality in the delivery, or their inability to command a room or audience with any type of personal charisma. Compare this level of boredom to a concert performer who manages to entertain a room of 300, or a stadium of 30,000, where and when they seem in complete control to make each participant feel connected and involved in the show. In this scenario, you are so engaged that falling asleep would be humanly impossible. Great performers work very hard at their "stage presence" because how they make an audience feel connected helps them communicate their music and provide an overall experience for the audience members. What makes some presenters captivating while others are, let's just say, forgettable? Mastering the art of facilitation can be the key to creating unforgettable memories and avoiding regrettable ones. Whereas the facilitator cannot make the audience believe in the content or message, they can make or break the aura surrounding the presentation of information in a way that leaves the audience either wanting more or wanting to leave.

认识到引导的艺术是一项需要打磨的技能，这很重要。这不是观众的任务，而是信息传递者的任务。对于表现者而言（无论他们是为一个班级授课还是发表演讲或进行培训），认识到他们所做的事情是一种表演是极具价值的。所有表演家都应该在表现技巧（包括舞台表现、声线投射、外表、传达等）上下功夫，以确保他们所呈现的信息和材料都是以一种最能被观众接受的方式进行传达，从而对他们产生尽可能大的影响。所谓引导，更多指的是清楚该"如何"讲，而不仅仅是"知道"要讲什么。

It is important to see the art of facilitation as a skill that needs to be perfected. It is not the job of the audience, but rather of the message giver. For the presenter (whether teaching a class or giving a speech or training), there is a value in seeing that what they do is a performance. All performers should work on their presentation craft (stage presence, projection voice, appearance, delivery, etc.) to ensure the message and material is given in a way it can best be received to make as strong an impact as possible. To facilitate is more than just "knowing" what it is you're are going to say - it is more about "how" you say it.

我是知名论坛"TED 演说"的粉丝。我很欣赏 TED 演说发言者的表现，由于时间有限，他们大多数人读的都是精心编排过的发言稿，以保证在严格的时间安排下完成演说。为了与观众迅速建立联系，这些"表演家"必须精心遣词造句并运用生动的故事讲述技巧。有些 TED 演说者能够成功地与观众建立连接，而另一些人则似乎在演说中融入了他们自己的杂音。那些能吸引人的演说之所以具有吸引力，可能在于他们的声音、他们的面部表情、故事本身或者他们用言语讲述故事的方式。他们的表现力决定了到底是建立与观众之间的连接，还是打破这种连接。遣词造句以及发言者讲话的方式是重要的引导因素。

I am a fan of the popular forums called "Ted Talks". I appreciate that a Ted Talk speaker has a limited time allotted and so most of them read their well-worded and rehearsed script in order to stay on a very strict time schedule. These "performers" must connect quickly with an audience through careful word choice and dynamic story telling skills. Some Ted Talk performers manage to connect, while others seem to blend into the noise of their own voice. For those speakers that I find engaging, it may be in their voice, their facial expressions, the story itself or in the way they tell the story they have constructed in spoken words. The power of their performance is what can make or break the speaker's connection with the audience. The words used and the way someone delivers the spoken word are important elements of facilitation.

我曾听过一个说法，说公开演讲是人们能经历的最可怕的事情之一。一想到要站在一群陌生人面前（甚至哪怕是朋友也一样），许多人都会心生恐惧。公开演讲从小学早期已经开始练习，"展示和讲述"活动、读书报告或在全班面前演讲的机会等等都是练习的方式。既然有这么多机会进行公开表演，为什么大多数人在必须这么做的时候还是觉得它们这么可怕呢？

I have heard it said that public speaking is one of the most frightening experiences anyone can have. The thought of standing in front of strangers (or even friends) strikes fear into the hearts of many. Public presentations are practiced from early elementary school days with "show & tell," book reports, or other opportunities to speak in front of the class. If these types of public performance exposures are so readily available, why do they continue to be so frightening for most people who must do them?

我最棒的经历之一，就是在我大学时期成立的摇滚乐队担任主唱。虽不能说舞台对我而言是最舒服的地方，但我的确有一种自我意识，在上台之前，它帮我把紧张感转化为一种自信。我心中的"恐惧"并不一定是对失败的恐惧，而是一种预期，即我是否能够找到一种方式，通过我的声乐和舞台表现，建立观众与我们的音乐和歌词之间的连接。当我们作为一个乐队走上舞台，把音乐表演好，把音符演唱和演奏控制好的时候，我（作为主唱）能否把观众带到到一个情感空间来倾听我的思想和想法呢？这一场景所展示的就是引导艺术的一种形式。对于一位表演者（或一群表演者），运用抒情的语言和舞台动作来传递信息就是一种独特的引导形式。

One of my best life experiences came from being the lead singer in a rock and roll band that I began back in college. I cannot say that the stage was always the most comfortable place for me to be, but I did have an ego, and that helped transform my nervous energy into a form of confidence before taking the stage. My "fear" was not necessarily the fear of failure, but rather it was the anticipation of whether or not I would be able to find a way to connect the audience to our music and lyrics through my vocal and stage performance. Could we as a band step on stage, perform the music well, singing and playing the right notes, while I (as the lead singer) tried to invite the audience into the emotional space of hearing my lyrical thoughts and ideas? This scenario exemplifies one form of the art of facilitation. For a performer (or group of performers) to use lyrical words and stage movements to project and communicate a message is a unique form of facilitation.

对我们而言，没有两场乐队表演是一样的。这也使得这种引导更加让人感到兴奋。每天晚上的观众都不一样，对音乐的反应也各不相同。我发现有些晚上我的表现比其他晚上好，有些晚上观众的活力水平也比其他晚上要高。虽然我认为我的活力水平一向都比较高，但它有时候还是会受到观众反应（或者是观众没啥反应）的影响，甚至观众数量也会对此产生影响。站在舞台上，我可以对观众的面部进行视觉解读，观察他们的反应，以确定我是否与他们建立起了连接，或者我是否需要更加努力地建立起这种连接。对我而言，舞台表演是最佳的训练，使我明白了自己作为群体引导者的角色。每天晚上都是一场表演，而我明白自己的角色，那就是向观众传达内容（歌词）并影响观众对演出的接受方式。我学会了拥抱这种角色，而不是对它心怀恐惧。

For us, no two band performances were ever the same. This also contributed to the excitement of this type of facilitation. Each night, the audience was different and would react in a variety of ways to the music offered. I realized that some nights I was better than others, and some nights the audience had a higher energy level than others. My energy level, though I thought it was always high, at times may have been affected by the response and reaction (or lack thereof) or even size of the audience. From the stage, I could visually read the faces, see the reactions and determine whether or not I was connecting with the audience or if I needed to do more to forge a connection. For me, the performance stage was my best training to understand my role as a group facilitator. Each night was a performance, and I understood my role in delivering the content (lyrics) and in influencing how the audience would receive the show. I learned to embrace that role, instead of fear it.

如果你是一名教师或领导，站在你管理或教育的人面前可能是一种可怕的经历。我认识一些老师，他们在自己的课堂非常出色，但一旦让他们进行一场培训，或者跟成年人或者甚至年龄大一些的学生说话都会让他们一下子吓得心惊肉跳。有些领导身上也有这种情况，当他们需要发表演讲或发布公司新的计划或方向时，他们连几句通顺的句子都说不出来，因为他们既缺乏自信，也不具备足够的舞台表现力，无法有效地传达自己需要传达的信息。那么，就算这些都是一次性的表演，少数登台的时刻也可能产生日常生活中无法感受的恐惧。当我讨论引导这个话题的时候，你面对的可能是认识的观众，环境也是让你觉得自在的，但你也有可能需要对一群从未见过面的陌生人进行培训。不管是哪种情况，在传达信息的时候，你都应该学会引导的艺术，只有这样，你要传达的信息才最有可能以你希望的方式被观众倾听。

If you are a teacher or a leader, getting up in front of those you manage or teach may be a frightening experience. I know teachers who are excellent teachers in their classrooms but ask them to give a training or talk to adults or even older students and they suddenly are gripped with fear. The same can be said of leaders who, when asked to deliver a speech or reveal a new company plan or direction, can barely speak a few fluid sentences because they do not have the confidence or stage presence to effectively deliver their message. Now, granted, these are more one-time performances, and it is possible that the rare moments on stage cause fear that is not felt on a daily basis. When I am talking about facilitation, it can either be with those participants you know, and in a setting in which you feel at home, or it could be the training you have to deliver to a new group of strangers whom you have never met. Whatever the case, the art of facilitation should be studied so that when you deliver your message, it has the best chance of being heard exactly has you hope it will be.

我发现许多老师仅仅把自己视为教授书本内容的人。而我认为这只是老师角色的一小部分，老师应被看作课堂的 CEO。老师不仅要教学生知识，也要教会他们如何学习知识。他们通过教授必要的内容来评估和教导学生如何进行批判性思考。但同时他们也具有引导者的角色。引导者的工作就是创造学习的空间和氛围。引导者要为参与者／学习者创造令他们身心都感到安全的场所。

I find that many teachers see themselves as simply those who teach content. I find this to be only a small part of the role of a teacher. I ascribe to the view that the teacher is a CEO of their classroom. As such, a teacher teaches students WHAT to know and HOW to know it. They teach content necessary to assess and teach students how to think critically. But they also play the role of facilitator. The facilitator creates the SPACE & ATMOSPHERE for learning. A facilitator creates an emotionally and psychologically safe place for the participant/learner.

根据定义，引导者指的是"帮助一个群体理解他们的共同目标并协助他们制定计划以达成这些目标"的人。但定义中并没有指出引导者该**如何"帮助"**群体理解。这是扮演引导者角色的关键部分，但也常常被忽视。这个部分往往没有得到充分的练习。

By definition, a facilitator is one who *"helps a group of people to understand their common objectives and assists them to plan how to achieve these objectives."* However, what is not implied is the significance of this role related to HOW a facilitator "HELPS" a group understand. This is a crucial part of embracing the full role of facilitator, and one that is often missed or overlooked. It tends to be the part that is not practiced or rehearsed enough.

在深入探讨老师／引导者的具体角色之前，让我们先看看引导者可能会扮演哪些角色。

Before we zero in on the specific role of a teacher/facilitator, let's look at the different types of roles a facilitator may play.

1. 中立调解——在一些情况下，如帮人解决个人矛盾时，引导者的角色更像一位客观的第三方。他们的任务就是倾听，确保当事各方都平等地获得被人倾听的机会。并且在必要的时候帮他们进行澄清。在这个角色中，他们的作用不是裁判，而是确保当事人之间进行清楚的沟通。有些人专职做这件事，而所有老师和领导在管理他们的团队时都时不时地需要这么做。调解员／引导者的技巧至关重要，能把这件事情做得很好的人在任何组织中都会是备受重视的成员。

1. Neutral Mediation - There are situations, like helping to resolve personal conflicts, where the facilitator is more like an objective third party. Their role is to listen, ensure all sides are given fair opportunity to be heard, and to provide clarification when the need arises. In this role, they are not there to judge, but to ensure clear communication is carried out with those involved. Some do this as a profession, and certainly all teachers and leaders do this occasionally in helping to manage those they lead. The skill of mediator/facilitator is very important and those who do it very well are valued team members in any organization.

2. 群体引导者——这一角色承担召集会议，以及会议或班级活动议程的责任。关于会议的目的，参加者可能知道，也可能不知道。在需要明确会议目的的情况下，引导者必须以恰当的方式设计和传达这一信息，确保参加人员能够明白。教师／领导力研讨会就是一个例子。很多时候，与会人员并不确定他们报名研讨的到底是什么内容。我在中国举办的研讨会，很多时候就是这个情况，与会人员只是被告知这是一个职业发展的机会，以及我是一个来自美国的教育家。作为引导者，了解这一点对我而言非常重要。同样，对于我与他们最初的互动，我必须仔细地列出我与他们共度的时间里我的目标是什么。通过这样做，我能让他们知道我们的研讨会将走向何方。一旦大家明白了"目的地"（预设目标），就可以进行（调整）"方向"这一过程，或者至少已经有了指导方向，让大家在引导者的带领下朝着预期的结果迈进。

2. Group facilitator - The role here is to take charge of the gathering and assume responsibility for the flow of the meeting or class. The objective for a gathering/meeting may or may not be known by the participants. In cases when the clarity of meeting purpose is required, the facilitator must design and deliver this message in such a way that the purpose can be known. An example of this may be teacher/leadership training seminars. Many times, those in attendance are not sure exactly what it is they have signed up for. Many times, as is the case with my workshops in China, they are simply told that it is a professional development opportunity and that I am an educator from the United States. Knowing this is quite important for me as the facilitator. As such, my initial interaction with them requires that I carefully lay out an overview of my objectives and goals for our time together. In doing so, I give them a sense of where we are headed. Once the "destination" (projected goal) is understood, the process of "direction" can be delivered, or at least guided, by the facilitator to help achieve the desired outcome. Most often, this is the role of a teacher, a supervisor, a trainer or someone chosen and placed in this role by position or appointment.

打磨你的引导技巧
Sharpening Your Facilitation Skills

在这一点上，你可能对于引导者的责任落到自己身上感到战战兢兢，或者你可能会摇摇头说，我已经知道这是我的职责了，但我怎么才能在这方面做得更好呢？我想说明的是，任何人都可以引导他人（可能是这么回事），但并不是每个人都能像其他人一样有效地做这件事。在引导的艺术中，为什么有些人比较高效，而其他人则不行呢？

At this point, you may be either shaking in your boots, fearing the responsibility that now rests with you as a facilitator, or possibly shaking your head saying, I already knew that was my role, but how do I get better at it? I would like to proclaim that anyone can facilitate (and that might be true) but not every facilitator is as effective as another. Why are some people effective and others are not as effective at the art of facilitation?

引导者的关键因素
Key Facilitator Factors

个性——一个很容易调动他人、显得真诚、有风度、能够与他们建立连接的引导者可以对人们形成强大地激励作用。这些个性特质可以帮助人们更容易地团结在一起。

举个例子，如果观众发现引导者具有吸引人的性格，他们就会更易接近引导者，并参与对话。这可以成为引导者在传递信息时的杠杆因素。

Personality - A facilitator who can easily engage others, appear genuine, personable, and able to relate to others can be a great motivator of people. These personality characteristics can help unify and bring people together more easily.

For example, audience members find it easier to approach facilitators and engage in conversation if they perceive their personalities to be inviting and engaging. This can be used as leverage by facilitators in communicating their messages.

自信——在考虑站到人群面前时，每一个引导者都应该具有一定的自信心，因为引导就是表演。虽然自信并没有固定的表现方式，但它有助于引导者找到他们表演的"最有效点"，并努力将其做好。

例如，一位害羞、内向的引导者可能会表现得缺乏自信，而这很容易削弱信息的正当性和完整性。

Confidence - Every facilitator needs to have a healthy dose of confidence when considering being in front of others because facilitating is performing. Whereas there is not one set way to show confidence, it is helpful for the facilitator to find their performance "sweet spot" and work at it to do it well.

For example, a shy, introverted facilitator may project a lack of self-confidence, which can easily diminish the legitimacy or integrity of the message.

高情商——引导者必须始终"解读整个房间"，以对观众的反应进行衡量。出色的引导者知道什么时候该发声，并根据感知到的反应做出改变。当有经验的引导者心中有一个明确的目标时，他们可以进行改变，而这并不会分散受众对信息的注意力。

举例，有时候我发现听众在午餐休息前的三十分钟很难集中注意力。于是我改变了自己的表达方式，加入了一个简短的互动游戏，帮助他们重新参与进来，而不偏离既定的目标。

Strong EQ - Facilitators must always "read the room" to gauge the response. Good facilitators know when to call the audible and make a change based on the perceived reaction. When the experienced facilitator has a clear destination in mind, changes may be used without causing a distraction from the message.

For example, sometimes I find audience members struggling to keep focused 30 minutes before the scheduled lunch break. I change my method of presentation to include a short interactive game that helps bring them back to engagement without detouring from the intended destination.

谦逊——作为一个引导者，具备一些自我意识固然很好，但过多展示自我只会让听众疏远你。如果自我意识能让你对你自己、你传达的信息或者你的表现能力感到自信，便是健康的自我意识。然而，如果你的自我意识暗示你比房间里任何人都优越，那便不过是一种软弱罢了。

举例，引导者会在他们的"表演"中营造气氛。如果一位引导者过多地谈论自己的专业知识、经验或成就，这种过度自信就可能让观众觉得他没有任何谦逊之心，并因此对他所传递的信息失去兴趣。

Humility - As much as it is good to have some ego as a facilitator, displaying too much of it can alienate you from your audience. Ego that gives you confidence in yourself, your message, or your ability to perform can be healthy. However, ego that implies you are better than anyone else in the room is a weakness.

For example, facilitators cast an aura during their performance. If one talks too much about their expertise, experience or accomplishments, the audience may perceive this over confidence as a total absence of humility and lose interest in the message.

弹性——在外国做引导时，我曾多次经历这样的情况：我想要的条件完全不是最优的。比如，当我需要活动空间时，我有时会被塞进一个比事先约好的小得多的空间。还有一些时候，对方明明承诺满足我的技术需求，但实际提供给我的却远远不够。恰恰就是在这种时候，你必须牢记（团队的）目标，根据眼前的实际情况调整方向，以确保自己仍然能按照原计划传达信息。这并非易事，有时这种情况确实还会影响内容的传达。然而这种情况很少会阻碍我产生影响或达成预期的结果。为什么呢？因我引导方面的经验让我具备了全面看问题的能力，所以在我无法控制的临时情况下，我依然可以灵活应对。面对挑战和适应预料之外的情况会让引导者获得更多经验，尽管他／她可能并没准备好，也不希望这种情况发生，但每一次挑战都是有益的课程。在逆境中迎接挑战需要一种健康的心态，而灵活应变永远是实现这一目标的一种途径。

Flexibility – When facilitating in a foreign country, I have experienced, on many occasions, a situation where the parameters of what I wanted for optimal conditions were anything but optimal. For instance, when I needed room space for activities, I would sometimes end up squeezing into a much smaller space than was agreed upon. In other instances, the stated technology demands, though clearly promised, were under-delivered by more than just a little bit. It is during these times that you must keep the destination (of the group) in mind, but alter the direction based on the circumstances, to ensure that you are still able to deliver the planned message. It is not easy, and at times it certainly impacts the delivery of the content. However, rarely does it stop me from having an impact or from achieving desired results. Why? Because experience in facilitation provides me with the ability to see in full perspective so I can be flexible in those circumstances that I cannot control. Challenges and unforeseen adaptations can quickly provide a facilitator with more experience than he/she may be ready for or deserve, but each challenge is a lesson. Meeting challenges in the face of adversity requires a healthy mindset, and flexibility will always be a means to that end.

塑造你的经验——提高引导技能是需要付出努力的。那到底是什么样的努力呢？如何迈出第一步？

Shape Your Experience – Improving facilitation skills takes effort. What does that effort look like? Where does one start?

1. 练习——为了在观众面前表现自如，你必须把自己置于"脆弱"的境地——这是一个扩展你舒适区的境地。这种练习很简单，比如在陌生人面前K歌，或者邀请一群听众，然后在他们面前演讲等。重要的是你需要通过练习来获得经验。认识到你的恐惧或过度自信，并勇于承认，然后直面挑战，解决问题。勇于直面恐惧是一项技能，恐惧并不会自动神奇消失，只有靠经验的积累来战胜它。同样，请他人提出建设性的批评意见也需要深刻和彻底的反省。你终将把恐惧从无能转化为健康、急切的兴奋感，就像你可以把过度自信转化为健康的平衡一样。这两者都是通过经验积累来实现的。

1. Get Practice - In order to appear comfortable in front of an audience, you must put yourself in vulnerable positions – positions that stretch your comfort zone. Getting practice could be as simple as doing Karaoke in front of strangers or presenting in front of an invited audience. The important message is that you need to GET PRACTICE in order to get experience. Identify and acknowledge any fear or over confidence and then face the challenge to fix it head on. Facing fear bravely is one skill that does not magically disappear with anything but experience. Likewise, inviting constructive criticism requires deep and thorough introspection. You can eventually turn the fear from incapacitation to a healthy, anxious excitement just like you can turn over-confidence into a healthy balance. Both are accomplished simply through gaining experience.

2. 发现你的"最有效传递点" ——引导者必须适应自己的个性和传递方式。可能你天生就不具备幽默感，但幽默是使听众放松的好办法，也能让他们在你营造的氛围中感觉自在。假设你实在无法在演讲中融入高雅或幽默的话语，请至少确保你的演讲和表达是自信、正确而鼓舞人心的。没有什么比听一个文法不通、语气单调的人讲话更糟糕的事情了。你的演讲中可能会有一些让你的听众听不明白或有些反感的方言或词语。有时候，发言者的口音就足以让听众抗拒他们传达的信息。在提升演讲风格的过程中，你应该试着去找到自己最好的演讲风格。一定要从公正的听众那里去获取诚实的反馈。记住，虽然肯定在某种意义上是有价值的东西，但你真正需要的其实是那些诚实的、建设性的批评意见。

2. Discover Your Delivery "Sweet Spot" - Facilitators must be comfortable with their own personality and delivery style. Maybe you are not funny by nature, but humor is a great way to put your audience at ease, and it is an inviting way for them to feel comfort in the atmosphere you create. Maybe you can find ways to add humor to your delivery approach, which may also put yourself at ease. If you cannot blend in tasteful and acceptable humor, at least make sure your speech and delivery is confident, correct and invigorating. There is nothing worse than listening to someone who uses poor grammar or speaking skills with a monotone voice delivery. Your speech may have identifiable dialects or phrases that are not understood or appreciated by your audience. Sometimes, just the accent of the speaker is enough to block the message. As you are perfecting your delivery style, you should also try to discover what your best delivery style is. Be sure to get some honest feedback from an impartial audience. Your friends, spouse, or family may not be the best source of feedback. Remember, though affirmation may be valuable in one sense, what you really need is honest, constructive criticism.

3. 获得自信——这可能是最简单的一项，它与第一条直接相关——经验是没有捷径的。自信源自经验的积累。糟糕的经历可能反而大有益处。好的经历可以建立自信。我想表达的意思很简单——只要走出去，大胆地做，你的自信就会提升！你表达得越多，你就能变得越自信。自信源自经验。

3. Gain Confidence - This may be the easiest one, and it is directly tied to number 1- there is no shortcut for experience. Experience breeds confidence. Bad experiences can be extremely instructive. Good experiences can build confidence. The message is simple - get out there and do it and your confidence can grow! The more you deliver, the more confidence you will gain. Experience begets confidence.

4. 寻找机会——一旦你发现了自己必须传达的信息，你就要尽可能多找机会去传达。要积极地寻找引导的机会。如果你想成为一名收费演说者，你有可能必须先进行免费演说，然后才能获得报酬。如果你想领导团队，那就去找一些团队来进行领导。关键是你要积极地寻找这样的机会，因为你的动力是成长为引导者，而这只能通过寻找机会、积累经验来实现。

4. Seek Opportunity - Once you find out what message you must give, seek out as many opportunities as you can to deliver your message. Actively seek out opportunities to facilitate. If you want to be a paid speaker, you may have to initially speak for free before you get some that will pay you for it later. If you want to lead groups, then find groups to lead. The key is that you actively seek out these opportunities because your motivation is to improve as a facilitator, and that can only happen with experience through opportunities.

5. 简洁的信息——这可能是最难提升的一点。我发现，随着经验积累得越来越多，我所传达的信息变得越来越简洁。根据我在经验积累的过程中收获的反馈，我对信息进行塑造。曾经要一个小时才能说完的内容，我现在只需要三十分钟，因为我已经找到了更好的表达方式。信息的巩固并不是突然获得启示的结果，而是来自经验积累的机会中获得的直接反馈。

5. Concise Message - This may be the hardest of all to develop. I found that my message became more concise with each additional experience. I shaped my message based on the feedback received through experience. What I once said in an hour, now takes me 30 minutes, because I have found better ways to say it. Consolidating my message was not the result of a sudden revelation, but rather listening to direct feedback gained over several experience-building opportunities.

尊重"引导者"职位的力量——引导者可以对任何群体产生巨大的力量和影响。如果你不小心维护的话，这种力量能够很快冲昏你的头脑。引导者能够很轻易地建立或打断一个群体的成长历程。通过拥抱和提升引导技能，教师可以提高每个学生的学业表现。善于引导的商业领袖则能提高公司的生产力和利润。在任何组织的每个层级上，训练有素、经验丰富的引导者都能够成为强大的资产。

Respect the Power of the Position - There is tremendous power and influence that a facilitator can have on any group. This power can quickly go to your head if you are not carefully guarded. A facilitator can easily make or break a group process. Teachers who embrace and sharpen their facilitation skills can elevate the learning of every student. The business leader who facilitates well can improve the productivity and profit of a company. At every level, a well-trained, and seasoned facilitator can be a powerful asset to any organization.

尊重你所扮演的角色以及你所能产生的影响力，因为一位扮演"引导者"角色的领导是会获得重视的。你的团队指望你能把这个角色做好！好了这个角色，团队成长过程将令人满意，而成果也将是显而易见的。这样你就能体会到通过影响他人而带来的甜蜜感。伟大的引导者身上的魅力在于他们愿意承担风险，然后通过努力和经验积累来强化他们要传达的信息。请抓住机会，最大程度地发挥你作为引导者的影响力吧，你可以改变许多人的人生。

Respect for the role, and influence you can have, as a facilitator leader is to be valued. Your group is counting on you to get it right! When you do, the process is satisfying, and the product is evident. That is the sweet spot of influence you want to experience. The magic in the power of a great facilitator is in the willingness to take the risk and then to sharpen the message through hard work and experience. Seize the opportunity to maximize your influence as a facilitator and you can change the lives of many.

保持好奇心
Be Curious

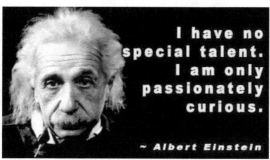

Image credit: www.thequotes.in

　　教师的影响力和工作内容远不止向学生传授知识内容。理想的情况是，教师应该激发学生的好奇心，让他们去钻研比教学内容更深入的内容。这样做将激发学生以一种更加丰富、深入和富于参与性的方式去探索知识。如果一个老师仅仅告诉学生应试所需要知道的东西，那他就剥夺了学生怀着好奇心探索未知而获得的乐趣。采用"应试教育"的教学方法不仅束缚了学生的学习，而且也使导师这一角色变得廉价。

　　The impact and job of a teacher extends far beyond just being the person responsible for delivering content knowledge to those who will listen. Ideally, the teacher should stimulate the curiosity of the learner so that they dig deeper than the extent of the content delivered. Doing so will invite the learner to explore learning in a rich, deep, and engaging way. A teacher who simply tells the students what they need to know for the examination robs the students of the joy that can be found through curious discovery. When a "teaching to the test" teaching method is used, it not only constricts the student learning but also cheapens the role of being a mentor.

通常，在开学的第一节课上，我会做一个开场白，大概告诉学生如下内容："*我知道对于你们中的很多人而言，在这门历史课里，并非所有内容都能让你们兴奋，甚至可能连兴趣都勾不起来。有时你们可能会讨厌这门课，但我希望在其他时候，它能激发你们保持好奇的兴趣。作为学习者，投入的方式之一便是始终努力保持好奇心。如果你们能对某个话题感到好奇，这种好新奇就会帮你找到有趣的视角、真相、思路或想法，并且也许会激励你进行更深入的挖掘。如果你们能这样做，它就能为你们开启额外的学习，并使得该话题以及学习过程与你们更加相关。*"我喜欢配图中这句爱因斯坦的名言，并且觉得我自己作为一个学习者颇为符合它的描述。（我并不是在拿自己和爱因斯坦比较！）当我自己还是一名学生的时候，我并不觉得自己有学习、记忆、解决问题或深入思考方面的过人天赋。我真正拥有的是好奇心。它促使我分析、阅读、学习、发问并对许多不同的话题有了更好的理解。请保持你的好奇心！

Typically, in my first class of the school year, I would give an opening message to my students that went something like this: *"I know many of you will not find all of the topics covered in this history class to be exciting or even interesting to you. At times, you may hate it, but I hope that at other times, it will pique your interest to be curious. One way to engage as a learner is to always strive to be curious. If you can be curious about the topic, it will help you look for an interesting angle, fact, thought, or idea about the topic and maybe inspire you to dig a little deeper. When you do that, it opens up additional learning and can help make the topic and the learning far more relevant to you."* I love the above Einstein quote, and felt it described me as a learner. (I am not drawing any personal comparison to Einstein!) As a student, I did not feel I had a special talent for learning, memorizing, problem-solving or deep thinking. What I did possess was an appreciation for curiosity. Curiosity has caused me to analyze, read, study, ask questions and better understand many diverse topics. Be curious!

教师如何激发学生的好奇心？
How can teachers inspire curiosity in the learner?

教师需要养成正确提问的技能。事实上，很多教师都不会正确提问，他们只会提容易的问题。如果是在法庭上，对方律师将会对引导性问题提出"反对意见"。许多老师只提显而易见的问题，而不是深刻的问题。知道如何构建问题将帮助你激发好奇心。

Teachers need to develop a skill for asking the right questions. In fact, many teachers do not ask the right questions, they ask the easy questions. If it were in a court of law, the "objection" outcry from the opposing attorney would be for a leading question. Many teachers simply ask the obvious question and not the deep question. Knowing how to scaffold questions can invite curiosity.

不过并非所有问题都能激发好奇心。有些问题属于最简单的那一类，只要它们能在适当的时候引出更高层次的思考，那就没有什么问题。最好的问题能够引出激烈见解和角度或者能够促进不同意见，这些意见可以帮助阐明主题或帮助正在倾听或投入其中的个人、群体或班级提升他们的理解。当然，有些问题可能直接就有正确或错误的答案，但还有许多层次的发问会导致诸多变化和选项，而这就是学生们参与的地方。教师应构建能够激发讨论、引发更深刻的思考且提升听课人好奇心的问题。

Not every question can inspire curiosity. Some questions are of the easiest kind, and there is nothing wrong with that, provided they lead to a higher level of thinking at the appropriate time. The best questions are those that invite a provocative opinion, angle, or promote a difference of opinion which can help elucidate the topic or increase understanding for an individual, group or class who may be listening and engaged. Sure, there is content that may have a direct right or wrong answer to it, but there are many levels of questioning that invite variations and options, and this is where student engagement can occur. Teachers should scaffold questions that provoke discussion and elicit deeper consideration to pique the curiosity of the listener.

问题类型应包括在小组讨论中引发思考并推动讨论的问题。问题的类型可以推动小型或大型的小组讨论或辩论。也许提出的问题更多地属于微观层面（比如让学生进行思考—结对—分享的交流），让他们独立思考，然后与同伴分享，再在一个更大的群体内进行讨论。教师应努力成为最好的提问者，因为这是激发学生好奇心的最佳方式之一，并能让学生更深层次地参与课堂内容，以及课堂本身。

Question styles could include those where a thought-provoking question provides fuel for small group discussions. The style of question asked can provide fuel for small or large group discussion or debate. Maybe the question asked is more at the micro-level (like having students engage in a think-pair-share exchange) to individually contemplate, then share with a partner before discussing it as a larger group. Teachers should work to become the best question askers because it is one of the best ways to inspire student curiosity and invite a deeper level of student engagement with the material, and in the class itself.

正确提问很重要，在正确的时间提问也同样重要。根据学生（或年级）水平的差异，学生可能已经掌握了某些知识基础，也可能没有掌握，而这些基础知识能够让他／她自如地回答探究或拓展他／她知识基础的问题。向没有足够知识基础的学生提困难的问题，可能非但不能激发他们的好奇心，反而会让他们心生恐惧。务必要熟悉你的学生。很多教师还没有有效地搭好舞台，就开启了"新"的话题或章节。他们可能会先宣布话题，然后就一头扎进内容讲解、背景阅读或回答问题的环节。然而，在引入一个新的话题或章节时，提出一些正确、引人深思的问题会带来全新的意义，并极大地激发学生的好奇心。这就是教师可以影响、赢得并激发学生参与、激发他们的好奇心——或者完全压抑他们好奇心

——的地方。

As important as it is to ask the right question, it is equally as important to ask a question at the right time. Depending on the learner (and maybe the grade level) a student may or may not have acquired a base of knowledge that would allow him/her to feel comfortable with answering questions that probe into, or expand, his/her knowledge base. Asking difficult questions to students without enough knowledge base may instill fear rather than pique the intended curiosity. Be sure to know your learners well. Many teachers start a "new" topic or chapter without setting the stage effectively. They may announce the topic and then proceed to dive headfirst into content, background reading or the answering of questions. However, asking the right, thought-provoking questions when introducing a new topic or chapter can take on an entirely new meaning and powerfully spike the curiosity of the student. This is where a teacher can influence, win, and inspire student engagement and pique their curiosity…or squelch it completely.

在引入一个新的单元或主题时，应考虑精心设计且具有创造性的策略。学生可以从这些方面看到教师的创造力，如果这些策略富于变化、难以预测，那么它们就可能引发学生更深的好奇心和兴趣。在引入一个需要背景知识的新话题时，教师可能要提供必要的知识信息让学生分类和整理。给学生一份"基础知识一览"可以快速有效地给学生提供基本事实或者所需的知识背景，让他们更快地参与进来。

Carefully designed and creative strategies should be considered when a new unit or topic is introduced. This is where teacher creativity can be visible to the students and, if varied and unpredictable, may lead to deeper student curiosity and interest. When introducing a new topic where background knowledge needs to be taught, maybe the teacher provides essential knowledge information that the students categorize and organize. Giving an "essential knowledge fact sheet" can quickly and effectively give students basic facts or a needed landscape of knowledge to allow for faster engagement.

　　有时候还可以通过学生来激发其他学生的好奇心。比如，让学生结对或者结成小组使用轮流分享的方式通常是有效的，学生们在这个过程中分享阅读、构建内容、提供可用于活动或作业的实际结构。通过这一策略，教师还可以事先给学生分组，把有学习困难的学生和高分学生安排在一起，让他们获得同伴的帮助。对于同一水平分组，它也可能起到帮助，因为高分学生分到一组的话，他们可以很快将材料过完，这就让你可以向他们提出更高的挑战，为他们安排更高水平的练习。无论你采用什么策略，都应该对学习者多加思考，给你教育的学生最好的管理和激励。你对新学习内容初始阶段的设定和任何单元评估测试同等重要。

　　Sometimes, students can be used to inspire the curiosity of other students. For instance, it is often effective to have students work in pairs or small groups and utilize rotating station work that involves shared reading, content building, and providing a factual fabric able to be used in activities or assignments. Using this strategy allows teachers to also design pre-selected student groupings that may put challenged students with high-achieving students for peer support. It may also lend itself to homogenous grouping because a group of high achieving learners can easily move through the material, allowing you to further challenge them by giving them additional work on a higher level. Whatever your strategy is, think about the learner and how to best manage and inspire those you teach. How you set the initial stage for new learning is as important as any end of unit assessment of knowledge.

　　我喜欢提问题，因为我喜欢认识新朋友，游历新地方。我发现自己最明显的人格特质之一就是我在提出疑问方面的能力和兴趣。每到一个新地方，或第一次遇见某人，我总会采取调查员进行任务的心态，先了解各项事实。我若是初来乍到，就会花时间观察其他人的行为。我喜欢看人。我着迷于观察别人的一举一动，因为这能帮助我深入了解自己所在之处，以及我如何才能适应这里。随着观察的进行，我可以进一步质疑自己先前的各种臆测，用各种相关问题来加以证实或否定。

My love of asking questions was born out of my interest in meeting new people or going to new places. I found that one of my prominent personality traits was my ability and interest in interrogation. When I go somewhere new, or meet someone for the first time, my mindset is more like that of an investigator on a quest to learn all the facts first. If I am in a new place, I spend a lot of time observing the behaviors of those around me. I love to people-watch. I find it fascinating to observe the behavior of others because it can help me learn more about where I am and what I should do to fit in. As I process these observations, I can then challenge my assumptions and validate or disprove them by asking pertinent questions.

我发现当我与某人初次见面时，我会遵循类似的模式。一段寒暄之后，我会问一些简单的引导性问题（你来自哪里？是做什么的？）而这只是为了激发我自己的兴趣，看看双方是否存在共同点。我锻炼倾听的技巧，因为通常而言，人们总是喜欢谈论他们自己。我也这样做，是为了测试我在某些领域，是否略知一二或者能给点意见。如果答案是肯定的，那么对话的过程将变得很容易，并且，基于我了解更多的知识、兴趣或好奇心，我的提问水平将变得更加深入。我希望自己的学生在学习过程中也有同样程度的参与感。通常，好奇心可以通过简单的提问过程达到顶点。在此过程中，学习者从纯粹的兴趣出发寻找信息，以找到共同点，而不是简单地，以必须存储知识，以便可以用在考试中为出发点，去寻找信息。好奇的人会提出有趣的问题，而这些问题通常源自于提问人的乐于倾听。

I find that I follow a similar pattern when I meet someone for the first time. After exchanging pleasantries, I find myself asking simple leading questions (Where are you from? What do you do?) simply to spark my own interests and to see if there are areas of commonality. I exercise the skill of listening because people usually like talking about themselves anyway. I also do it to discover if there are areas on which I may have some knowledge or opinions. If so, conversation flow is easy, and my level of questioning will become deeper based on my knowledge, interest, or curiosity to learn more. This is the same level of engagement I would like my students to use when learning. Often, curiosity can be piqued through the simple process of question asking. In this process, the learner seeks information from a place of pure interest to find things in common, rather than from a place of simply having to store the knowledge so it can be regurgitated back on an exam. Curious people ask intriguing questions, often born out of the willingness to listen first.

好奇心会引起更深入的个人探索。我喜爱那些让我充满好奇心的年代，那时我会突然间发现自己在询问信息。我回想起有一次家庭旅行，那次旅程中的流行语是"这背后是什么故事呢？"那时我们正在进行穿越美国西南部的长途旅行，当我们经过历史事件或地标时，或者只是谈论某个随机话题时，我们自发地会问："那背后是什么故事呢？"如果我的学生也问这个问题，我会很乐意的，因为这个问题可能带领他们进行深入的自我探索，进而寻求真实而有意义的知识。不幸的是，太多的教育把注意力集中在了考试成绩上。教育的目的应该是激发每个人的好奇心，而不是非得规定，评估或测试应记住哪些内容。这限制了学习并扼杀了好奇心。

Curiosity can then lead to deeper personal investigation. I love those times when my curiosity is engaged, and I suddenly find myself on a quest for information. I recall a family road trip when the catch phrase on the trip became *what's the story with that?* We were on an extended trip through the American southwest and when we would pass a road marker about a historical event or place, or when simply talking about random topics, we found ourselves saying, *what is the story with that?* I would love it if my students

34

would ask that question because it could lead them to a deep self-discovery quest for true and meaningful knowledge. Unfortunately, too much of education is focused on the exam results. The goal of education should be to inspire curiosity in each individual, and not necessarily to mandate which content should be remembered for the assessment or test. That limits learning and stifles curiosity.

我已经见过很多好心的老师用他们无聊的演讲、糟糕的内容传达方式、无力的提问、乏味的"舞台表演"，甚至是因为他们那缺乏个性的性格而将生命力从教室中抽走，从而压制和破坏学生的好奇心。许多老师关注学生的成绩，而非他们的好奇心。他们没能激发学生好奇心，因为他们自己就没有好奇心。并不是每个老师都应该成为老师的。我认为，一位老师和一位伟大的老师之间的区别在于，伟大的老师可以从学生身上唤起学生的参与度。每位老师都必须是一个坚定的终身学习者，而且还应致力于提高他们的沟通、陈述和传达能力。他们需要树立纯粹的好奇心榜样，以激发学生们也这样做。

I have seen so many well-meaning teachers squelch and destroy student curiosity through boring presentations, poor content delivery methods, weak questioning, dull "stage presence", or even because of a disengaged personality that sucks the life out of a classroom. Many teachers focus on student results and not student curiosity. They fail to inspire curiosity because they themselves are not curious. Not every teacher should be a teacher. In my opinion, the difference between a teacher and a GREAT teacher is the level of student engagement that great teachers can evoke from students. Every teacher needs to be a committed lifelong learner, but also committed to sharpening their skills of communication, presentation and delivery. They need to model pure curiosity, themselves, in order to inspire their students to do the same.

团队变革的挑战
The Challenges of Group Change

Image credit: CyberPR

改变一个人已经不易，而试图改变整个群体或团队时，挑战将更大！有时，领导者需要改变的不仅仅是一个人，因为需要的是对更大的"团队文化"的改变。当认识到所需的变革之路在于他们能否影响一大批人时，许多领导者会感到不安。

Bringing about change in just one person is difficult. The challenge becomes significantly greater when trying to change an entire group or team! Sometimes leaders need to change more than just one person because it is a change in the larger "team culture" that is required. Many leaders face trepidation when they consider that the path of change needed rests in whether or not a large group of people can be affected.

每个群体、阶级或工作场所都会发展出自己独特的文化。每年，我的班级都会因其内在的性格而形成独特的群体文化。这种文化由习惯、习俗、规范和行为构成，它们在任何群体中都作为标准出现。即使对于最具影响力的领导者而言，改变任何一个团队的文化也是一项艰巨的任务，因为要使团队成员在变革方面保持一致是很难的。通常，群体会因适应了常态而抵制变化。适应变化需要牺牲固有己见，需要牺牲自我权利。变革是艰难的，而看到变革需要的领导者，应该为前方的艰难道路做好准备。

Each group, class, or workplace develops its own unique culture. Each year my class has a distinctly unique group culture that forms, based on the personalities within. This culture is made up of habits, customs, norms, and behaviors that emerge as standards within any group. Changing the culture of any group is a daunting task, even for the most influential leaders, because getting the members of the group on the same page, with respect to change, is difficult. Often, groups are resistant to change because they have become comfortable in their norms. Yielding to change requires a sacrifice of autonomy and self-reliance. Change is hard, and the leader who sees the need for change should be prepared for the tough road ahead.

少数人可能将变革视为令人兴奋的冒险，但同时，大多数人却将其视为对自身稳定性的攻击。每个人对改变的想法或需求的反应和反响都不尽相同。每个人接受改变的决定更多地取决于心态，而非此种改变本身的环境。不得不接受改变通常是一个逆耳的提醒，因为这等于在告诉团队中的成员，他们根本就做不了主。他们的独立性和自治权受到威胁，因为他们可能看不到个人或团体的改变需求。如果采取这种态度，那么领导者的工作就困难得多。许多人会仅仅因为难以改变而抵制改变。

Where a few may see change as an exciting new adventure, most see it as an assault on their stability. Everyone reacts and responds differently to the thought or need for change. Everyone's decision to embrace change is more dependent on mindset than it is about the circumstances surrounding the change itself. Having to accept change is often a stinging reminder that individuals within the group are not in charge at all. Their independence and autonomy feel threatened because they may not see the personal or group need for change. When this is the attitude, the leader's job is significantly more difficult. Many will resist change simply because making change is hard.

为什么有些人能够像接受新的令人兴奋的冒险旅行一样拥抱变化，而另一些人却将其视为对其自主性和自我导向的威胁呢？当然，变化可能会令人不舒服且令人不安，因为我们已知的标准正在被修改，而任何不同的内容都意味着需要做更多的工作。但是，我发现许多面对变化时刻的人，只要得知学习新事物可能最终更有价值或者能带来改善，他们都拥，有或可以发现，忽视不适或经受不适的能力。我们必须对变革的需求和过程有一个清晰的愿景，以便团队知道、理解并能够接受预期的方向。这便是成长型心态可以在变化过程起作用的地方。

Why is it that some individuals can embrace change as if it is an invitation to go on a new and exciting adventure trip, whereas others see change as a threat to their autonomy and self-direction? Granted, change can be uncomfortable and disconcerting because what we knew as standard is now being modified, and anything that is different means more work is needed. Yet, I find many people who are facing moments of change have, or can find, the ability to look past or through the discomfort, if reminded that the prospects of learning something new may ultimately be more valuable and bring about improvement. A clear vision for the need and process for change must be cast so that the group knows, understands and can embrace the intended direction. This is where a GROWTH MINDSET can help the process of change.

美国心理学家、斯坦福大学教授卡尔. 得怀克撰写了《心态》一书，通过更好地理解思维方式的力量，帮助改变了数百万人的生活。在她的精彩著作中，她简明扼要地展示了人们对自身才干和能力的认识和看待方式，如何极大地影响着人类在各领域的成功。德怀克的研究表明，那些拥有固化思维模式的人-认为人的能力是固定的人，相较于拥有成长型思维模式的人——认为能力可以发展的人，发展起来的可能性更小。这不仅仅是乐观和悲观的问题。它是自我反思的镜子，可以成为人生方向和经验的有力灯塔。领导者需要认识到，当涉及到变化这个问题时，人们需要一种成长型思维模式，固化思维模式是有害的。对于团队文化变革，领导者必须了解团队成员的思维模式。

American Psychologist and Stanford Professor, Carol Dweck, wrote the book, *MINDSET*, which has helped transform millions of lives by giving a better understanding of the power of mindset. In her brilliant book, she simplistically shows how success in every area of human endeavor can be dramatically influenced by how we think and view our talents and abilities. Dweck's research shows that those people with a *fixed mindset*—those who believe that abilities are fixed—are less likely to flourish than those with a *growth mindset*—those who believe that abilities can be developed. It is more than just optimism versus pessimism. It is a lens of self-reflection that can be a powerful beacon for life's direction and experiences. Leaders need to understand that when it comes to change, a growth mindset is needed and a fixed mindset is detrimental. For a collective group culture change, the leader must understand the mindset of those in the group.

我认为德怀克的书是我读过的最具变革性的书之一。在我的家庭中，我有一对慈爱的父母，我是五个孩子中最小的一个。我父亲是一位牧师，作为一个人，一位父亲和一位丈夫，尽管他非常出色，但他不一定抱有什么大梦想。他喜欢自己的例行工作，也喜欢那种知道自己是谁、做过什么以及为什么选择这样做的一贯性。甚至确切知道自己的收入也令他感到满意。这种一贯性给了他安全感和放心的感觉。在我成长的过程中，我发现这种心态对他似乎是有用的，因此，我认为它对我也有用。然而，我的心态被重塑了，首先是因为绝望，然后是出于自己的选择。

I found Dweck's book to be one of the most transformational books I have ever read. I grew up the youngest of five kids to a loving mother and father. My dad was a preacher, and in all his greatness as a person, father, and husband, he did not necessarily dream big for himself. He loved his routine and the consistency of knowing who he was, what he did, and why he chose to do it. He even found comfort in knowing exactly what he would earn for his work. This consistency gave him a sense of security and a feeling of reassurance to his psyche. As I was growing up, I could see that that mentality seemed to work for him, and therefore, I thought it would also work for me. However, I think my mindset began to reshape first out of desperation and then out of choice.

当我向妻子求婚时，她已经是两个小女孩的母亲。我们之前在大学期间约会过，之后分手，后来我们重新建立了关系，唯一不同的是这次有两个小生命要加到我们的关系中。当然，我不知道如何成为父亲，那时我认为我只有和 1 岁和 2 岁的孩子一起学习"育儿之道"，而没法返回到她们婴儿时开始学习。像许多新婚夫妇一样，至少可以说我们的财务状况十分艰难。当时我并没有从事什么视为"长远职业"的工作，结婚后三个月内，我被解雇，在一家餐馆当服务员谋生。但那时，我很快发现自己（那之后很久我才读到德怀克的书）有很强的成长型心态。

When I proposed to my wife, she was already a mother to two little girls. Having dated previously, we reconnected and picked up our relationship where we left off from our college dating days, except this time there were 2 little lives to add to the relationship mix. Granted, I had no idea how to be a father, but I assumed I would just learn the "parenting thing" with kids who were already 1 and 2 years old, versus starting out with them when they were babies. Like many newlyweds, our financial start was rocky to say the least. I did not have a "career" job at the time and, within 3 months of being married, I found myself laid off and waiting tables in a restaurant for economic survival. What I soon discovered about myself (long before I had read Dweck's book) was that my growth mindset was strong.

这些早期的经济困难使得我改变的需求变得显而易见。要说服自己并不难，我已经有了一个四口之家，不得不迅速做出一些重要的改变。

我知道我可以找到很多谋生的方法。我打零工（多谢卡尔姆巴赫太太和克雷恩太太），我的妻子也同样努力工作，我们就这样度过了艰难的早期岁月。通过这些奋斗，我们俩都具备了更坚强的心态，这种心态让我们明白自己可以做到什么。这些情况需要个人进行改变。改变很困难，但却是必须做的事情。具有成长型心态使我们能够接受变化带来的不适，因为我们可以看到变化带来的好处。对我而言，最不为人知的是，那些早期岁月塑造了我的企业家直觉，以及我一生中关于变革的思考。

These early economic struggles made the need for personal change rather obvious. It was not hard to convince myself that with a new instant family of four, I was going to have to make some critical changes quickly. I knew I could find lots of ways to survive and make a living. I picked up odd jobs (thank you Mrs. Kalmbach and Mrs. Crane) and my wife worked equally hard to survive some tough, early, lean years. Through those struggles, we both developed stronger mindsets that showed us that we could accomplish things. Those circumstances required personal change. Change was hard but had to be done. Having a growth mindset allowed us to embrace the discomfort of change because we could see the benefits of the change on the horizon. Unbeknownst to me, those early years were shaping my entrepreneurial instincts and how I thought about change for the rest of my life.

短短几周之后，我有被餐馆解雇，这促使我申请了教师的工作（这是我最初在大学学习的内容）。意识到改变的必要性后，我更加努力地做出改变，以创造更光明的未来。幸运的是，我找到了一所小型私立学校，非常适合我当老师。我很快发现自己跟随父亲的步伐，走上了稳定舒适的道路。

After just a few short weeks, I was fired from my restaurant job, which pushed me into applying for teaching jobs (which is what I had been trained for in college in the first place). Realizing the need for change, I pushed harder to make the change necessary for a brighter future. Fortunately,

I found a small private school that was a great fit for me as a teacher. I soon found myself following my father's footsteps into the comfort of consistency.

我的教学生涯虽然算不上特别挣钱，但为我提供了财务上的稳定性，并且非常充实，使我处于一个可以永远塑造我的企业家精神的环境中。当我开始从事不同的业务时，我发现自己遵循着与以往一样的职业道德。这些追求可能是出于养育全家五个孩子的需要，但更深层的动机并非财务方面的，而是追求成就。

My teaching career, though not particularly lucrative, provided me with financial consistency and proved very fulfilling, placing me into an environment that would forever shape my entrepreneurial spirit. I found myself applying the same work ethic that I had noticed previously, as I began to start different business pursuits. These pursuits may have arisen out of the need to provide for my family of five children, but the deeper motivation was not as much about finances, as is was about finding fulfillment.

伴随 20 年的全职教学生涯中，我也发展了其他业务。我接受了成长型思维模式——这是机遇使然，并从全职教学中走了出来，将更多的精力投入到发展我的商业兴趣上。具有讽刺意味的是，父亲此时将我的许多选择视为"风险"，但在我看来，我认为这些改变是有必要的。这就是我证明德怀克所描述的思维差异的证据。我拥有一种成长型思维模式，而我父亲是典型的固化思维模式。（我得说，我并不认为一种思维模式一定是正确的，而另一种思维模式是错误的。我父亲是一个非常忠实自律的人。我的纪律性可能远不如他，但是在某些领域缺乏纪律使我在其他领域蓬勃发展。我因为他的稳定性带给我的一切而深爱着他。）

During my 20 years of full-time teaching, I simultaneously developed other business pursuits. I embraced the growth mindset that opportunity presented and stepped away from full-time teaching to pour more efforts into developing my business interests. Ironically, my father saw many of my choices at this time as "risky", yet in my mind, I saw them as necessary change. This was my proof of what Dweck would describe as *the mindset difference*. Mine was a growth mindset, whereas my dad's was a classic fixed mindset. *(Let me say that I do not think one mindset is necessarily right and the other wrong. My dad was an incredibly faithful and disciplined man. I am probably far less disciplined than he, but that lack of discipline in some areas makes me thrive in other areas. I loved him for everything his consistency did for me.)*

我所必须经历的改变对我而言至关重要。它完全唤醒了我的企业家精神，并开始了我作为商务人士的第二职业。对我来说，改变只是因为遵循了我的成长型思维模式。它并非没有风险，但我的风险承受能力远大于我父亲。

The change I had to go through was essential for me. It fully awakened my full entrepreneurial spirit and started me on my second career as a businessman….of sorts. For me, change resulted from simply following my growth mindset. It was not void of risk, but my risk tolerance was far greater than my father's.

我讲这个故事是因为这与个人改变有关。我必须进行一些艰难的个人改变。由于我的成长型思维模式和对风险的承受能力，这些变化得以发生。改变一个人（尤其是自己）并不总像改变多个人那样具有挑战性。如果教师将班级的性格视为有害或破坏性的，则他必须以成长型思维模式来努力实现群体的改变。需要改变公司文化的公司领导者或经理也需要一种成长型思维模式，以便为所需的文化变革设定清晰的愿景和过程。我们都可以发现变革是艰难的，有时甚至是让人不适的。但是，如果可以训练成长型思维模式，并且将经历的不适视为实现成长之必需，那么自我或团队的成功改变就有可能发生。

I tell this story because this is about personal change. I had to make some difficult personal changes. These changes were propagated because of my shaping growth mindset and emerging tolerance for risk. Changing one person (especially oneself) is not always as challenging as changing more than one person. A teacher who sees the personality of the class as one that is detrimental or destructive must embrace a growth mindset to work towards group change. A company leader or manager that needs to change a company culture will also need a growth mindset to set out a clear vision and process for the culture change desired. We can all recognize that change is hard and, at times, uncomfortable. But, if a growth mindset can be trained, and the discomfort experienced seen as necessary for fulfilling growth, then successful change in self or the group is possible.

带领团队走向变革
Leading a Group Toward Change

当团队领导认为有必要进行变革时，还必须仔细考虑如何要求成员接受变革。具有成长型思维模式的领导者不能期望团队中的每个人都具有相同的思想和接受度。许多人看不到变革带来好处的可能性，而认为变革是对稳定性和舒适性的恶化或威胁。领导如果不能让团队成员在感情上为即将发生的变革做好准备，那他们会发现团队成员在任何时候都可能对变革产生智力上的抵制。

The group leader who sees change as necessary must also give careful consideration to how to ask for members to embrace the change. A leader who has the growth mindset cannot expect everyone within the group to be of the same mind and acceptance. Many people see change not for the possibilities they may present, but rather as a deterioration or threat to stability and comfort of consistency. Leaders who fail to *emotionally* prepare the group for the impending change can expect *intellectual* resistance to the change at every turn.

认真树立变革愿景至关重要。对于团队成员而言，重要的是能够听到并且尽可能要看到变更的过程和结果是怎么样的。在进行变革之前，他们必须清楚表达愿景，这一点很重要。最初，那些拥有固化思维模式（甚至可能是成长型思维模式）的人可能会对变革的想法产生负面反应。他们可能在变革的方式方法上存在分歧，或者一开始就抵制需要变革这个观点。领导者不能无视这些反应，也不能简单地要求做出改变，而不设身处地地理解团队中的每个人对改变的想法。优秀的领导者会找到办法来验证和表达对变革可能有多困难的理解，并且这样做有助于塑造或至少揭示思维模式在这个过程中所起的作用。

Carefully casting a vision for change is essential. It is important for members of the group to hear, and probably see, the vision of what the change process and results may look like. It is important that they know the articulated vision before thrusting into change. Initially, those with a fixed mindset (or maybe even a growth mindset) may react negatively to the idea of change. They may disagree on the means, method and mode of change, or resist the philosophical vision that change is needed in the first place. Leaders cannot ignore these reactions, nor can they simply mandate the change without showing empathy for how individuals in the group will deal with the idea of change. Good leaders find ways to validate and express understanding for how difficult change can be, and in doing so, they help shape, or at least reveal, how mindset plays a role in the process.

有时，通过简单地对成员表明改变的需求或让其发声来化解变革阻力。富有同情心地表达关切，这代表了领导层的关心和考虑，这种做法可能会使许多人感到安慰，同时也分散了其他人的担忧。但是，如果希望获得全面的理解和支持，可能仍需更多的保证和说服。

Sometimes resistance can be headed off at the pass by simply providing an acknowledgment or vocalization for the range of feelings members are likely to have. Empathetically stating this reflects care and consideration on behalf of the leadership and doing so may give comfort to many while also diffusing the concerns of others. But more reassurance may still be needed if you hope to get full buy-in and support.

　　我们可以考虑的一种有效的策略，就是和对团队有明显影响的主要领导人（团队的推动者和参与者）私下会面。与主要领导人会面可能使得他们支持你的计划。指导和管理他们的反应可能有助于团队整体对变革的看法和接受度。希望他们能将它传递给他们所能影响的人。至少，这个举措将帮助他们了解团队的想法。

　　One effective strategy to consider would be to meet privately with key leaders (the group movers and shakers) who have a clear & obvious impact on the group. Meeting with key leaders may empower them to support your initiatives. Guiding and managing their reactions may help the overall tone and acceptance of the message, vis-à-vis the larger group. The hope is that they would pass it on to those they influence. At the very least, it will help them get a sense of the pulse of the group.

　　在教室中，这可能意味着与一些具社交影响力的学生坐在一起，他们可能会利用自己的身份来帮助传播信息。在工作场所中，这可能意味着需要找到一些能准确反映整个团队想法的有影响力的人员。这也就是"分而治之"的策略。领导者必须给策略以足够的时间，以考虑如何提出所需进行的变革，并在被问起时预知团队成员的潜在反应。优秀的领导者会把准团队的思想脉搏，很少会因团队的反应而感到震惊，因为他们了解那些他们领导的人的个性。

　　In a classroom, this may involve sitting with a few socially influential students who might use their status to help spread the message. In the workplace, this might include finding a few influential workers who could accurately reflect the overall group pulse. This is the "divide and conquer" strategy. It is necessary for the leader(s) to give quality strategy time to considering how to ask for the change needed and anticipate the potential reaction of group members when asked. Good leaders have their finger on the group pulse and are rarely shocked or surprised by the range of responses because they know and understand the personalities of those they lead.

　　另一个需要考虑的关键因素是团队成员有多少时间来消化变革的想法。在某些情况下，变革的发生必须比任何人所希望的都快得多。按照先前提出的先发制人的方法，可以简单地进行感同身受式的承认，即尽管大家都希望团队成员有更多的时间来吸收和处理即将发生的变化，但时间紧迫，根本没有办法这样做。因此，不得不立即发生改变，而这比任何人愿意接受的速度都更快。传达这一信息仍然可以验证你的感受，但几乎没有动摇和表示异议的空间。大多数团队成员希望做的，就是知道领导者能够验证并认识到团队对变化的感受。一个团队中，不是所有人都是成长型思维模式或固定思维模式，两者永远是融合在一起的。请尊重所有感受，并就如何在整个过程中共享、实施和处理变化提出周到的计划。这将有助于团队成员更好地消化和吸收变化。他们可能仍然不全都喜欢变化，但是相比于独裁的方法，感同身受的方法可能更让人乐意接受。

　　Another key consideration is how much processing time the group members are given to digest the idea of change. There are always situations that arise when change must happen more quickly than anyone may prefer. Following the same preemptive approach previously suggested could simply include an empathetic acknowledgement that although more time for members to absorb and process the impending change is the desire, the time constriction simply does not permit it. Therefore, immediate change must happen faster than anyone will necessarily be comfortable with. Giving this message still validates the feelings, but gives little room to wiggle and show dissent. A key thing that most group members want is to know that the leader validates and recognizes the group's range of feelings about change. No group has a membership of all growth mindset or fixed mindset members. There will always be a blend of both. Treat all feelings with respect and present a thoughtful plan as to how the news of change will be shared, implemented, and handled throughout the process. This will help the group members to digest and absorb change better. They still may not all like it, but it may be more palatable with an empathetic approach versus a dictatorial approach.

最终，团队成员希望信任领导他们的人。领导者不仅因拥有领导职位而赢得尊重。团队成员希望因自己的感情以及他们的服务而受到赞赏和重视。甚至连那些成长型思维模式的成员也可能在一定程度上因变革的想法而感到威胁。许多领导者认为变革的必要性一直是显而易见的，而被要求改变的人们却认为变革是有害且令人恐惧的。当然，领导者并非总是能够让团队中 100％ 的人信服改变可能是一件好事。但是，领导者应努力确保在必须进行改变之前，团队中 100％ 的人感受到倾听和重视。

Ultimately, group members want to trust those who are leading them. Leaders do not just earn that respect because of the leadership title they possess. Group members want to feel appreciated and valued for their feelings, as well as for their service. Even those growth mindset members may feel threatened by the idea of change, to a degree. Many leaders see the change needed as clear as day, while those being asked to change view it as detrimental and frightening. Granted, it is not always possible for a leader to convince 100% of the group that change may be a good thing but, the leader should work hard to ensure that 100% of the feelings of those represented are heard and valued before forcing change to occur.

认真考虑如何引入或实施变革是值得做的，并且需要花费时间。把准"团队成员脉搏"的领导者可能知道大多数团队成员将如何接受或拒绝这种变化，但是对于大型公司而言，获得关键部门领导的倾听可能对于获得真实观点至关重要。只有当将受到影响的接收者至少能够分享愿景和改变背后的原因时，才是实施变革的最佳方式。了解团队成员的成长型或固化思维模式将使变革的信息能够以更体贴的方式呈现。

Careful consideration as to how change is introduced or rolled out is worthwhile, and it requires an investment of time. Leaders who have the "pulse of the people" may know how it will be received or rejected by most of the group members, but for larger companies, hearing from key divisional leaders is probably crucial to have a true perspective. Change is best implemented when the recipients who will be impacted can at least share in the vision and in the reason behind the change. Knowing the growth and fixed mindset perspective of those in the group will allow the message of change to be presented in a more thoughtful and considerate way.

一些简单的思路
Simple Thoughts of Consideration

1. **精益求变**——我曾经听过"精益求变"一词。 我真的很喜欢听到这个词语时想到的画面。倾向于变革的公司或领导者通常会组建一支充满关键成长型思维的领导者团队。不是因为改变而改变，而是为了相关性和创新而改变。显而易见，苹果、阿里巴巴、腾讯、微软、亚马逊都是变革的伟大范例。而西尔斯公司则是一个反面案例。曾经在某个时期里，美国公司西尔斯凭借其 PRODIGY 产品的创新合作而有望成为亚马逊那样的公司。但是，由于西尔斯并不倾向于变革，因此它对时代文化的演变没有作出反应。如今，西尔斯仅剩不到 500 家门店，并且由于相关性的缺乏和对创新的抵制而逐渐走向衰败。

1. Lean Into Change - I once heard the term, "lean into change". I really like the image that comes to my mind when I hear that. Companies, or leaders, who lean into change usually build teams full of key growth mindset leaders. It is not that they change for the sake of change but instead for the sake of relevancy and innovation. Apple, Alibaba, Tencent, Microsoft,

Amazon are all clear mega-examples of leaning into change. Sears would be an example of the opposite. At one time, the American company – SEARS - was in the driver's seat to become Amazon with their innovative collaboration with their PRODIGY product. But, because Sears was not leaning into change, it did not react to the evolving culture of the times. Today, Sears has fewer than 500 stores remaining and is slowly being suffocated due to lack of relevancy and resistance to innovation.

2. 变革文化——我已经分享过很多人像躲避像瘟疫一样避免改变本身。很多时候，改变被视为对一致性、舒适性和独立性的的攻击。文化变革的基础源于领导者在聘用或引入团队时所做出的选择。文化往往是由人格塑造的，而不是程序。领导者应着重于让合适的人"上车"，即使领导者不能完全确定"汽车的去向"。在旅途中寻找可以适应并做出改变的人员要比让每个人都了解目的地但无法到达目的地要好得多。对于老师来说，应该意识到变革的文化是发生在每个班级成员的个性之内的。

2. The Culture of Change - I already shared that many people avoid change like the plague. Very often, change is viewed as an assault on everything that stands for consistency, comfort and independence. The foundation of culture change emanates from the choices leaders make in whom they hire or add to the group. Culture is most often shaped by personalities, more than procedures. Leaders should focus on getting the right people on the bus, even if the leader is not totally sure where the bus is headed. Acquiring people who can adapt and make modifications during the trip is far better than having everyone understand the destination, but not be able to get there. For the teacher, realize the culture of change is within the personalities of who is in the class.

3. 心态很重要——除了把《心态》这本书作为所有员工的必读书籍

之外，那些招聘人员或直接负责团队建设和培训的领导者还应该精通了解谁在塑造文化的"车"上。固定思维模式的人可以改变，但他们可能会以不同的方法来看到这样做的价值和需要。同样，成长型思维模式的人可能更容易接受改变，但是当需要整合文化时，他们也可能更容易分心。最重要的是，业务的开展既需要成长型又需要固定思维的个体才能组成团队。了解与你你一起工作的人的心态很重要。

3. Mindset Matters - Aside from making the book *Mindset* mandatory reading for all employees, those who do the hiring, or the leaders directly responsible for team building and training should be well versed in knowing who is on the culture-shaping bus. Fixed mindset individuals can change, but it may just take a different approach for them to see the value or need to do so. In the same way, growth mindset people may change more easily, but they can also become more easily distracted when culture consolidation is necessary. The bottom line is that business requires both growth and fixed mindset individuals to be a part of the team. Understanding the mindset of those you work with does matter.

总结
Summary

领导者对变革的看法可以通过口头进行表达，但需要确定的是，那些接受领导的人需要在听到变革之前先观察到变革。除少数例外，领导者需要生动表达自己对改变的感受。领导者应始终为期望的行为树立榜样，因此，他们必须愿意成为变革的第一部分。公司或团队的文化始于高层，领导者为变革和进步奠定基调。如果领导者自己的成长型思维模式都不灵活、适应力不强也不流畅，那么对于周围的人来说，这是肉眼可观察的。这些领导者时刻关注着团队的动向，因此他们通常知道传达变革有多么困难或轻松。即使在沟通良好的愿景中出色地提出变革，除非该团队成员认为对变革的诚意和支持始于提出变革要求的人，否则他们将对变革进行抵制。如果你想领导团队，请表现出同理心，但也要完全透明，并且自己也要愿意接受改变。如果你要让人们放弃稳定性、独立性、自治性和舒适性，那么请验证他们的感受。让他们知道变革是困难的，但是在过程和结果中他们会获得成长。

A leader's own opinion about change can be verbally communicated, but, most assuredly, those they are leading need to observe it before they hear it. With few exceptions, leaders will vividly portray their own feelings about change in how they conduct themselves. A leader should always model desired behaviors and, therefore, must be willing to be the first part of change. The company or group culture starts at the top, and those who lead set the tone for change and progress. If leaders are not flexible, adaptable, and fluid in their own growth mindset, that will be obvious to those around them. These leaders have their finger on the pulse of the group so they often know how hard or easy communicating change will be. Even when change is brilliantly laid out in a well-communicated vision, it will be resisted unless the group feels that sincerity and support for change starts with those who are asking for it. If you want to lead, show empathy, but also be fully transparent and willing to embrace the change yourself. Validate the feelings of those you are asking to give up independence, autonomy, and comfort in consistency. Let them know you understand change is hard, but that there is growth waiting for them in the process and in the results.

教师需要注意课堂文化。集体中的每个个体的性格塑造了这种文化。大多数情况下，班级氛围是无法通过剔除一个或几个成员而去除或改变的。与工作场所不同你无法轻易开除学生。改变班级文化是具有挑战性的。改变班级文化通常是全年进行的过程，具体而言，它是通过提出和执行明确的期望和后果而得到强化的。改变班级文化是最早教育孩子成长型和固定思维模式的机会之一。这是他们一生的宝贵教育。

Teachers need to be mindful of the class culture. It is shaped by the individual personalities that make up the collective whole. Most times, removing or changing the dynamics by removing one or a few members is not possible. Unlike in the workplace, you can't easily just fire a student. Changing a class culture is challenging. The process of changing the class culture is often a yearlong process strengthened by presenting and enforcing clear expectations and consequences. Changing class culture is one of the earliest opportunities to educate children on the ideals of the growth and fixed mindset. This is valuable education for their life.

关于影响的名言
Impact Quotes

- "成长是痛苦的。变化是痛苦的。 但是没有什么比停留在不属于你的地方更痛苦的了。"

  "Growth is painful. Change is painful. But nothing is as painful as staying stuck somewhere you don't belong."

- "那些不能改变主意的人，不能改变任何东西。"

  "Those who cannot change their minds cannot change anything."

- "万事唯有先难，方能后易。"

  "All things are difficult before they are easy."

- "未来的事情比我们抛在身后的要好得多。" ——孔子

  "There are far better things ahead than any we leave behind." -- Confucius

- "改🔲 是不可避免的。成🔲 是可🔲 🔲 的。"——🔲 翰.C.麦克斯🔲

  "Change is inevitable. Growth is optional" -- John C. Maxwell

It 要素
The "It" Factor

Image credit: The It Factor @ itfactorbiz

你是否想过，为什么成年之后你能记得一部分老师，而其他老师则记得不清楚呢？我对许多老师有一些基本的记忆，但对少数老师有强烈的记忆。我三年级的时候有一个老师，这个老师一定是很出色的，因为作为一个"活跃的"男孩，我在她的课堂上感到自己是有能力的。我还可以轻松地想起我的打字老师（阅读这篇文章的年轻人根本不知道打字机是什么东西），因为她在严格、友好和愉快之间找到了很好的平衡。对于那些以前听过我故事的人来说，我一直很在意一位老师——唐.马丁代尔所扮演的角色，他在我的生活中扮演着有影响力和改变一生的角色。尽管我在高中的学习成绩不佳，但他还是设法提高了我的运动能力和领导能力，并给了我从事教育事业的希望。他的鼓励，可以说，改变了我的人生道路。为什么我还记得这些老师对我的影响，但却无法记住所有的老师呢？我认为，有影响力的老师会因为具有"it"因素而与他们的学生建立连接。

Do you ever wonder why, as an adult, you can remember some of your teachers more than others? I have some basic recall memories of many of my teachers but intense memories of a select few. I had a 3rd grade teacher that must have been rather exceptional because, as an "active" boy, she made me feel capable in the classroom. I can also easily recall my typing teacher (young people reading this have no idea what a typewriter even is) because she managed a beautiful balance between being strict, yet friendly and pleasant. For those who have heard my story before, I have been very vocal about one teacher - Don Martindale - who played an influential and life-changing role in my life. Despite my less than stellar academic high school performance, he managed to encourage my athletic and leadership skills and gave me hope for a possible career in education. His encouragement literally altered the path of my life. Why do I remember the impact these teachers had on me, but I do not recall all my teachers the same way? I think impactful teachers make a connection with a student because of having the "it" factor.

在顺利完成本科、研究生学习并走上我的第一份教学岗位后，我的生活飞速前进，在那里我发现自己全神贯注于与学生的联系。像大多数老师一样，尽管我尝试对所有学生进行相同的教学，但我发现我与一些学生相处得比其他学生更好。我尽力以"影响"学生的方式教学生，就像我的老师影响我那样，我知道我作为老师的性格（常常以讽刺挖苦的方式来让自己显得有趣）对某些学生而言并不具有吸引力，但我敢肯定，这有助于建立一种舒适感和联系感，使我的角色超出教授学科知识的老师，让他们知道有对他们有更大的帮助，能够帮助他们成长并适应中学时代。当我考虑如何描述或定义"it"因素是什么时，我认为"it"在于教师如何与学生建立有意义的联系并产生影响，超越其所教授的课堂内容。学生和老师之间的联系成功地达到更高的水平，这使老师能够对学生进行有力的指导、建议、爱护和时不时地帮助和管教他们，使学生能够为人生做好准备。

Flash forward my life after having navigated successfully through college, grad school and into my first teaching job where I found myself focusing heavily on my connection to the students. Like most teachers, although trying to teach all students the same, I found that I got along with some students better than others. As hard as I tried to "impact" students the same way that my teachers had influenced me, I knew that my personality as a teacher (often using sarcasm to be funny) was not a personality style that some of my students probably found appealing. But I am sure for some, it helped to create a comfort and connection that allowed my role to be less about the subject taught and more about me helping them to grow up and navigate through their middle school years. When I think about how to describe or define what the "it" factor is, I think that "it" rests in how the teacher makes that meaningful connection with students and having that impact extend beyond the material that is being taught. The student and teacher connection that successfully hits a different level puts the teacher in a powerful position to guide, advise, love, and at times help discipline the student, enabling the student to be better prepared for life.

为什么有些老师似乎有"it"因素而有些老师却没有呢？我认为，这个问题的答案更多与师生关系的"化学反应"有关。我肯定记得自己和有些学生的联系比其他学生更加牢固。由于这种联系，我认为我们之间建立了更深的信任和尊重，进而形成了有意义的经历和联系。对于其他人，如果我们的性格不合，则尽管他们可能已经学习了我在班上所教的学科内容，但他们可能没有将我添加到具有"it"因素的老师名单中。与尽可能多的学生建立真诚的联系对我而言是即艰巨又理想的目标。作为老师，除了和与我们相处融洽的学生建立联系之外，我们应尽量不只选择和我们更为接近的人，而要竭尽全力确保与所有学生建立潜在的联系。我们的工作始终是教育每一名学生。为此，我们必须了解他们，并以他们作为一个人和学习者的身份对待他们。

Why do some teachers seem to have it and others don't? I think the answer to that question has more to do with the "chemistry" of the relationship between teacher and student. There were certainly students I can recall with whom I had stronger personality connections than with others. And because of that connection, I think a deeper trust and respect developed between us and, in turn, forged a meaningful memory and connection. For others, if our personalities did not mesh, then although they may have learned subject information taught in my class, they may not have added me to their list of teachers who had the "it" factor. Building authentic connections with as many students as possible was my difficult, yet desired, goal. We as teachers should try NOT to pick and choose who we want to be drawn closer too, but rather stretch ourselves to ensure we tap into potential connections with all students, not just those we seem to get along better with than others. Our job is always to teach each individual student. To do so, we must get to know them and meet them where they are as a person and as a learner.

　　我在一所学校工作了 20 年。在那段时间里，我可以诚实地说我爱我曾经教过的几乎所有班级的学生。当然，有个别学生让我的记忆尤其深刻，但是当我回顾我的整个职业生涯时，除了一个班级的学生之外，我几乎对所有学生都有愉快的回忆。这个班级的特点被少数几个男孩造成了负面的影响。那是一所小规模的学校，课堂比正常班级小（这可能表明这几个男孩消极情绪，迫使其他学生选择了转校）。他们蔑视权威，特别是对老师。他们彼此讨厌，也讨厌周围的人，对试图靠近他们的老师也心怀讨厌。简而言之，由于这几个男孩的行为方式，没有人喜欢他们。

　　I worked at one school for 20 years. During that time, I can honestly say I loved almost all the classes of students I ever taught. I remember specific students more than others, but when I survey my entire career, I have pleasant memories of all but one class of students. This class was negatively characterized and manipulated by a small handful of boys. Being a small school anyway, this class happened to be a smaller than normal class (probably indicative of the negativity within these few boys which may have forced other students to find another school). They carried a persona of contempt for authority and especially towards the teachers. They were nasty to each other, nasty to those around them, and nasty to the teachers who tried to draw close to them. In simple terms, because of how a few boys acted, they were unlikeable.

按照我们的一贯传统，我们每个学年都从 8 年级的过夜露营之旅开始，以帮助学生们彼此建立联系。这次旅行是在户外进行的，学生们在帐篷里睡觉，做饭，在大自然里徒步旅行，参加高空绳索课程，当我们作为老师与学生互动时，这也是非常重要的"沉淀时间"。这么多年来，在每次的露营旅行后，结果始终是相同的———一段美好的时光将学生们凝聚在一起，并为整个学年奠定积极的基调。但是，今年将会有所不同。

As was our longstanding tradition, we began each school year with an 8th grade overnight camping trip to help bond students together. The trip was done outdoors, complete with students sleeping in tents, making our own food, hiking in nature, participating in a high ropes course, and it also had the very important "down time" when we, as teachers, could interact with the students. In all the previous and subsequent years of this trip, the result was always the same - a spectacular time that bonded students together and set a positive tone for the rest of the school year. However, this year would be different.

学生们总是享受这段休息时光，在此期间，老师与学生们一起踢足球或打篮球。这段时光总是充满乐趣和欢笑，它使学生有机会在我们不那么严肃的时候通过"娱乐与游戏"的方式看待他们的老师。但是，在这个特殊的年份里，有一群男孩不仅试图赢得比赛，而且在此过程中羞辱了我们。我们甚至感到他们似乎试图殴打我们！

Students always enjoyed this downtime during which we teachers would play football or basketball together with the students. It was always filled with fun and laughter, and it gave the students a chance to see us, as teachers, in a "fun & games" element when we were not so serious. But, in this particular year, there was a group of boys who were not just trying to win the game but to humiliate us in the process. We felt as if they were trying to beat us physically!

大约 20 分钟后，我们就提前结束了橄榄球比赛，因此没有人受伤。我们认为篮球可能不如橄榄球那么具有战斗性，所以尝试了这项运动，但结果很快意识到他们把篮球打得更像橄榄球！那场比赛也很快结束了，以避免我们受到伤害。在两场比赛中，这群男孩都在嘲笑我们。本来初衷是与我们建立联系，但却迫使我们之间陷入了令人讨厌的困境。在之前和之后的所有年月里，我们从来没有一群学生有他们那样的表现。因此，像以前的所有野营旅行一样，这一年也为一整年奠定了基调。但是，与前几年不同，这种基调给人以非常消极和令人讨厌的感觉，并且从未消失。

We ended the football game after only about 20 minutes, so we did not get hurt. Feeling that basketball might be less combative than the football was proving to be, we tried that sport only to quickly realize they were making basketball look more like football! That game also ended rather quickly, to avoid us getting hurt. During both games, this group of boys was snickering and mocking us. What was meant to bond us, drove a nasty wedge between us, instead. In all the years before, and after, we never had a group of students behave the way that they did. Consequently, like all the prior camping trips, this one also set the tone firmly for the entire year. However, unlike all the previous years, this tone had a very negative and nasty feel to it that never went away.

即使在撰写本文时，我仍可以轻易回忆起班上少数可耻又讨厌的学生的名字和面孔！我也可以回想起同一个班级里的一些快乐、积极而又可爱的学生，但不幸的是，由于种种错误的原因，这些男孩的面孔更加令人难忘。

Even now as I write, I can easily recall the names and faces of the few members of that class who were mean and nasty! I can recall a few of the happy, positive, and sweet students within that same class, but unfortunately, the faces of those boys are far too memorable, for all the wrong reasons.

我非常努力地与他们建立联系。与八年级学生有很多联系，这让我感到很荣幸：我教了他们美国历史、卫生、体育以及足球和篮球。我也担任班主任和辅导员，因此与其中一些学生在度过了宝贵的时光。我以为他们可能只是不喜欢学术课程，如果是这样，那么我当然可以与他们建立联系，成为他们的篮球或足球教练。不，他们还是相同的反应！这也是我27年的教练生涯中唯一的一次在比赛结束时不得不将一支球队从地板上拉下来并且不与对手握手的原因，因为我的一些球员已经准备好与另一支球队的成员打架了。（请记住，他们是来自郊区一所富人中学的八年级学生。）作为教练和老师，我很尴尬，因为这些男孩子的表现与以往毫无二致。那支球队在两项运动中只赢了区区几场比赛，这一点也不奇怪。

I had tried very hard to bond with them. I had the luxury of having many points of contact with 8th grade students: I taught many of them US History, Health, PE, and coached soccer and basketball. I was also homeroom teacher and an advisor, so the time spent with some of these students was significant. I thought maybe they just didn't like academic classes and, if that was the case, then surely I could bond with them as their basketball or soccer coach. Nope! Same response. This would also be the only time in my 27-year coaching career that I had to pull a team off the floor at the end of the game and not shake the opponent's hands because some of my players were ready to fight members of the other team. (Remember, these were 8th graders from a wealthy, well-to-do middle school in suburbia.) I was very embarrassed, as a coach and as teacher, that these boys acted the way they did. Not surprisingly, that team only won a few games…in both sports.

在这种情况下，一个班级的特征遭到少数可悲的人的统治，他们以消极的态度对待他人，这破坏了许多老师及其同学的整个学年。我肯定看不到"it"因素。我可以肯定地说，这些难忘的男孩中没有一个把我列入对他们有影响的老师。要具有"it"因素，必须存在对等联系，而不是单向联系。就像老师可以尝试差异化的教学方式一样，我们也必须尝试差异化的联系方式。如果不能建立联系，那么整体而言，影响力就微乎其微。

In this case, the class was powerfully characterized and dominated by a few miserable individuals who treated others with negativity and, in doing so, ruined a school year for a lot of teachers and their classmates. The "it" factor was not visible in me for sure. I feel safe to say that none of these memorable boys would have me on their list of impactful teachers. To have the "it" factor, there must be a reciprocal connection, not a one-way connection. Just like the teacher may try differentiated teaching styles, so too must we try differentiated connection styles. If the connection is not made, the overall impact is minimalized.

培养关系
Cultivating Relationships

我喜欢教中学生的原因之一，是他们希望与老师建立积极的联系。我认为许多学生，甚至工作场所的许多员工都是如此。人们被人际关系所吸引，因此，大多数人在感受到连接时就会喜欢上它。我们都有一种与生俱来的强烈愿望，希望能感受到特别的事物。这就是为什么家庭感觉在人生中有如此强大的影响力。人类都想属于某一个群体。如果老师可以与学生建立联系并帮助其建立健康而有影响力的关系，那么老师便能够改变学生的人生。

One reason I loved teaching middle school students was that they wanted to have positive connections with their teachers. I think that is true of many students and even many employees in the workplace. Humans are drawn to personal connections and, therefore, most love it when they feel connected. We all have an innate and powerful desire to feel a part of something special. It is why the feeling of family is such a powerful influencer in life. Humans want to belong to a group. If a teacher can connect with a student and help forge a healthy and impactful relationship, that teacher can literally change the life of a student.

这是为我做的！它不是一夜之间发生的，而是老师坚定不移地以极大的爱心、耐心和努力来指导我的信念。值得庆幸的是，老师认为值得在我身上花时间，与我建立联系，帮助我的发展。作为一名成功的教练，他了解连接的影响力。对他而言，重要的是，我感受到了某种东西，这反过来又使我对自己的信仰比以往任何时候都更强。他促进了这种联系，反过来又促进了我的个人成长和自信。

This was done for me! It didn't happen overnight, but it was cultivated by one teacher's steady commitment to mentoring me with much love, patience, and effort. Thankfully he believed that I was worth the time spent investing in a relationship that would help me to develop. As a successful coach, he understood the impact that connection can have. It was important to him that I felt a part of something and, in turn, it helped me believe in myself more than I had before. He cultivated that connection and in turn, cultivated my personal growth and self-confidence.

建立联系需要时间，而老师需要与他们面对面的学生进行真实而体贴的努力。我发现我与中学生相处融洽，因为，老实说，我只比他们成熟一点点！我喜欢开玩笑、玩游戏，并且和我的学生玩得开心。当然，我也尝试在课堂上教他们重要的东西，但是我一直觉得我更重要的角色是与他们建立联系。对我而言，满足感的提高并不是因为我教授的内容，而是因为建立了良好的关系。这些关系使我能够为这些学生的初中学习提供帮助，并希望他们未来能过上幸福的生活。这对他们和我而言都是无比珍贵的。（这是附带的故事，显示了一位老师可以对学生产生的影响。我开始像我的老师曾为我所做的那样去影响我自己的学生。）

Connection takes time and it takes an authentic and sensitive effort on the part of a teacher to meet the students where they are. I found that I got along well with middle school because, truthfully, I was only slightly more mature than they were! I loved to joke, play games and have fun with my students. Certainly, I tried to teach them important things in the classroom too, but I always felt my more important role was finding ways to connect with them. I felt my fulfillment came less because of the content I taught, and more because of the relationships that were forged. Those relationships allowed me to help these middle school students navigate through middle school and hopefully, toward a happy future life. That was invaluable, both to them and to me. *(The side story to this is it shows the impact one teacher can have on a student. I set out to influence students exactly as my teacher had done for me).*

一些老师／领导者担心与他们领导的人"走得太近"，担心这会削弱他们的权威或影响力。他们认为，如果他们与自己领导的人过于亲密、友善或自在，那么他们将无法有效地领导这些人。是的，总是存在走得太近的危险，这可能导致双方都无法遵守界线。其他人则避免了与教师和学生之间某一方处于弱势地位的关系。在有些故事中，一些恶言相向的老师利用了这种师生关系，使其他人处于高度戒备的状态。为了达到平衡，一些老师避免任何建立联系的尝试，而只作为书本内容的传授者。这样可以避免学生与老师之间出现任何混乱，甚至也可避免错误的指控，因为这可能会破坏专业人士的声誉和职业生涯。

Some teacher/leaders are apprehensive about getting "too close" to those they lead for fear it diminishes their authority or influence. They think if they are too close, friendly or comfortable with those they lead, then they won't be able to lead them effectively. Yes, there is always a danger of someone getting too close, possibly resulting in either party not being able to respect the boundary line. Others avoid a relationship for the vulnerable position in which it puts the teacher and the student. There are stories where some abusive teachers have taken advantage of such student-teacher relationships, which put others on high alert. To counterbalance, some teachers avoid any attempt at connection, and simply remain as the giver of content. This avoids any possibility of confusion between the student and the teacher, as well as even the false accusation, which can ruin the reputation and career of a dedicated professional.

在确定"联系"对你意味着什么时，请务必仔细评估你的领导风格。我认为我的领导风格就是基于联系的。我想与自己的学生和员工保持联系，因为我希望他们知道我在乎他们，因为他们以及他们热爱从事的事情对我而言很有价值，所以我认为对这种关系的投入至关重要，因为这表明人们珍惜他们作为一个人的价值。我认为这种联系不会削弱我的教学或领导能力。实际上，我想说它的效果正好相反。我相信，因为我了解他们，所以我可以利用这种深厚的关系并提高他们对工作绩效的期望值。我认为，与接受领导的人建立健康关系的领导者不会因此失去影响力或尊重。

When deciding about what "connection" means to you, be sure to carefully evaluate your leadership style. I identify my leadership style as relationship-based. I want to have a relationship with my students and employees because I want them to know I care about them. Because who they are, and what they like to do is valuable to me, I see the investment in the relationship to be of the utmost importance because it shows them that I value who they are as a person. I do not feel this connection weakens my ability to teach or lead. In fact, I would say it has the opposite effect. I believe that because I know them personally, I can leverage that cultivated relationship and raise their own level of expectation about their job performance. I do not think a leader who builds healthy relationships with those they lead loses leverage or respect by doing so.

总结
Summary

当老师（领导者）愿意为培养人际关系进行投入时，对于学生或他们领导的人来说，结果可能是强有力的。由于建立起来的关系，老师／领导者可以以更有意义的方式进行教导、带领、建议、指示和管教。成为老师的意义不仅仅在于教授学科内容，就像领导不只是发号施令一样。努力建立健康和真实的关系需要老师／领导者付出努力。成功取决于你的个性和领导风格。如果做得好，它可以改善所有参与者的人生，使老师更有效，领导者更有力，也能使接受者的感受得到重视和联系。

When teachers (who are leaders) are willing to invest in cultivating a connection relationship, the results can be powerful for students or those they lead. The teacher/leader can mentor, guide, advise, instruct, and discipline in a much more meaningful way because of the relationship established. The significance of being a teacher is not just about delivering the information in the subject they teach, just like leading is not just about giving orders or commands. Working to build healthy and authentic relationships requires effort on the part of the teacher/leader. Success depends on your personality and leadership style. When done correctly, it enhances the life of all involved, making the teacher more effective, the leader stronger and the recipient feeling valued and connected.

因为一位老师与我建立了联系，所以我的人生方向发生了变化。他使我感到与人联系并受到重视，从而永远改变了我的人生。反过来，我也希望延续这种东西，并且对至少一名学生——当然我希望不只是一名学生——做到同样的事情。

Because one teacher cultivated a connecting relationship with me, the direction of my life was changed. He made me feel connected and valued, thereby altering my life forever. In turn, I hope I paid it forward and did the same for at least one, but hopefully more than just one, student.

领导他人就是影响他人。 我的老师是领导者，因为他对我产生了深远的影响。他不仅将自己的角色看作是教授历史、健康和体育知识的知识提供者，而且还担任人生导师。他担任我的篮球和足球教练，不仅传授了我每天使用的运动技能，而且还帮助我培养了领导才能。因此，我最终走上了历史，健康和体育教学的道路也就不足为奇了。另外，我也执教足球和篮球，和他完全一样。 因为他在我身上进行了投入，所以我也致力于对其他人进行投入。建立联系对于我现在所做的一切至关重要，因此，我既谦虚又心怀感激。

To lead is to influence. My teacher was a leader because he influenced me in a profound way. He saw his role as not only the knowledge-giver hired to teach History, Health, and PE, but also as a life mentor. He served as my basketball and soccer coach, which helped instill not only sports skills, but also leadership skills, that I use every day of my life. It should be no surprise that I also ended up teaching History, Health and PE. In addition, I coached soccer and basketball exactly as he did. Because he invested in me, I sought to invest in others. Cultivating a connecting relationship is essential to everything I now do and, as a result, I am both humbled and grateful.

我的课堂很无聊吗？
Is My Classroom boring?

Image credit: So Bored Smiley

我不记得任何老师说过他们的课堂很无聊。但是，在我与无数的学生交谈中，他们告诉我他们的许多课程都无聊透顶。怎么会这样呢？学生只是不切实际或脱离现实吗？还是说真正不切实际或脱离现实的是老师们自己？

I cannot recall a time when I spoke with a teacher who professed that his/her classroom was a boring place for students. Yet, I talk to countless students who tell me many of their classes are boring. How could this be? Are students simply unrealistic or disengaged? Or, could the teachers themselves be unrealistic or disengaged?

现实是，作为老师，我们每个人都或多或少有无聊的时候。甚至可以肯定的是，当我们很无聊、我们的课程或者我们设计的学生活动很无聊的时候，我们是能认识到的。作为教师，我们可以认识到我们无法使每个课程计划都让人充满兴奋和精力，以此保持所有学生的充分参与。我们并没有将"无聊"作为任何课程计划的目标，但是我们有时难免都会这样。尽管我们应该让无聊的时刻限制在最低水平，但对许多人而言，无聊已成为习惯，而对学生来说，无聊*的确*已经是习以为常了。

The reality is, as teachers, we all have times when we are, or have been, boring. It may even be true that we recognize when we are boring, our lesson is boring, or our designed student activity is boring. As teachers, we recognize it is impossible to make every single lesson plan filled with excitement and energy to keep all students fully engaged. We do not set "boring" as the target objective of any lesson plan, but we all have those moments. Whereas we should seek to limit the boring moments to a "rare occasion" basis, for many, being boring becomes a routine, and for students, boring *is* the routine.

面对现实吧，对于生活中的大多数事情，简单地在工作中开启"自动驾驶"模式要容易得多。在这些时刻里，例行公事的感觉舒适而轻松，而我们通常可以毫不费力地如此前行。无论我们从事什么职业，陷入常规都会轻易导致惯例的形成。停留在惯例中成为了一种生活方式。我们需要问自己的问题是："我是愿意停留在目前的惯例中，还是愿意付出努力摆脱惯例呢？"要走出惯例需要大量的努力，但是对于你和你的学生而言，结果将是值得的。停留在某种领导惯例中会降低我们的效率，并降低我们对所领导的人的影响。我们将变得懒惰，因为停留在惯例中是无比轻松的事情。

Let's face it, for most things in life, it is so much easier to simply put our work efforts on autopilot. In these moments, routine feels comfortable and easy, and we can often move along with little to no effort. Regardless of our occupation, falling into the routine can easily lead to a rut. Remaining in that rut then becomes a lifestyle. The question we need to ask ourselves is, "Is the rut we are currently in where we plan to remain, or are we willing to put in the effort needed to steer out of it?" To steer out is going to involve a lot of hard work and effort, but the results will be well worth it for you and your students. Remaining in a leadership rut reduces our effectiveness, and it reduces the influence we have on those we lead. We become lazy because the routine rut is an easy place to remain.

作为一名教师，设计独特而有创意的教学计划是一项艰巨的工作，需要牺牲时间、精力和资源。在中国，许多老师每天的工作时间很长，几乎没有时间花在家庭或备课上。此外，一天中老师需要准备的课程往往不只一堂。我还记得以前教书的日子里，我不得不在同一天备五堂不同的课。当然，不能期望我在同一天把五堂课都上得很棒！确保学生在课堂上的每一次经历都令人兴奋、引人入胜且令人难忘的工作和奉献精神基本上是无法维持的。即使老师们有这样做的动力，执行这一计划所需的时间管理和计划也需要付出巨大的努力。

As a teacher, designing unique and creative lesson plans is extremely hard work and requires a sacrifice of time, energy, and resources. Many teachers in China work very long hours in a day, leaving little time for family or lesson preparation. In addition, teachers have more than just 1 lesson to prepare for in a day. I remember days of teaching when I had to deliver 5 unique lesson preps in the same day. Surely it could not be expected of me to deliver five great lessons on the same day! The amount of work and dedication it takes to ensure that every classroom experience for the students is exciting, engaging, and memorable is almost impossible to sustain. Even if the motivation to do so were present, the time management and planning needed to execute it would take a heroic effort.

当我反思教学生涯的头两年时，我清晰地记得我只是想比学生领先两到三个课时。在最初的几年里，我基本上只是在学生学习之前进行学习而已！老实说，有时候我发现自己在用"辅导"活动来拖延或占用教学时间，因为我不确定接下来该教什么内容。这是好的教学吗？当然不是！我不过是在尽力而为罢了。我是第一个承认有时候我的课对我的学生而言很无聊的老师。从那以后，我就宽恕了那些曾在早年让我觉得无聊的老师。我缺乏的是经验。

When I reflect on my first two years of teaching, I remember vividly that I was just trying to stay two or three class periods ahead of the students. In those early years, I was basically learning the material just a little before they were! Honestly, there were times when I found myself making up some "filler" activities to stall or take up instructional time because I was unsure of what content I had to teach next. Was this good teaching? Of course not! I was managing the best that I could. I am the first to admit that sometimes my class was a boring place for my students. I have since forgiven myself for being a boring teacher in those early years. What I lacked was experience.

如果你是一位年轻的老师，那么我希望你做的第一件事，就是原谅自己课堂无聊的时候。当然，你也可以记住这种情况，我不怪你。现在，你需要原谅自己。 像我当初一样，你可能也是一名刚走上教学岗位的老师，只比你的学生领先几节课而已。这是可以理解的，并且与提高所需的经验直接相关。如果你的课堂是由于这种情况而无聊，那么要宽恕就并非难事了。但是，如果你认为自己是一位经验丰富的老师，但你的教室仍然很无聊，那么宽恕就可能需要花费额外的精力。

If you are reading this as a young teacher, the first thing I want you to do is forgive yourself for the times you, too, are boring in the classroom. Surely, you can remember a time when this has happened to you. I forgive you. Now you need to forgive yourself. Like me, you may be a new teacher prepping and staying just a few lessons ahead of your students. This is understandable and directly related to experience needed in order to improve. If your classroom is boring due to this type of scenario, then forgiveness should not be difficult. However, if you consider yourself an experienced teacher and your classroom is still boring, then forgiveness might take additional effort.

"教育的成本很高，但是与无知的成本相比，却显得微不足道。"（本.富兰克林）我认为无知的一种表现就是忽略你本已知道的事实，而不是对无知的更传统的定义——不做或不知道你尚未学到的东西。根据这一定义，如果你还没有学到某些东西，可以认为你是无知的。但是，当你明明知道某些东西但却不采取任何措施时，你可以被视为冷漠。只有掌握了知识，你才能变得冷漠。随着我们获得宝贵的经验，我们有责任对它做点什么。随着经验的积累，我变得更加善于利用课堂时间，同时我在课程设计方面也变得更好了，以便适应学生的需求和我的目标。

"The cost of an education is high, but that pales in comparison to the cost of ignorance." (Ben Franklin) I think one perception of ignorance involves ignoring what you know to be true, as opposed to the more classic definition of ignorance - not doing or knowing what you have not yet learned. By definition, you can be considered ignorant if you have not yet learned something. But you can be considered *indifferent* when you know something, but do nothing about it. Only after you have knowledge can you be indifferent. As we gain valuable experience, we are then responsible to do something with it. As I gained experience, I became much better at making the most out of the classroom time, but I also became better at designing lessons to fit my students' needs and my objectives.

在老师／领导者培训课程上，我经常谈到对教学或领导很重要的两个关键词：**目的地和方向**（请参阅"目的地和方向"一章）。简而言之，目的地描述的是学习目标。这可以是需要学习的技能或内容，也可以是团队的领导目标。不管怎么说，目的地是我希望我的学生完成的"十字准心"的中心。就方向而言，我指的是到达目的地的指导策略。光指明道路还不够。老师和领导者在学习过程中需要进行仔细而周到的指导。这就是为什么引导技巧对于任何老师或领导者都是必不可少的。

In my teacher/leader training workshops, I often talk about two key words that are important to teaching or leading: **destination and direction.**

(Refer to "Destination and Direction" chapter)   Simply stated, destination describes the targeted learning objectives. These objectives could be the skills or content needed to be learned, or they could be the leadership objectives for the group. Nonetheless, destination is at the center, in the "crosshairs", of where I wanted my students to end up. By direction, I am referring to the guided strategies used to reach the destination. Pointing the way is not enough. Teachers and leaders need to be a careful and calculated guide in the process of learning. This is why facilitation skills are essential to any teacher or leader.

为了指引方向，人们利用并设计活动来引导自己到达目的地。对于老师而言，应始终设计和选择定向活动，以保持学生的参与度并强化预期的学习效果。有效地开展这些活动需要出色的引导技巧。成为一名优秀的引导者是无法替代的。拥引导者经验意味着你可以更好地指导你所领导的人，因为你具备信心、技能和专业知识来预测可能的发展趋势。作为老师获得的经验越多，我的目标和方向就变得越清晰、越有效，因为我可以预测它可能会如何发展。我知道如何提出更好的问题，并通过问答来提高学生的参与度，甚至在短时间内就设计一些学生活动，这些活动对我来说可能仍然是出于填充时间的目的，但对于学生来说却仍然是健康的学习经历。当"目的地"明确时，我的指导"方向"会更好。当老师可以设计创造性的活动来增加学生的参与度时，便减少了学生感到无聊的机会。

To guide the direction, activities are utilized and designed to help lead toward the destination. For a teacher, directional activities should always be designed and chosen that keep the students engaged and reinforce the intended learning. Carrying out these activities effectively requires excellent facilitation skills. There is no replacement for experience in being a good facilitator. Having experience as a facilitator means you can better direct those you lead because you have the confidence, skill, and expertise to anticipate how it is likely to go. The more experience I got as a teacher, the sharper and more effective my destination and direction became, because I could predict how it was likely to go. I knew how to ask better questions, get more student engagement through responses, or, even on short notice, design some student activities that may have been filling time for me, but still healthy learning experiences for the students. When my destination was clear, my direction was better. When a teacher can design creative directional activities that increase student engagement, the result is reduced opportunities for student boredom.

有时，由于对"方向"的渴求，学生的参与度会达到难忘的程度。有时被认为占用课堂时间的活动，反而催生出最好的学生活动。我记得上一堂课时，"方向"错误反而变成了令人难忘的方向性时刻，学生们在期间展现了极高的参与度。

Sometimes, memorable moments of student engagement came as a result of directional desperation. There were times when the need to fill class time spawned some of my best student engagements. I remember one class when directional disaster was turned into a memorable directional moment of high student engagement.

在一个漫长的假期来临之前的两天，我们完成了一个大单元的学习，比起在假期前夕尝试引入新的学习材料，这不是一个好主意。很明显，学生们心里已经开始放假了。在一次快速而疯狂创意搜索活动的过程中，我发现了签署《美国独立宣言》的历史人物传记的资源包。知道我们最终将要了解有关该传奇文档的历史，一个场景突然出现在我的脑海中。我想象我的学生坐在星巴克那样的氛围中，喝热可可，吃零食，随意讨论这份文档的价值。我知道学生会喜欢星巴克这个主意，但是他们会接受关于历史想法的讨论吗？

Having finished a large unit of study 2 days prior to a lengthy holiday break, I knew better than to try to introduce new material on the eve of a vacation. It was clear the students were already on a mental holiday. In a fast & frantic search to creatively fill time, I stumbled across a resource packet of biographies of historical figures who signed the American Declaration of Independence. Knowing we were going to eventually learn about the history surrounding this legendary document, an image of a scene popped into my mind. I imagined my students sitting in a Starbucks-like atmosphere, drinking hot cocoa, eating snacks and casually discussing the value of the document. I knew the students would like the Starbucks idea, but would they embrace the discussion of history idea?

趁着把水烧热的时间，我找到了一个茶水壶，一些在野营时留下的热巧克力小包，并准备足量的签署者传记的复印讲义。上课的时候，我热情地向学生们宣布我们正在举办**历史咖啡厅**！仅凭我的语气，就听起来神奇而有趣，几乎使我相信这是经过仔细考虑和计划的"方向"活动。令我惊讶的是，每个学生都急着开始阅读自己手上的传记。他们甚至还主动提出为明天的"课堂咖啡厅"活动带零食！

With barely enough time to get the water hot, I located a hot water urn, some hot chocolate packets that were left from a class camping trip and made enough copies of the signer's biographies. As I entered class, I enthusiastically announced to students we were having a HISTORY CAFÉ! The tone of my voice alone made it sound magical and fun, almost convincing myself that it was a carefully thought out and planned directional activity. To my surprise, each student anxiously started reading their given biographies. They also started offering to bring in snacks for tomorrow's café!

第二天（学校放假前的最后一天），学生们迅速涌入教室。每个人都做了一个名字标签，有些甚至带来了一些简单的道具来宣传他们的签署人物。我让他们阅读并充分了解他们的人物性格，以便第一人称视角讲述他们各自的历史角色以及他们当初签署此历史性文件时所冒的风险。

茶水越来越热的同时，我不禁看到了学生明显高涨的参与度。

The next day (the final day of school before holiday break) the students flooded quickly into the room. Each had made a nametag, some even brought in some simple props to promote their signer. I had tasked them to read and understand enough about their character to speak in the first person about their historical role and about the risk they took to sign this historic document. While the water was heating up, I couldn't help but see the obvious level of student engagement.

当水烧热时，学生们开始享受热可可的温暖，并假装文件的原始签署者已经通过他们的声音复活了。正如我之前在忙乱时刻的灵光一现中所想象的那样，大家分享小吃，进行历史对话。完美吗？算不上！难忘吗？当然！无聊吗？没那回事！你不知道吗，当我在学年结束对学生进行调查时，大多数学生都将历史咖啡厅视为那学期最喜欢的课程之一！

By the time the water was hot, students began to enjoy the warmth of the hot cocoa as they pretended as if the original signers of the document had come back to life through their voices. Snacks were shared and historical conversation took place, just as I imagined in my moment of desperation. Was it perfect? Not at all! Was it memorable? For sure! Was it boring? Not even close! Wouldn't you know it, when I surveyed students at the end of the year, most students commented on the history café as being one of their favorite classes of the term!

并非每个计划外的方向性时刻都会产生一个难忘的时刻，但在当时那个情况下，我受到了上天的眷顾，因此我将历史咖啡厅延续了多年。在每个咖啡厅的场合，我都想办法来对它进行改进。我想让你学习的课程不是关于"即兴表演"并把某些东西堆在一起，而是要冒险尝试一些可能与常规不同的东西。例行程序很无聊。 要确保始终挑战自己，以摆脱常规。

Not every unplanned directional moment spawns a memorable one, but in this case, the universe came together in my favor, and I continued the History Café for many years. With each café occasion, I tried to find ways to improve it from the time before. The lesson I want you to learn is not so much about "winging it" and throw something together, as it is about being willing to take the risk to try something that might be different and well outside the routine. The routine is boring. Push yourself to steer out of the routine by making sure you always challenge yourself.

在中国的培训中，我结识了许多才华横溢且经验丰富的老师。当我发现学生们苦于**"无聊的常规课堂"**时，我可以看到他们有多么不自在。我问他们："你的学生入学时是否能保证，他们每天都会坐在同一座位上？你构建的课堂流程是否很好预测？你是否是按设计规律来授课和安排课程的？用来衡量他们学习水平的问题是否也遵循类似的模式或风格？你的测评仅仅是以前测评的复制吗？"当我的问题完成解答时，我可以看到许多老师认罪似的蔫在座位上。同时，年轻的老师们开始坐得更高，好像松了一口气似的，因为他们意识到经验丰富的老师们也像他们一样在无聊的课堂里苦苦挣扎。两者之间的区别在于，年轻的老师渴望适应和修改他们的教学方法，而经验丰富的老师则意识到，摆脱常规的束缚需要进行大量的工作。我发现新老师比有经验的老师更渴望摆脱常规。

I have met many talented and experienced teachers in my trainings throughout China. I can see their level of discomfort when I reveal that students find "**the routine to be boring**." I ask them, "Do your students enter your class with reasonable assurance that they will sit in the same seats each day? Do you structure your class procedures with great predictability? Are your lessons delivered and framed with regularity of design? Do the questions asked to gauge their learning follow a similar pattern or style? Are your assessments mere clones of the previous?" As I finish the line of questions, I can see many teachers sheepishly slouch in their seats in an admission of guilt.

At the same time, young teachers begin to sit up taller in their seats, seemingly relieved because they realize experienced teachers struggle with a boring classroom just like they do. The difference between the two is that the younger teachers are anxious to adapt and modify their teaching methodology, whereas the experienced teachers realize the amount of work needed to steer out of the routine rut is significant. I find new teachers more eager to steer out of the rut routine than experienced teachers.

我真诚地分享了我在常规教学中的挣扎。我大方地承认我曾经在"自动驾驶模式"上惯性滑行／上课。在有些时候,这是由于我的懒惰,而其他情况则是由于缺乏经验。青年教师只需要经验,而经验丰富的教师则需要找到动力来诚心地寻求变革。对他们来说,惯例似乎已经成为一种生活方式,摆脱惯例所需的努力比留在惯例中要困难得多。人们正是由于这两个非常不同的原因而留在了相同的常规惯例中。

I share, honestly, about my struggle teaching in the rut routine. I freely admit that I had times of coasting on autopilot. In some of those times, it was because I was lazy, while other instances were from lack of experience. Young teachers simply need experience, whereas experienced teachers need to find the motivation to launch a sincere effort to change. For them, the rut routine seems to have become a lifestyle, because the effort required to get out of the rut is harder than staying in it. These are two very different reasons for being in the same routine rut.

努力创造富有参与性的课堂体验
Strive to Create an Engaged Classroom Experience

"参与"这个词一直吸引着我。在美国文化中,当一对恋爱中的年轻夫妇决定准备好结婚时,他们就会"订婚"(译者注:英文中"参与"与"订婚"是同一个词)。从文化上讲,这时男子要给未婚妻戴上戒指,表示她已经有主了。戒指是一种视觉标志，显示出他们之间的关系与寻常人相比处于不同的水平。我想表明两者的相似之处是，真正的学生参与意味着老师和学生之间的教学处于与别人不同的水平。参与意味着老师不仅负责传授考试所需的知识，更意味着就相关材料进行更高程度的互动。

The word ENGAGEMENT is something that has always appealed to me. In the United States culture, when a young couple in love decides they are ready to commit to marriage, they "get engaged." The culturally common practice is for the man to present his fiancé with a ring, signifying that she is now taken. The ring is a visual display that the relationship they have is at a different level as compared to anyone else with whom they may be seen. The parallel I want to establish is that authentic student engagement signifies a different level of learning between teacher and student. Instead of the teacher being solely and simply responsible for communicating knowledge needed for test results, engagement implies a higher level of interaction with the material.

现代教学法鼓励老师谨慎地结合针对学习而进行的测评和为了学习而进行的测评。有些测评关注知识习得，而其他测评则着眼于提升知识水平。参与式课堂是教师设计方向（活动）的方式之一，可以达到广泛的学习风格，并同时训练硬性和软性（影响）技能。参与式学习是指学生对学习负有主动权甚至承担相应责任。当学生参与课堂时，他们不仅非常活跃、高度参与，而且彼此之间也在互相学习。

Modern pedagogy practice encourages teachers to use a careful blend of assessment OF learning and assessment FOR learning. Some assessments assess knowledge gained where other assessments are given to increase the knowledge. An engaged classroom is one where the teacher is designing the direction (activities) that reach a broad spectrum of learning styles, as well as training both hard and soft (impact) skills. Engaged learning is when the student has some ownership and even responsibility for learning. When students are engaged, they are not only highly active and involved, but they are also teaching each other.

我希望避免让教室陷入无聊，这也促使我有能力找到其他方法来吸引或重新吸引我的学生。为此，我使用简单的游戏来打破常规，并保持课堂环境的活跃和新鲜。我注意到，即使只这样做3到4分钟也足以加快学生大脑血液流动并重新吸引他们的注意力和脑力。对于那些触觉学习者来说，连续坐8分钟太久了（我当学生的时候也是一样），我发现他们通过活动，重新投入了学习状态，并激发了他们的兴趣和好奇心。当然，稍微偏了一会儿题，但我认为这是宝贵的过渡时间，从长远来看，这为我提供了更富有成效的教学时间。我相信这项的投资是值得的。

My personal desire to avoid having a boring classroom also empowered me to find other ways to engage or re-engage my students. To do so, I used simple games to break up the routine and to keep the environment active and fresh. I noticed that even doing this for 3-4 minutes was enough to get the blood flowing and re-engage both their focus and their brains. For those tactile learners for whom sitting more than 8 minutes was too long (like I was as a student), I found they re-engaged and reinvigorated their interest and curiosity. Sure, it took a little bit of time away from instruction, but I looked at it as valuable transitional time, which provided me with more productive instructional time in the long run. I believe it was an investment well spent.

老师如何摆脱常规？
How Can a Teacher Get Out of the Routine Rut?

变革需要建立新的健康模式。你不能继续做导致你陷入习惯性的例行教学中的事情。你是否曾经看过讲述某人戏剧化的减肥历程的电视节目呢？减去400磅用不着的脂肪并不是短期内就能轻松完成的任务。其间的转变是精神和身体两方面的，需要耗费时间和精力。实际上，如果没有正确的精神状态，想要的身体转变将不会如愿发生。减重的工作实际上比增重还要多。如果一个人不对自己进行重大改变，那么他想要的改变就不会发生。

Change requires the establishment of new healthy patterns. You cannot continue to do the things that led you to teach in a rut routine. Did you ever watch television shows highlighting an individual's dramatic weight loss journey? Losing 400 pounds of unneeded body fat is no quick fix or easy task. The transformation is mental and physical, and it takes time and commitment. In fact, if the mental attitude is not properly fixed, the physical transformation desired will not follow. The work to lose the weight is substantially more effort than it was to add it on. A change cannot occur if the person does not make drastic changes.

改变生活方式。一个人为了实现向所需的结果的完全转变（你的目的地），必须破坏既定的模式。要改变既定模式，只能通过引入能够养成良好习惯的新习惯（方向）来实现。如果你在常规的模式中开展教学，请了解当前状况以及把你引入该状况的模式。这谁都怨不了，只能怨你自己。要认识到是你任由不健康的模式发展，才最终导致了当前的结果。产生新结果的承诺将要求进行转型变革，包括建立全新的、仅由你的行动支持的健康模式。改变需要由你自身做起。 要下定决心，以便在思维上创建新模式。

Changing lifestyle patterns. For a person to achieve a total transformation for the desired results (your destination), established patterns must be disrupted. Patterns can only be changed by the introduction of new habits (direction) that lead to healthy routines. If you are teaching in a rut routine, take ownership of the current condition and the patterns that got you there. It is nobody's fault but your own. Recognize that you allowed unhealthy patterns to develop that produced the current results. The commitment to producing new results is going to require a transformational change involving establishing new, healthy patterns supported only by your actions. You need to be the change. Get your mind set so that you mentally create new patterns.

原谅你自己。我发现原谅他人比原谅自己要容易得多。承认是你放任自己的模式导致了当前的结果。不要再责怪"体制"、学生、行政部门、教育局、个人情况...结果源自你自己所做的选择。承认这一点，然后找到一种原谅自己的方法吧。经过这个过程，你可以获得解放并大声说："我原谅自己的懒惰模式。"

Forgive yourself. I personally find it easier to forgive others faster than I can forgive myself. Recognize that the patterns you have allowed have produced the current results. Stop blaming the "system," the students, the administration, the education bureau, personal circumstances, etc. The results are based on choices you made. Own up to it and find a way to forgive yourself. The process can be liberating and empowering to say out loud, "I forgive myself for my lazy patterns."

制定一个计划。有句话说得好："人们并不计划失败。他们失败源于没有计划划！"有一点很容易理解，那就是你所追寻的目的地需要明确的方向指引。如果要到达任何地方，你不仅必须将终点位置可视化，而且还必须识别出沿途需要转弯的地方。在制定完善的教学计划之前，要先制定一个自我改进的计划。找出不良习惯（写下来），然后列出能使你摆脱不良习惯的新习惯（也写下来）。执行此过程中，你将拥有一份书面记录，以帮助你衡量自己的成长并提升你的责任感。你的教学改进应遵循相同的计划。写下使你陷入困境的不良习惯，并写下新的方向，以引导你到达新的理想目的地。

Make a Plan. There is a great saying, "People don't plan to fail. They fail to plan!" It is simple enough to understand that the destination you seek requires clear direction. If you want to get anywhere, you must not only visualize where you want to end up, but also be able to identify the necessary turns to make along the way. Make a self-improvement plan before making an improved teaching plan. Identify the bad habits (write them down) and then list the new habits that will get you out of it (write them down as well). When you do this, you will have a written record to help you measure your growth and provide you with some accountability. Your teaching improvement plan should follow the same plan. Write down the poor habits that got you in the rut, and write down the new directions that will lead you to reach your new and desired destination.

责任。 "一个人力量太小，不足以实现卓越。" （约翰. 伍登）没有人可以独自改变世界。进行持久改变需要一些帮助和责任感。有效的问责可以通过愿意成为问责伙伴的导师形式出现。导师可以在需要时提供指导、肯定和建设性的批评。你的问责伙伴务必仔细选择。通常，朋友或配偶不是最好的选择，因为他们离你太亲近了，并且只会给你鼓劲，而不是向你提出挑战。你的导师不能是只微笑并同意你所说或所做的一切的橡皮图章。只有选择了合适的导师，你才会有机会。 选择错误的导师将保证你的失败。

Accountability. "One is too small a number to achieve greatness."(John Wooden) No one person changed the world on his/her own. Making lasting changes requires some assistance and accountability. Effective accountability can come in the form of a mentor who is willing to be an accountability partner. Mentors can provide guidance, affirmation, and constructive criticism when needed. Your accountability partner needs to be carefully chosen. Usually a friend or spouse is not the best choice because they are too close to you and will simply enable you, as opposed to challenge you. Your mentor cannot be a rubber stamper who only smiles and agrees with everything you say or do. Pick the right mentor and you have a chance. Pick the wrong mentor and you guarantee your failure.

可衡量的目标。如果人们认为一项任务太艰巨，许多人会选择回避而不是冒险失败。如果你设定了不切实际且无法衡量的目标，那么你每次都会失败。把你想要达到的目标写下来。合适的导师可以帮你开始挑战和修正目标，但前期工作必须你自己来做。有些人认为养成新习惯需要 21 天。我不相信这个说法，但我确实认为练习和制定按时间衡量的目标时，3 周是合理的时间。将它们分成这样的时间长度可以让人有足够的时间来关注结果，同时又没有太多的时间可以忽略目标。此外，限定时间范围可以使你的思考和评估保持清醒状态。

Measurable Targets. If humans think a task is too hard, many will opt for avoidance rather than risk the possibility of failure. If you set unrealistic and immeasurable targets, you will succeed in failing every time. Write down goals and targets you want to reach. The right mentor can help challenge and revise your goals, but you must do the initial work. Some believe it takes 21 days to establish a new habit. I am not convinced that is true, but I do think 3 weeks is a reasonable length of time to practice and develop time-measured goals. Breaking them into this length of time allows for enough time to pass to notice results, but not so much time to lose sight of your goals. Plus, limiting your time frame allows you to keep your reflections and assessments fresh.

面对风险——不采取行动不是风险。它是另一个坏习惯。有些人因为害怕失败而不采取行动。你必须认识到不作为的风险比失败的风险要大得多，并且会打败自我。最初，一个新的课堂活动可能会失败，但是你至少要承担这个风险。不要因为担心失败而害怕风险。相反，你要怕的应该是连失败的机会都没有抓住过。通过失败，我们在分析结果时，将学到宝贵的经验和知识。将你的计划付诸实践是有风险的，但保持例行程序也是有风险的。通过练习，对风险的适应将变得越来越容易。

Face the Risk - Inaction is not a risk. It's another bad habit. Some people do not act because they fear failure. You must feel that the risk of inaction is far greater and self-defeating than the risk of falling short. A new classroom activity may fail, initially, but at least you took the risk. Do not fear the risk because you fear failure. Rather, fear never having taken the opportunity to fail. Through failure, we learn valuable lessons and knowledge when we analyze the results. Putting your plan into action is risky, but so too is continuing in the rut routine. Adjusting to the feeling of risk becomes easier with practice.

在设计方面进行协作——如果你想成为最好的房地产开发商，那就不要试图向其他行业的人学习房地产知识。相反，要做到最好，找到在自己领域内被公认为最好的人，并请求与他们会面，以便请他们给你提些建议。同样，如果想要成为最好的老师，你可以去找最伟大、最受尊敬的老师，并邀请他们共进午餐。告诉他们你正在制定一个改变自己教学习惯的新计划，并且希望他们帮助你弄清楚使他们成为伟大老师的原因。（如果你这样说，午餐甚至可能会由他们买单！）你和什么样的人来往，就会成为什么样的人。想致富吗？那就与有钱人来往。想破产，那就和破产的人来往。想成为一名出色的老师？那就与出色的老师来往吧，这样你就可以目睹他们的工作。请求他们让你看能提高学生参与度的课程计划。问他们哪些活动在学生中很受欢迎？询问他们的学业测评，针对学习的测评和为了学习而进行的测评都要。询问他们是否愿意在项目上与你合作，以便你可以向他们学习。直击他们的自我是获得他们知识的一种好方法。关键是与你尊敬的人合作，以帮助你改进教学模式。

Collaborate on the design - If you want to be the best real-estate developer, you do not try to learn about real estate from someone in a different industry. Instead, to be the best, find people who are considered to be the best in their field and ask them to meet with you so you can ask their advice. Likewise, to become the best teacher, find the best and most respected GREAT teacher you can and offer to take them to lunch. Tell them you are making a new plan for changing your teaching habits, and you want their help in discovering what has made them a great teacher. (If you say it that way, they will probably even pick up the lunch tab!) You become like those you hang around. Want to be rich? Hang out with the rich. Want to be broke, hang out with those who are broke. Want to be a great teacher? Hang out with the great teachers so you can see what they do. Ask to see lesson plans that produce high student engagement. Ask them what activities they find popular among the students? Ask about their assessments, both FOR and OF learning. Ask them if they would be willing to collaborate with you on a project so that you can learn from them. A stroke of the ego is a great way to gain access to their knowledge. The key here is to collaborate with someone you respect in order to help produce improved patterns in your teaching.

绘制结果图表。 在教学（或生活）中尝试新的具有挑战性的方向后，请绘制结果图表。你可以将其作为日记来完成，也可以仅作为私人成长图来完成，但是稍后进行反思是颇有价值的。拿出你几个月或几年前写的东西，就可以对成长有健康的看法。无论你是回顾新课程还是方向性活动，该过程都极具价值。无论是每周一次还是每两周一次都可以，最重要的是确保持续书面成长记录。快速回顾可以揭示新的模式，或者让你发现旧习惯的死灰复燃。绘制结果图表可以成倍地提高你的成功率。

Chart Your Results. After you try new and challenging directions in your teaching (or life), chart your results. You may accomplish this as a diary or simply as a private growth chart, but it is valuable to reflect on it later. Pulling out something you have written months or years earlier provides healthy perspective on growth. Whether you review each new lesson or directional activity you try, the process is valuable. Whether you do it on a weekly or bi-weekly basis isn't as important as making sure you keep a written record of your growth. A quick look back can reveal the new patterns or allow you to spot old habits resurfacing. Charting the results increases your success rate exponentially.

总结
Summary

当你思考"我的课堂很无聊吗？"这个问题时，请对自己保持诚实，如实回答。我不认为有谁一开始就想让自己的课程无聊。没有歌手／作曲家一开始就打算写一首糟糕的歌。没有任何领导者希望自己效率低下。没有任何运动员把最后一名作为目标。我们可能不会以无聊为出发点，但是，很可能我们所有人都有无聊的时候，虽然自己不愿承认，很大程度上那是已经存在的不良习惯导致的。

When you contemplate the original question, "Is my classroom boring?", be honest with yourself and answer the question truthfully. I really do not think anyone sets out to be boring. No singer/songwriter sets out to write a bad song. No leader wants to be ineffective. No athlete sets a goal to come in last. We may not set out with the intention of being boring but, it is possible that we all move in and out of being boring more than we care to admit, largely because of pre-existing bad habits.

你可能已经知道问题的答案。你可以根据学生的反应来衡量自己的课程是否无聊。如果他们看起来并没融入课堂或者看起来很无聊，那么答案已经显而易见。如果你不确定自己的课堂是否无聊，那么请对学生进行调查，无须为此感到羞耻。诚实和反思的自我检查是一项宝贵而有价值的任务。

There is a chance you already know the answer to the question. You can gauge whether you are boring by the reaction of your students. If they appear disengaged or look like they are bored, then the answer is obvious. There is no shame in taking a survey of students if you seem to be unsure whether or not your classroom is a boring place to be. Honest and reflective self-examination is a valuable and worthwhile task.

如果你在教学中陷入了"例行公事"的模式，那就必须决定是保持现状还是勇敢前进。与养成"惯例"比起来，挣脱"惯例"需要付出更多的工作。要下决心认识到，要对既定的习惯和模式进行彻底的改变，因为它们完全不利于打造一个令人兴奋的课堂。你将需要制定改善计划。可以从原谅自己开始。然后，列出不健康的习惯，并愿意冒险尝试新事物。寻求导师与你合作并帮助你设定可衡量的目标。绘制结果和进度图表，以便你可以看到自己在该过程中的成长和奋斗。这都需要付出努力。如果你付出了必要的努力和奉献，结果自然会到来。当你挣脱常规时，你终将能够用一个明确的"不是！"来回答最初的问题"我的课堂很无聊吗？"。

If you have slipped into the rut routine in your teaching, you must decide whether you want to remain in the rut or steer out of it. Getting out is going to be more work than it took to get into the rut. Set your mind to the realization that steering out will require a drastic change in the established habits and patterns that were not conducive to the creation of a stimulating classroom. You will need to make a plan to change. Begin by forgiving yourself. Then, list the unhealthy habits and be willing to take more risks to try new things. Seek out a mentor to collaborate with and to help you set measurable goals. Chart your results and progress so you can see the growth and struggle of the process. It will require hard work. But if you put in the necessary hard work and dedication, the results will emerge. When you steer out of the rut routine, you will emphatically be able to answer the initial question, "Is my classroom boring?", with an emphatic "NO!"

动机的魔力
The Magic of Motivation

Image credit: Forbes

我发现人们对年底的反应是对人类行为的非常有趣的心理学研究课题。在美国，我们在 11 月的最后一个星期四庆祝感恩节。假期的传统包括一顿丰盛的家庭聚餐（"宴席"这个词要准确得多），这含有大量的卡路里。实际上，仅此一餐，美国成年人平均就摄入了超过 3,000 卡路里的热量！加上几片山核桃或南瓜派，一顿饭可以将其增加到 4,000 卡路里。如果还不够的话，感恩节就预示着"节假日美食季"的开始，该季节将持续 4 周，直到新年前夜来临。

I find people's reactions to the end of the calendar year to be a very interesting psychological field study of human behavior. In the United States, we celebrate Thanksgiving on the last Thursday in November. The holiday tradition includes a large family meal (the term feast is far more accurate) that has a ridiculous number of calories attached to it. In fact, the average American adult consumes in excess of 3,000 calories on that one meal alone! Add a few slices of pecan or pumpkin pie and one can push that to 4,000 calories in one single meal. If that weren't bad enough, Thanksgiving signals the start of the "holiday eating season" that will last for the next 4 weeks leading up to New

Year's Eve.

在这个假期里，将有无数的家庭和工作派对，人们会吃得更多，以至于到最后，你觉得自己别说吃，就是看食物都不想看了！然后，新年来临，就像宿醉一样，美国人开始清醒地思考个人的健康习惯。他们突然试图恢复镇定，并不可避免地宣称自己想要恢复健康！对新目标的大胆宣言就是所谓的"新年决心"。由于之前4周大吃特吃，在身体上留下了多余的脂肪，因此大多数人的决心都是将身体重新塑造成原来的样子，甚至想比以前的身材更好。这些决心会导致健身房会员人数激增，因为节假日后减肥已成为大家痴迷的新潮流。这些决心大多数都不能实现，到了2月底就更不用说了，因为人内心的动机消失的速度比假日大餐所吃的最后一块馅饼要快。

During this holiday season, there will be countless family and work parties that involve more eating, to the point you almost never want to see or eat food again! Then, as soon as the New Year kicks in, like a bad hangover, Americans start to sober up regarding personal health habits. They suddenly try to regain composure and inevitably proclaim they want to get back into shape! This bold proclamation of a new goal is what we call a New Year's Resolution. Because the previous 4-week feeding frenzy has left unwanted fat all over the body, most of these resolutions are about sculpting the body back into what it once was, or even making it better than ever before. These resolutions cause a significant spike in gym memberships, as losing the holiday weight becomes the new personal obsession. Most of these resolutions fail to make it to fruition, let alone the end of February, as the internal motivation needed soon vanishes faster than the last piece of pie eaten at the holiday meal.

许多人起初是有动力的，但很少有人能够有自律的精神去坚持实现真实而持久的改变。为什么有些人可以下定一个新年决心并最终实现，而另一些下了相同决心的人却惨败收场？一些人的动力比其他人强吗？导致变化的动机是对人类行为的有趣研究。有些人可以设定目标，然后通过必要的步骤来采取行动，而其他人则做不到。理解这背后的原因可能有助于我们更好地了解学生的课堂表现。

Many people start out motivated, but few sustain the discipline needed to effectuate true and lasting change. Why is it that some people can make a New Year's resolution and follow it through to fulfillment, but others, who may start out with the same objective, fail miserably? Do some people have better motivation than others? Motivation that results in change is an interesting study in human behavior. Some individuals can set a goal and then take the necessary steps to follow it through with action, but others cannot. Understanding why this is true may help us understand our students' classroom performance better.

我不认为动机中有什么"魔法"。动机不是要喝下的魔力药水，也不是发生在某些人身上却不发生在其他人身上的奇迹。请任何人解释他们的自我动机，我保证你听到的回答不会包含"魔法"或"奇迹"这样的字眼。典型的答案可能包括诸如自律、问责、决心、毅力、专注之类的词语。所有这些词语被视为确保维持动力所需采取的绝佳指标。是什么使某些人能够维持动力而其他人却惨败收场？回答这个问题需要更多的自省。

I do not believe there is "magic" in motivation. Motivation is not a magical potion to be consumed or a miraculous occurrence that happens to some, but not to others. Ask anyone to explain their self-motivation and I guarantee responses will not include the word "magic" or "miracle". Typical answers are likely to include words such as: self-discipline, accountability, determination, perseverance, focus, or others. All these words would be considered excellent indicators of what it takes to ensure that motivation is maintained. What makes some able to sustain motivation while others fail miserably? Answering that question requires a bit more philosophical self-examination.

像许多人一样，我发现动机的起源有内在的和外在的。确定成功是内在力量还是外在力量导致的结果并非易事。实际上，起初似乎是清晰的，内在的动机可能是由不那么明显的外部因素所推动的。作为老师和父母，我们将外在动机应用于学生和孩子，并认为我们正在帮助他们将其转化为内在动机。在某些情况下可能会发生这种情况，但我们自认为激发内在动机的努力可能只是在灌输对失败的恐惧而已。

Like many, I see the origins of motivation coming from intrinsic and extrinsic sources. Determining if success is the result of intrinsic or extrinsic forces is not a simple task. What may have started out as clear, intrinsic motivation may have, in fact, been fueled more by less obvious external factors. As teachers and parents, we apply extrinsic motivation on our students and children, thinking we are helping them channel that into intrinsic motivation. That may happen in some cases, but it is likely that our effort to inspire intrinsic motivation simply instills fear of failure.

我最近问了一位年轻的中国大学生，是什么促使她保持自己忙碌的日程。除了成为全日制医学生之外，她还想办法打工。她说："我做服务生赚钱，以便继续接受大学教育，成为儿科医生。"通过询问，我发现她至少还要学习六年，并且还需要花很多钱才能实现自己的目标。我问她，当目的地距离遥远时，她如何让自己聚焦于最终的目标。她回答说："因为这就是我选择的人生。"

I recently asked a young Chinese university student what motivates her to keep the very hectic schedule she endures. In addition to her being a full-time medical student, she is also managing to work a job. She said, "I work as a waitress to earn money, so I can continue my university education to become a pediatric doctor." Through questioning, I found out she has at least 6 more years of study and a lot of money yet to spend in order to reach her goal. I asked her how she keeps the end-goal in focus, when the destination is so far off in the distance. She replied, "Because it is what I have chosen to do with my life."

我想知道她是否能够维持必要的动力，以支撑这漫长而艰难的求索之路，最终实现目标。她的动机中有多少是内在的，外在的又有多少？我知道她为了实现这个梦想而肩负着家庭的重担。她还有两对祖父母和一对辛劳的父母，他们付出大量财力以确保实现自己的人生目标。我想知道这种外在动机是否比她想要做儿科医生的个人目标更能激发她的奋斗。她害怕失败吗？如果她不能让家人感到自豪怎么办？如果她失败了，那么他们投入在她身上的所有时间和金钱都会付诸东流！我遇到过很多像她一样的学生。可悲的是，我遇到的许多人都还在上初中和高中，所以他们还要承受很多年的压力。外部动机并不总是能激发内部动机。

I left wondering if she can sustain the required motivation to stay the long and difficult course towards achieving her goal. How much of her motivation was internal, and how much was external? I know she was bearing the heavy weight of family expectations to fulfill this dream. She also had 2 sets of grandparents and 1 set of hard-working parents directing lots of financial resources to ensure she accomplishes her goal. I wondered if this external motivation fueled her more than her personal goal of wanting to do the work of a pediatric doctor. Did she fear failure? What if she cannot make her family proud? If she fails, then all the time and money they poured into her would be lost! I have met many students just like her. Sadly, many I meet are in middle school and high school, so they still have many more years of this pressure yet to endure. External motivation does not always inspire internal motivation.

在最近的一些阅读中，我遇到了这样的说法："思想产生感觉，感觉导致行动，而行为带来结果。"我认为，这是维持个人动机、实现既定目标的秘诀。在采取行动并取得成果之前，我们需要深刻地感受。感觉—行动—结果。那些认为自己选择的饮食习惯和生活方式导致不必要增重的人，在采取行动之前，要先有需要改变的感觉。当然，人们只有在努力工作和改变生活方式后才能获得结果。首先必须深刻地意识到需要改变。内部和外部动机会影响这些感觉，但是如果人们没有需要改变的感觉，这种动机就注定不会持久。

In some recent reading, I came across the statement that "thoughts lead to feelings, feelings lead to action, and actions lead to results." I think, herein lies the recipe for being able to sustain the personal motivation to accomplish set goals. We need to have deep feelings impacted before action can be taken and results can be achieved. Feelings-Actions-Results. The individual who feels their eating habits and lifestyle choices are leading to unwanted weight gain would need to FEEL that change is needed before ACTION can be taken. Certainly, RESULTS can only be obtained after the hard work and lifestyle changes are implemented. One must first FEEL deeply that change is needed. Internal and external motivation can impact those feelings, but without the individual feeling that change is needed, the motivation will not be sustained.

我在教育中注意到的一个巨大危险，学生对学习的热爱被成功的"动力"压得喘不过气。当我采访学生为什么喜欢或不喜欢学校时，他们的不喜欢很少与"工作"相关，而通常与成功之类的"压力"有关。这种动机不是来自内心（内部），而是来自外部。许多学生感到学习不愉快，因为他们试图满足他人对其学业表现的期望。获得某些结果的压力成为了焦点，而不是真实、好奇或参与性学习。在最近的一项研究中，74％的5年级学生感到他们参与了自己的学习过程。可悲的是，只有32％的11年级学生回答说他们参与了自己的学习过程。学校（和父母）是否应该激发孩子们的好奇心和对学习的热爱，使他们感到对学习的参与呢？初中和高中学生参与度的下降应该是令人震惊的，并且应该警示人们注意到整个教育体系的变化，而不仅仅是低质量的教学或表现欠佳的学生。我认为问题出在学生为了的高分而感到压力，这个动机是不对的。

One great danger I see in education is when the love of learning in the student is suffocated by the imposed "motivation" to succeed. When I interview students about why they like or dislike school, their dislike is rarely related to "the work" and more often linked to the "pressure" felt to succeed. This motivation is NOT coming from within (internal), but rather from external sources. Many students do not FEEL learning is enjoyable because they are trying to meet someone else's expectations for their educational performance. The pressure to achieve certain results becomes the focus, not authentic, curious, or engaged learning. In a recent study, 74% of 5th graders felt engaged in their learning. Sadly, only 32% of 11th graders responded that they are engaged in the learning process. Shouldn't schools (and parents) be inspiring children's curiosity and love of learning so that they feel engaged in learning? The decline in student engagement in middle and high schools should be alarming and indicative of something systemic to the overall educational process, not just poor-quality teaching or poorly performing students. I think the problem lies within the misaligned motivation of pressure students feel to score high marks.

错位的动机起初可能是无辜的，但由于成绩表现驱动的期望可能会使学生产生冷漠，因此它可能会适得其反。结果是缓慢而痛苦地扑灭了学生们的好奇心，让他们无法为了热爱学习而学习。在一个好心的老师都说他们想激励学生成就卓越的时代，许多人无意间参与了对梦想有条不紊的粉碎。我们突然之间发现，学生学习不再因为热爱，而是为了结果而学习。成绩成为学生的个人标识，而竞争成为激发学生努力的最有力的动力。加上父母对学生在高中"努力学习"的压力，以便将来上一所伟大的大学、获得一份高薪的工作、享受幸福的生活等。这样，曾经在早期学习过程中享受到的纯粹就被破坏性的外部压力所取代，这些压力消灭了真正的内在动力。

The misaligned motivation may start out innocent enough, but it can quickly backfire, as performance-driven expectations potentially create apathy in the student. The result is a slow and painful extinguishing of personal curiosity, making it impossible for the student to learn for the love of learning. In a time when well-meaning teachers all say they want to inspire their students to become something great, many inadvertently participate in the methodical crushing of dreams. Suddenly, learning is not for the love of it, but for the results of it. Grades become the personal student identifier, and competition emerges as the most powerful motivator to inspire student effort. That can be coupled with the parental pressure for students to "work hard" in high school, so they may attend a great university, get a good-paying job, enjoy a happy life, etc. With this, the pureness once enjoyed in the early learning process is replaced by damaging external pressures that kill true internal motivation.

我忘记了在高中时学到的很多东西，但是由于某种原因，我还记得几个比较奇怪的话题，它们在当时激发了我的好奇心。我记得十年级时的公民项目课程，我们在那个课程里学习了威廉一世。我似乎记得我们曾做过一些独立研究，关于威廉一世的历史或故事引起了我的兴趣。最终，我抱着极大的兴趣学习了这个课题，但对我的学习成绩却丝毫没有考虑。

I do not remember many things I learned in high school, but for some reason, I remember a couple of rather odd topics, which even back then, sparked my curiosity. I remember a 10th grade civics project where we studied Wilhelm I. I seem to recall that we did some independent study, and something about the history or story of Wilhelm piqued my interest. It ended up being a topic that I studied with great interest, but with little consideration about the grade I might receive for my learning.

在研究生院时，我参加了全班研究美国内战的项目，但是老师并为要求我们进行传统的（无聊的）研究，而是要求我们设计一个以内战为主题的虚拟乐园。不论出于何种原因，这都让我感到非常震惊，我深入研究了分配给我的两个主题：地下铁路和安德森维尔监狱。我对这些主题进行了深入的研究，以至于项目完成近十年后，我从教学工作中休假时，选择了驾车前往美国南部。你最好相信这次自由行的一个主要目的地便是在安德森维尔监狱。

In graduate school, I was part of a class-wide project to study the American Civil War, but instead of the traditional (boring) research, we were asked to design a fictitious Civil War-themed fun park. For whatever reason, that struck a chord with me, causing me to dive deeply into my 2 assigned topics: The Underground Railroad and Andersonville Prison. I dug so deeply into those topics that, nearly 10 years post project completion, I took a sabbatical from my teaching job and opted for a driving tour into the American south. You better believe one major destination on this self-directed tour was a stop at the site of Andersonville Prison.

老师是如何向我介绍这两个主题，并激发我的内在动力，在它们上进行了比其他课题更深入的探究呢？我没有只是为了获得好成绩而进行深入研究。我发现了一些有趣的东西，所以我学它完全就是因为这对我来说很有趣。这便是内在的动力。

What was it about the way the teacher presented these 2 topics to me that inspired my intrinsic motivation to explore deeper than other topics? I did not dig deeply because I wanted a good grade. I found something so interesting that I learned it because it was interesting to me. That is intrinsic motivation.

我并不认为老师在项目介绍中做了任何独特或有创意的事情，但确实有些"魔发配料"使我对学习产生了好奇。它始于一种兴趣。这种感觉驱使我好奇地学习更多，并做出了有效的行动。我的行动导致了结果。动机来自于我学习的欲望，而不是成绩这一外在动力。这种感觉来自我内心，而不是来自成绩差的威胁。我最终学习并培养了一种兴趣，这种兴趣因我的感受而激起并得到了增强。这就是我动力的源泉。 教育者具有影响学生好奇心的巨大能量。如果成功，好奇心可以激发被称作动机的内部行动。

I do not think the teachers did anything unique or creative in their project presentation, but there was some "magic sauce" that spiked my curiosity to learn. It started with a feeling of interest. That feeling drove my curiosity to learn more and produced effective action on my part. My actions led to results. The motivation came from my desire to learn, not the external force of grades. The feeling came from within me, not from the threat of a bad grade. I ended up learning and nurturing an interest that was piqued and enhanced through my feelings. This was the source of my motivation. Educators have tremendous power to influence student curiosity. If successful, that curiosity can provide the internal action called motivation.

有一天，爱因斯坦 4 岁或 5 岁的时候，他不得不因病缺课。为了不被生病的爱因斯坦所困扰，他的父亲给他带来了一个指南针以分散他的注意力，后来回忆起此事时，他说这令他兴奋不已。爱因斯坦产生了浓厚的兴趣，想知道是什么魔力让指南针工作的。这魔力是指南针的显示吗？恐怕不是。真正的魔力是他的好奇心，只是这个物件揭开了他的好奇心而已。爱因斯坦对驱使这个物体工作的奥秘感到无比好奇。他后来写道，他内心深处隐藏着某种东西，迫使他去发现它起作用的原因。产生这种感觉的原因并不像引起和唤醒他的好奇心的感觉那么重要。一旦觉醒，这种感觉就会导致行动，从而带来结果。在这种情况下，爱因斯坦的真正内在动机已经被激发出来，并没有被任何学习测评压到窒息。

One day, when Albert Einstein was 4 or 5 years old, he had to stay home sick from school. So as not to be bothered by the sick child, his father brought Albert a compass to distract him, which he later recalled made him tremble with excitement. Einstein was magically taken into an overwhelming feeling of interest and connection with the hidden force that made the compass work. Was it the presentation of the compass? Probably not. The magic was his curiosity that was uncovered by the object itself. Einstein was curious as to the mystery behind what made that object work. He later wrote that there was something deeply hidden in him that compelled him to discover the reason why it worked. What created that feeling was not as important as the feeling that stirred and awakened his curiosity. Once awakened, the feeling led to action, which led to results. In this case, Einstein's true intrinsic motivation had been elicited, and not suffocated by any assessment of learning.

处理感觉绝非易事，它需要强大的情商来维持。识别、管理和控制我们的情绪需要内心强大。我们都经历过情绪的"低谷"和绝望的时刻。这些时刻使我们重新剥开自己情绪的洋葱皮，以找出我们所相信的，我们所感受到的和我们想要的事物的核心到底是什么。有时候你会想放弃，但是如果你深知并理解自己的感受，那么与低谷的情绪进行谈判也是可以忍受的。

Managing feelings is not at all easy or simplistic, and it requires strong emotional intelligence to sustain. To recognize, manage and control our emotions is not for the faint of heart. We all experience emotional "valleys" and times of despair. These times are trying, and they make us peal back the onion layers of our emotions to find out what is at the core of what we believe, how we feel, and what we want. There are going to be times you want to give up, but if you intimately know and understand your feelings, then negotiating the valley is bearable.

一个人注册成为健身房会员之后，并不愿意因为不想改变自己的身体而放弃锻炼。他们之所以放弃，是因为"失望低谷"和真正的身体转变所需的努力很难。他们不能让自己的感觉支配他们的行动。为了保持敏锐的情商，必须不断地监控和管理自己的情感。恢复体形所需的艰苦工作只是努力的一部分。这些最初会使我们感动的深刻感受，只是朝着目标迈出的一步而已，而非事情的全部。即使你遇到诸如艰苦挣扎、自我怀疑或恐惧之类的障碍，你也有能力战胜这些情绪并保持执着，这将决定你成功的广度。当你面对这些时刻的挑战时，管理你的情商至关重要，因为你的成功和整体效率就在于这一点。

A person does not sign up for a gym membership and then give up working out because they don't want to change their bodies. They give up because the "valley of disappointment" and effort needed for true body transformation is difficult. They fail to let their feeling dictate their actions. Feelings must be constantly monitored and managed in order to keep a sharp EQ (emotional quotient). The hard work necessary to get back into shape is only part of the endeavor. Those deep feelings, which may initially get us moving, are just one step toward the goal, not the whole journey. Your ability to channel those emotions and remain committed, even when you come up against obstacles like hard work, self-doubt or fear, will determine the breadth of your success. When you are challenged by these moments, managing your EQ is crucial because your success and overall effectiveness lie within.

彼得．伯格曼（2012年1月）在《哈佛评论》的一篇文章中指出："思想对于动机而言至关重要。"尽管头脑会激发动机，但头脑在后续过程中什么也不做了。后续行动结合的是毅力和决心。创造参与变革欲望的情感首先来自我们的思想。"渡过低谷"的决心来自我们的头脑，它表达着我们成功或失败的意愿。我们的学生正在设法弄清并管理他们对不符合外部期望产生的恐惧情绪。许多学生无法对自己的成功或失败产生连接。他们的情商很低，因为没有人教他们如何识别或管理自己的情商。他们只是被告知要"努力学习并做到最好，这样你才能拥有良好的工作和幸福的生活。"同时，那个学生看着这一信息的传达者（老师或父母），可能会问为什么这会使他／她感到高兴？"他们内部没有主动权或动机。只有好意而已，但外部压力可能会也可能不会产生结果，它们往往无法提升学生充分参与学习的好奇心。

In a Harvard Review article, Peter Bergman (January 2012) points out that "The mind is essential to motivation." Though the mind initiates motivation, the mind does nothing on the follow-through. The follow-through is an action that combines grit and determination. The feelings that create the desire to engage in change come first from our mind. The determination to "weather the valley" comes from our mind telling our will to succeed or fail. Our students are trying to figure out and manage their fear of not meeting external expectations. Many students have no connection to the feelings of their own success or failure. They have very low emotional intelligence because no one is teaching them how to recognize or manage their EQ. They are simply being told to "work hard, study hard, and be the best so you can have a good job and good life." Meanwhile, that student looks around at the message giver (teacher or parent) and may question why that would make him/her happy?" There is no ownership or motivation from within. There is just well meaning, but external, pressure that may or may not produce results, but often fails to increase a student's curiosity to engage fully in their learning.

教师必须尽可能地呼吁学习者并帮助他们管理和驾驭他们对成功和失败的情绪洪流，但他们也必须通过激发学生的好奇心来帮助他们充分参与学习。如果他们能够激发好奇心，那么学习的动机就会从学习者的内心生长。这将产生高度投入的学习者，因为他们会对学习的前景感到兴奋。这种兴奋将产生行动进而带来结果。因此，教师不是以学业等级或成绩为动机，而是以学习者的好奇心为动机。随着好奇心的增长，老师需要谨慎地帮助学生识别和处理情绪，毫无疑问，学生之间的打分和比较将是不可避免的事情。这也就是为什么从教师到学生的情商开发和管理是教师／导师角色中至关重要的部分的原因。

Teachers must appeal to the learner where they can to help them manage and navigate the flood of emotions they have about success and failure, but they must also help them engage fully in the learning by spiking their curiosity. If they can ignite the curiosity, the motivation to learn will grow from within the learner. This will produce a highly engaged learner because they will feel excited about the prospect of learning. This excitement will produce actions that lead to results. The teacher, therefore, is not using academic grades or results as the motivator, but rather the learner's curiosity. As the curiosity grows, the teacher needs to be mindful of helping the student identify and manage the emotions along the way because, undoubtedly, grading and student-to-student comparison are going to be inevitable. This is why the EQ development and management from the teacher to the student is such an important and critical part of the teacher/mentor role.

对于教师来说，一个好的起点是自己首先成为高情商的好榜样。认识、理解和管理自己的情绪，这样你才可以帮助他人认识、理解和管理他们的情绪。这就是影响力！情商低的老师不会影响学生的好奇心，他们也不知如何影响学习者的人生。这些老师只是简单地翻阅书本材料，以便学生们下次考试的时候用得上这些东西。这就延续了不明智"学习"的恶性循环。学习者没有参与度，也没有好奇心。这恰好迎合了记忆型的学习者。学生认为他在"学习"，但他却错过了教育的真正本质，教育的本质始于好奇心和内在动机，并以拥有完整的教育经历为满足的。

A good starting point for teachers is to first be a shining example of high EQ. Recognize, understand and manage your own emotions so that you can help others recognize, understand and manage their own emotions. That is influence! Teachers with low EQ do not impact student curiosity and have no idea how to influence the life of a learner. Those teachers simply plow through the material so the student can regurgitate information on another exam. This continues the vicious cycle of disingenuous "learning". There is no learner engagement and no curiosity spike. This just caters to the learner who happens to be a good memorizer. The student thinks he is "learning", but he is missing out on the true essence of education, which involves the pathway beginning with curiosity and intrinsic motivation, and ending with the fulfillment of having a complete educational experience.

总结
Summary

为什么有些人拥有坚持追求目标的动力，而有些人却没能实现相同的目标？真正的内在动力源于感觉。感觉会导致行动，进而带来结果。内在动机是最好的动机类型，因为有内在动机的人会感受到渴望，付出努力并创造结果。外部动机可以产生结果，但也附带损害，例如让人害怕失败和承受巨大压力。理想的情况下，为了获得最佳的学习效果，应激发学生的好奇心，然后让他们挑战自己，以便出于内在兴趣而不是为了成绩而学习。教师需要有多种测评方法，以确保他们教育并且全面影响学习者的风格，而不仅仅是让他们死记硬背。这是艰苦的工作，但学生的幸福和成功都取决于它。

Why do some people sustain their motivation towards a goal while others with the same goal fail to achieve? True internal motivation is born out of feelings. Feelings will lead to actions that produce results. Intrinsic motivation is the best type of motivation because the individual feels the desire, puts forth the effort and accepts the results. External motivation can produce results, but has collateral damage as well, such as fear of failure and intense pressure. Ideally, for optimal learning, a student's curiosity is piqued, and they then challenge themselves so learning is achieved from intrinsic interest and not grades earned. Teachers need to have multiple methods of assessment to ensure they are teaching and reaching all styles of learner, not just the memorizer. It is hard work, but the happiness and success of your students depend on it.

那么我们如何激励学生呢？首先要认识到他们的感觉会导致行动并

带来结果。这些感觉的来源必须来自每个学生内心。太多的人没有个人动机，只不过是善意的父母和老师给他们施加了义务和压力的动机。老师需要熟练地关心和教导学生如何管理他们自己的情商。帮助他们认识并表达自己的感受，以便他们可以更好地表达和管理它们。老师和校长必须帮助父母了解如何教育子女，以免给他们造成不必要的压力，这些压力会令学生的参与逐渐降低。如果我们想让学生参与学习并且感到快乐的话，我们必须帮助他们拥抱并认识他们自己的感受。 这将导致行动并带来结果。

So how can we motivate our students? Recognize that their feelings will lead to actions that produce results. The source of those feelings must come from within each student. Too many have no personal motivations, only the motivations of obligation and pressure put on them from well-meaning parents and teachers. Teachers need to be proficient at caring for and teaching students how to manage their EQ. Help them recognize and verbalize their feelings, so they can be better versed at expressing and managing them. Teachers and Headmasters must help parents understand how to support their children, so that unwanted pressures, which contribute to stress and suffocate true student engagement, are not placed upon them. If we want students to be engaged and happy learners, we must help them embrace and recognize their feelings. This will lead to actions and results.

- 彼得. 伯格曼，"你的问题不是动机"，《哈佛评论》，2012 年 1 月 4 日。
  Peter Bregman, "Your Problem Isn't Motivation", *Harvard Review*, January 4, 2012. (https://hbr.org/search?term=peter bregman)

勇气、胆量还是运气？
Grit, Guts or Luck?

Image credit: Tirzah Libert

勇气＝勇敢和决心；性格的力量
Grit = Courage and resolve; strength of character
胆量＝不屈不挠
Guts = Fortitude
运气＝幸运事件的发生几率
Luck =The chance happenings of fortunate events

　　我经常反思自己的人生，并思考其间的一些重要事件，情况、选择和发生过的事情，这些都有助于构成我的人生故事。我们每个人都有一个"故事"，请了解并欣赏它与你的身份的独特联系，这一点非常重要。你的人生故事是由塑造你生活的重要事件组成的。我意识到我的人生故事并不引人注目，但它是"我的"故事，并且由于它对我来说是独一无二的，所以我常常想知道我是如何走到这一步的？我绝不是在暗示我已经成功了，或者说我有什么特别之处，但是我的确有一些很棒的人生经历，它们帮助我成为了如今的我。实际上，它们是定义和促使我成为我的一些事件。由于我将要讨论"成功"的概念，因此，我首先将其定义为：*最大限度地发挥才能、技能、努力、奋斗和环境，以取得令个人满意、愉悦和满足的结果。*

I often reflect on my life and consider significant events, circumstances, choices, and happenings that help make up my story. Each of us has a "story" and it is important to know and appreciate it for being uniquely connected to who you are. Your story is composed of the contributing events that shape your life. I realize my story is not spectacular, but it is "my" story and since it is unique to me, I often wonder how it is that I got here? I am in no way suggesting that I have "made it", or that I am anything special, but I have had some great life experiences that have all helped shape me into the person I have become. These are, in fact, defining and contributing events that made me who I am. Since I am going to be discussing the concept of "success", let me first lay out my definition as: *maximizing one's talents, skills, hard work, efforts, and circumstances to achieve results that, in combination, bring personal satisfaction, pleasure and contentment.*

在去旅行或开始新的工作项目之前，我曾多次听到朋友或祝愿者的"祝你好运"一词。在这种情况下，"祝你好运"一词既常见又适当。我知道他们是一番好意，但我也会喜欢听到这样的话："愿你的辛勤工作带给你想要的结果。"或"继续完全按照自己的意愿做，你会做得很棒的。"但是，当人们说"祝你好运"时，几乎就好像在暗示成功或失败是取决于随机几率的，并且成功和失败对技能的依赖程度还不如对偶然性的依赖程度。运气对个人取得成功能起到多大的作用呢？

Many times, I have heard the words, "good luck" from friends, or well-wishers, before I leave for a trip or start a new work project. The words "good luck" are both common and appropriate in situations like these. I know they mean well, but I would also enjoy hearing phrases such as: "May your hard work produce the results you want." or, "Continue to do exactly what you have been doing and you will be great." But, when people say, "good luck", it is almost as if they are implying that the only chance of success or failure rests on a random set of circumstances and, that success and failure are less dependent upon skill than upon happenstance. How much of a role does luck play on an individual achieving success?

作为一个喜欢看体育比赛的人，我在体育运动中见过很多好运的例子。例如，让我们想象一位篮球运动员，他在 84 英尺外绝望地投篮，只有篮球完美入网他们才能赢得比赛。那个球员可能练了 84 次，一次都没成功。在这种情况下，完美的轨迹和距离产生了幸运的结果。我曾在一个足球场上见识过运气，一个球员失了球（所谓的笨手笨脚），而那个长椭球形（所谓的橄榄球）由于其几何形状而开始随机弹跳。一番弹跳之后球恰好完美地飞入了一名防守球员的怀抱，后者将其接达得分。运气体现在哪里？ 那个球员以正确的角度和速度靠近球，干净利落地接住球，然后带球奔跑，这当然离不开技巧，但是"反弹的运气"与人的努力、技巧或计划都没有关系。当你玩的彩票游戏从 100 个乒乓球中吸出 6 个，上面印有随机数字时，也会发生同样的运气。幸运的是，你恰好就选了那六个获奖的数字。 随机抽取数字球的过程没有任何技巧可言。有人可能会争辩说，选出获奖数字也没有什么技巧可言。如果体育赛事和彩票中有运气，那是否意味着人生中也有运气呢？

As one who enjoys watching sports, I have seen many examples of luck in athletics. For example, consider the basketball player who heaves a desperation shot from 84 feet away, only to have it swish in the net perfectly to win the game. That player can practice that shot 84 times and never make it once. On this occasion, the perfect trajectory and distance produced lucky results. I have seen luck on a football field when one player drops the ball (called a fumble) and the *prolate spheroid* (a.k.a football) begins to bounce randomly because of its geometrical shape. One of these bounces happens to elevate perfectly into the arms of a pursuing defensive player who runs it in for a touchdown (score). Where is the luck here? Having that player take the correct angle and speed towards the ball, grasping it cleanly and then running with it certainly has skill involved, but the "luck of the bounce" had nothing to do with human effort, skill, or planning. The same sample of luck occurs when the lottery game you are playing sucks up 6 out of 100 ping pong balls with random numbers printed on them. As luck would have it, these are the same exact 6 numbers you chose for the win. There was no skill in the random draft of the balls. Some may argue there wasn't any human skill in even picking the winning numbers. If there is luck in sports and in the lottery, does that mean there is also luck in life?

作为一个有信仰的人，我不确定我是否相信运气。但我觉得，许多并非我应得的事情，也不在我计划之内的事情，可能发生在我身上。作为这些事件的接受者，我感到非常幸运并且心存感激。但是事实上，很多时候我们都将运气归因于一种情况，那就是我们已经付出了真诚的努力和练习，减轻了失败的可能性。实际上，我们所投入的练习和计划让我们值得好的结果。成功或失败取决于心态。

As a person of faith, I am not sure I believe in luck. But I feel that many undeserved things may happen to me that I did not earn or otherwise plan. As the recipient in these times, I feel quite lucky and grateful. However, there are many times we attribute luck to a situation when, in fact, we have put sincere effort and rehearsal into mitigating the possibilities of failure. The practice and planning invested has in fact earned a result. Success or failure depends on a mindset perspective.

我到中国旅行已经十多年了。我的第一次中国之行仅仅是为了拜访几个把孩子送到我夏令营的家庭。从那时开始，人们把我介绍了出去。我继续回到中国，结识更多的人，扩大人脉，这些年来，我很幸运地造访了 10 个不同省份的 100 多个城市。我不再为自己的夏令营做宣传，但是我的业务已经扩展到了教育咨询、演讲嘉宾和教师培训。我是否要将这种业务增长和机遇仅仅归因于运气呢？不！我更愿意认为这是毅力和勇气的结果，是它们帮助我建立了这些联系。

I have been traveling to China for more than 10 years now. My first trip to China was simply to visit a few families who had sent their children to my summer camp. From there, introductions were made. I continued to return to meet more people, expand connections and, all these years later, I have been fortunate enough to visit over 100 cities in 10 different provinces. I no longer find myself promoting my summer camp, but I have expanded into education consulting, guest speaking, and teacher training. Do I attribute this business growth and opportunity simply to luck? No! I would give more authority to the notion that it was a result of grit and guts that helped me to forge and build these connections.

我深夜在路上开车，轮胎扁了，这是运气吗？如果 我碰巧在行李箱里放了我的备胎、手电筒和安全照明弹，这是运气吗？我正好扎到那颗钉子，它的位置很合适，恰好可以刺破轮胎，这是"运气"使然，但是可以说，我预先做好了一些计划，以确保无论何时发生这种情况，即使我感到不便，我都已经做好了准备，这里面就包含着技巧和勇气。

Is it luck that I am driving down the road late at night and I get a flat tire? I happen to have my spare in the trunk along with a flashlight and a safety flare. Is it luck? It may be luck that the nail I ran over was perfectly positioned to puncture the tire, but, arguably, there was some element of skill and grit that I invested in pre-planning to make sure when that scenario occurred, even though I was inconvenienced, I was still prepared.

运气里面确实没有任何人为的计划或技能。这是随机发生的事情，例如足球，篮球或彩票数字球都与技能无关。当我获得"好运"（无论好运到何种程度）时，我当然会感到高兴，但我宁愿不依靠运气过自己的生活。相反，我宁愿希望自己的勇气和胆量能产生我想要的结果，而不是指望它偶然发生。

Luck is really the absence of any human planning or skill. It is a random happening, like the bounce of a football, basketball or lottery ball that skill had nothing to do with. I am certainly happy when I am the recipient of "good luck" (to whatever extend it may be luck) but I would prefer not to live my life relying on luck. Instead, I prefer to live a life where my grit and guts produce the results I desire, and not leave it to happenstance.

有时，当与一位朋友聊天，发现他们刚从温暖的热带地区度假后归来时，我听到自己说："哇，你真幸运！"我试图抓住自己，并意识到运气可能与此无关。要省下所需的钱需要勇气和技巧，需要制定必要的计划，也需要假期以便他们可以去他们选择的目的地。仔细的预先计划与运气无关。一个好运的例子是，如果在假期结束时，当他们去支付酒店账单时，他们被告知他们"碰巧"（运气）是第20,000入住该酒店的客人，而酒店为此选择的庆祝方式是给他们免去全部住宿费，这次住宿将是完全免费的！没有计划，技巧或毅力可以帮助他们获得这种奖励。这就纯粹是运气！

Sometimes, when speaking to a friend who reveals they recently returned from a vacation in a warm, tropical place, I have heard myself say, "Wow, you're so lucky!" I try to catch myself and realize that luck probably had nothing to do with it. It required grit and skill to save the necessary money, make the necessary plans, and take the desired vacation to the destination of their choice. Careful pre-planning had nothing to do with luck. An example of luck would be if, at the end of the vacation, when they went to pay the hotel bill, they were told they "happen to be" (luck) the 20,000th guest to ever visit that hotel. To celebrate, the hotel is awarding them by covering the entire cost of the stay. The stay would be completely free! No planning, skill, or grit would have been used to receive this reward. This would be pure luck!

当我们使用"运气"这个词时，便忽略了我们所投入的勇气和胆量。这两个词我都喜欢。勇气的定义之一是"勇气和决心，性格坚强"。勇气即是韧性。它需要决心、毅力，有时还需要克服不利条件。我希望人们认为我是一个有勇气和胆量的人，而不是一个幸运的人。我希望成为一个愿意付出必要的努力的人，当遇到不利条件时，我希望自己表现出毅力和决心。这样，我就可以接受可能出现的结果。也许我还是需要一些运气，但因为我有勇气和胆量，我可以更容易地对任何运气心存感激，同时也对自己的决心和努力感到满意。我愿意相信自己的努力，而不是运气。

When we use the word luck, we overlook the grit and guts that were invested. I love both of these words. One of the definitions for grit is "courage and resolve; strength of character". Grit is toughness. It requires determination, perseverance and, at times, going up against unfavorable odds. I want people to think of me as a person who possesses grit and guts, rather than luck. I want to be one who is willing to put in the necessary hard work and effort, and when up against unfavorable odds, shows perseverance and determination. In doing so, I can then accept the results that may come along. Maybe there is still some luck involved, but because I have grit and guts, I can more easily be grateful for any luck involved, but also satisfied with the determination and effort I put forth. I want to trust my effort, not my luck.

如果体育界存在运气，那么教育界也存在运气吗?作为一名教育工作者，当我试图教导我的学生在准备个人的学习和生活时，要依靠自己的勇气和胆量。我不希望他们抱着考好成绩的幻想而松懈下来。我敦促他们采取必要的准备措施，以获得更多的成功机会。有了勇气和胆量，学生可以从任何运气中受益，也不会在遭遇"坏运气"时崩溃。老师应该鼓励学生尽可能地学习和准备（也就是教给学生毅力），这样当学生被问到一个意料之外的考试问题（运气不好）时，他们不会崩溃。

If there is luck in the world of sports, can there also be luck in the world of education? As an educator, I tried to teach students to rely on developed grit and guts in their personal preparation for studies and for life. I did not want them to sit back and hope for a good grade. I urged them to take the necessary preparatory steps to keep the odds of success favorable to them. With grit and guts, the student can be the beneficiary of any luck involved, and also not be devastated when "bad luck" occurs. Teachers should encourage students to study and prepare as best they can (that is teaching grit), so that when an unexpected exam question (bad luck) is asked, students are not devastated.

有了坚定的决心，就有了毅力。有了胆量，处理意外情况就成为了可能。当勇气和胆量都很明显的时候（不管遇到好运气还是坏运气），结果都可以被更好的接受。培养勇气和胆量是人生中的伟大计划。依赖运气只能带来徒劳的挫败感，最终无法让人满意或得到信任。等待运气不能成为计划。

With well-established grit, perseverance is present. With the demonstration of guts, dealing with the unexpected is possible. When both grit and guts are evident (even if good or bad luck is involved) the results can be better accepted. Developing grit and guts is a great game plan for life. Relying on luck is a futile frustration that ultimately cannot satisfy or be trusted. Waiting for luck is not a plan.

向学生传授勇气和胆量并不容易，因为要同时学习两者，就必须经历挫败带来的失望。太多的家长不希望他们的孩子经历挫折、失败或坎坷，所以他们会立即介入，责怪老师或学校。父母担心孩子的不适感会给他们的一生留下创伤。传递给家长的适当信息应该是，支持老师将更好地帮助孩子理解他们可能需要在哪些方面做得更好，以减轻厄运发生时的情况，或在好运发生时心存感激。克服失望需要勇气和胆量。太多的学生在这两方面都缺乏。

Teaching grit and guts to students is not easy because, to learn both, one must experience the disappointment of failure. Too many parents do not want their child to experience frustration, failure, or a set back, so they immediately step in to blame the teacher or the school. Parents fear the discomfort in their child will scar them for life. The appropriate message to parents should be that supporting the teacher will better help the child understand where they may need to do a better job to mitigate instances when bad luck happens or appreciate it when good luck occurs. Overcoming the disappointment requires grit and guts. Too many students lack evidence of either.

结果导向的教育与勇气和胆量的教育背道而驰。学生成绩越来越重要，并最终决定学生、教师和学校的成败。由于教育的重点在于结果，我们并不能正确地教授勇气和胆量。家长和学生都不愿承受挣扎带来的不适，而这对于勇气和胆量的教育是必不可少的。即使是那些非常努力的学生，他们花了大量的时间准备，他们可能显示出了胆量，但依然缺乏勇气。任何轻微的成绩下滑（或出现坏运气）都会使学生和家长崩溃。Results-driven education is heading in the opposite direction from teaching grit and guts. Student grade results are taking on a greater importance and ultimately are used to determine the success of the student, teacher, and school. With the focal point of education being on the results, we fail to properly teach grit and guts. Parents and students do not want to endure the discomfort of the struggle, which is needed to teach grit and guts. Even for those very hardworking students who spend tremendous time preparing, they may show guts but lack grit. Any slight deterioration in results (or the presence of bad luck) renders the student and parents devastated.

总结
Summary

我很幸运地教导了一些非常坚毅而勤奋的学生，然而他们的成绩从来没有高过"B"。虽然他们的一些同学可能获得了更高的分数，但他们并没有发展或学习到与我的这些 B 级学生一样的勇气和胆量。结果，B 级的学生学到了勇气和胆量，而高分学生则只是得到了更高的分数。如今，那些 B 级学生（以及其他像他们一样的学生）经营着成功的企业，这些企业之所以变得强大，是因为他们的勇气和胆量，而非他们的成绩。

I was fortunate to teach some very gritty, hardworking students who never earned higher than a "B" for a grade. Although some of their classmates may have earned higher grades, they did not develop or learn the same level of grit and guts as some of my "B" students. As a result, the B students learned grit & guts, whereas the higher scoring students simply got higher grades. Today, those B students (and others like them) are now running successful businesses that have grown strong because of their grit and guts, not because of the grades they received.

尽管我自己的高中成绩很差，但我确实学到了勇气和胆量。这种教育是通过体育运动和比赛而得来的，这些都为未来的商业投资和计划打下了基础。当然，好运和厄运都时有发生，但我的勇气和胆量帮助我忍受、坚持，让我对好运和厄运都心存感激，并让我因为自己的努力工作而获得满足感和成就感。我学到的勇气也来自于无数次的失败。业务失败和糟糕的决策则导致了业务计划和新想法的改进。失败并没有把我毁掉。它激励我做得更好或改变我现有的方法。是勇气和胆量让我做到了这一点，而不是运气。

In spite of my own poor high school academic record, I did learn grit & guts. This education came through athletics and competition, which then parlayed into future business investments and initiatives. Sure, there are times that both good and bad luck events occur, but my grit and guts help me endure, persevere and appreciate the good and the bad, as well as give me satisfaction and fulfillment because of my hard work. My learned grit also grew out of a lot of failure. Business failures and poor decisions led to improved business plans and new ideas. Failure did not ruin me. It inspired me to do it better or shift my approach. Grit and guts did this, not luck.

教学生如何培养勇气和胆量，同时对好运气和坏运气都心存感激。它们一个涉及到可行的计划，另一个只是依赖于偶发事件。一个可以打磨或摧毁你的勇气和影响你的胆量。培养勇气需要胆量，但付出的努力都是值得的。这样一来，当幸运降临时，你就可以简单地心存感激。如果你有勇气，那么任何坏运气都只会让你变得更有胆量。如果你有勇气，又赶上了好运气，那么你会更加心怀感激地迎接它。

Teach students how to develop grit and guts while also appreciating both good and bad luck. One involves a workable plan and the other simply relies on happenstance. One can sharpen or destroy your grit and impact your guts. Developing grit takes guts, but it is worth the effort. Then you can simply appreciate luck when it happens. If you have grit, then any bad luck simply teaches you to have even more guts. If you have grit, and good luck happens, then you appreciate and welcome that even more.

每个人都需要一个行动计划来培养个人的勇气和胆量。学生和老师都同样需要它。强大的领导型教师需要在学生身上进行投入，引导和指导他们，这样他们才能两个方面同时获得发展。相信自己的勇气和胆量可以带你到达个人发展的新高度。依赖运气会让你变得脆弱、软弱，最终壮志难酬。

Each person needs a game plan to develop personal grit and guts. Students and teachers need it equally as much. Strong lead teachers need to make the investment in their students to guide and mentor them so they can develop both. Trusting in grit and guts can take you to new heights of personal development. Relying on luck leaves you vulnerable, weak, and ultimately unfulfilled.

目的地 vs. 方向
Destination vs. Direction

Image credit: Home Professionals

　　我可以轻松地回忆起我第一份教学工作早期的情形。我从大学毕业并获得了学位和证书，表明我已有资质走上教学岗位，我认为我已经准备好在经验丰富的资深老师的信任下开展我的第一份课堂教学工作！好吧，并不是这么回事！我所拥有的只是一些教学的理论知识罢了，我的实践教学（大学期间完成了两次实习）让我获得了一点课堂经验，获得了大学学位、教师资格证以及过度的自信。现在回想起来，我显然缺乏了最重要的东西——经验。我可能已经合格并很兴奋，但是我显然是缺乏经验的！像大多数其他一年级老师一样，我发现那年的教学工作非常困难，有很多过渡学习内容。就像我父亲说的那样，那是"艰苦的磨练"，天哪，我被磨练得七荤八素的！

　　I can easily recall the initial days of my first teaching job. Having graduated from the university with a degree and certificate indicating I was authorized to teach, I assumed I had been prepared to enter my first classroom job with the confidence of an experienced veteran teacher! Well, I was NOT! What I had was some teaching theory knowledge, a little bit of classroom experience because of my practice teaching (having completed two placements in schools), a degree from a university, a teaching certificate, and a heavy dose of overconfidence. As I look back now, I clearly lacked the most important thing of all - experience. I may have been qualified and excited, but I was certainly not experienced! Like most other first year teachers, I found that year of teaching quite difficult, with a lot of transitional learning. As my father said, it was the "school of hard knocks" and boy did I get knocked around!

如果我能向你形象地描述我当时感受的话，请想象一个人在海洋中颤抖，陷入水流的漩涡，同时拼命地抓着一个物体，但却还是几乎呛水。每次我都以为自己能屏住呼吸，但当我更加努力地保持漂浮时，另一轮波浪拍过来，将我吞没。那真是令人筋疲力尽的事情，我的教学生涯就这么开始了！

If I could give you an image illustration of how I felt, it would be a person bobbing in the ocean while desperately clinging to an object barely able to keep my head above the swirling waves. Each time I thought I would catch my breath, another wave would wash over me as I tried even harder to stay afloat. That would be exhausting and terrifying, and thus my teaching career was launched!

那一年的大部分时间里，我发现自己和学生相比，就提前学了1到2个课时的内容。基于我的经验，我疯狂地计划着最好的课程。我进行了勇敢的尝试，以增加创造力，我认为它们可能会激起学生对学习体育和美国历史的好奇心和必要的参与度。那时，我认为我的目标是上完每一章和每个单元的内容，最终完成期末考试。我把考试作为目标。我并没有看到我的课程将如何作为预备课程，帮他们适应高中时期更为广泛的学习，更不用说如何帮助他们为人生做好准备。最终，我心里并没有一个正确的目的地。

Most of that year, I found myself staying 1-2 book lessons ahead of my students. Based on my inexperience, I was frantically planning the best lessons I could. I was making a valiant attempt to add the creativity that I thought might inspire the engagement necessary to make middle school students curious about learning PE and US History. At that time, I thought my destination was to complete each chapter and each unit that would culminate with a final exam. The exam was my destination. I did not see the bigger picture of how my course would fit into their bigger picture of high school preparation, let alone how I could better help them prepare for life. Ultimately, I did not have the correct destination in mind.

　　回想起来，我当时心里很难有正确的**目的地**，因为我并不知道如何开发教学的这一个方面。我希望我的学生了解历史事件与相关人员的行为之间的因果关系。但是，由于没有必要的经验来提供构思周到的课程和测评，我发现自己的教学效率很低。那时，我不得不把自己评为一名典型的新手老师。用口头语来说，我当时是"跟着感觉走！"幸运的是，经过短短几年的经验积累，我开始理解**目的地和方向**的真正含义，以及这些词语在塑造我的教学风格和方法方面的重要性。

In retrospect, it was hard for me to have the correct **destination** in mind because I had no idea how to develop that aspect of my teaching. I wanted my students to understand the cause/effect relationship between events in History and the actions of people involved. However, without the necessary experience to deliver well-conceived lessons and assessments, I believe I was ineffective. I would have to rate myself, back then, as a typical rookie teacher. In colloquial terms, I was "flying by the seat of my pants!" Fortunately, after a few short years of experience, I began to understand the true meaning of **destination and direction** and how important those terms are in shaping my teaching style and methods.

　　请允许我用两个词深入探讨我想表达的意思：目的地和方向。**目的地**是老师教授任何学科内容的最终结果或宏观目标。（目的地不是测试或评估。）例如，也许当我讲授有关美国内战的内容时，我真正打算让学生们了解的是战争的社会、政治和经济原因，以及战争的结果如何塑造了美国这个现代化国家。目的地归根到底是我们希望在我们所教的课程中得到的结果。如果比作一张地图，那它就是你旅程的最终目的地。

Let me dive deeper into what I mean using the two words: destination and direction. **Destination** is the end-result, or macro objective, a teacher has for teaching any subject content. (The destination is NOT a test or assessment.) For example, perhaps when I taught the content about the American Civil War, my intended destination for my students was to understand the social, political, and economic reasons for the war and how the results shaped the United States as a modern nation. Destination is ultimately the WHERE we hope to end up in WHAT we are teaching. If it were a map, it would be the final destination of your trip.

要到达目的地需要很多转弯。这就是对"方向"这个词的理解。如果将其与教学联系起来，方向指的是教育者用来实现其宏观目标的日常技巧。如果目的地是**哪里**和**什么**的话，那么方向便是**这个**和**那个**。它们共同作用，相互依存。方向性项目可以是任何设计的团队活动，方向性问题、工作表、项目、辩论，甚至是将知识推向目的地的视频片段。

Getting to the destination requires many turns along the way. This is how to understand **direction.** To relate it to teaching, direction is the day-to-day techniques educators will use to reach their macro objective. If destination is the WHERE and WHAT, then direction is the THIS and THAT. They go together and are dysfunctional without each other. Directional items could be any designed small group activities, guiding questions, worksheets, projects, debates or even video segments that move the knowledge toward the destination.

参加我的工作坊的老师总是能得到"职位晋升"！在培训的开始，

我总会很高兴地告诉他们，他们都已经得到了晋升。他们不再仅仅被称为老师，而已经被提拔为课堂里的 CEO。在这个领导职位上，老师将承担教室之内所有活动的"建筑师"和"设计师"的职责。建筑师设计一栋建筑物时，他们知道项目最终完成后的样子。为此，他们还要决定使用的材料以及构建过程的步骤顺序，以便按正确的工序完成工作。在课堂里，CEO（老师）选择开展哪些方向性活动以及何时开展这些活动，因为他们心里清楚最终产品是什么样的。和任何优秀的建筑师一样，他们借助包含所有建筑物详细信息和所含系统的蓝图开展工作。以此类推，蓝图便是课程和目的地。方向则是完成建筑所需的材料和步骤。而 CEO 显然是老师。

Teachers who attend my workshops are always promoted! Early in my training session, I happily inform them that they have all been promoted. No longer are they just known as a teacher, but rather they are promoted to the position of CEO of their classroom. In this leadership position, the teacher assumes the responsibility as the architect and designer of all that gets built inside those classroom walls. The architect designs a building knowing what the final project will look like when completed. To accomplish that, they also decide the materials used as well as the sequential steps in the building process so that things are completed in the proper order. In the classroom, the CEO (teacher) chooses which directional activities to use and when they should happen, because they know what the finished product should look like. Like any good architect, they work from a blueprint that contains all the building details and systems to be included. In this analogy, the blueprint is the curriculum and destination. The materials and steps taken to complete the building are the direction. The CEO is obviously the teacher.

当我从经验不足的新人转变为经验丰富的 CEO 时，我注意到我为学生学习而设定的"目的地"已经有所改善。当我对他们有所了解并明白了如何利用自己的领导力时，我对如何阅读自己试图建立的蓝图有了更好的理解。随着对最终产品理解的提升，我得以改进自己的建筑设计，以便用正确的材料和体系促进成长和学习。有了更清晰的视野，我对方向有了更好的了解，于是得以改善学生的学习体验。我开始明白，教学不仅仅是为学生提供考试要记住的内容和信息而已。我需要他们了解和理解这些信息，但更重要的是，要让他们知道如何应用学到的信息，以便他们不会在学了三天之后就把它们忘记。目的地和方向对于每位老师来说都至关重要。请始终把它们置于日常计划的最前端，以便在你作为"首席建筑师"，打造课堂杰作时，它们始终处于学生学习经验的最前端。

As I transformed from an inexperienced rookie to a more experienced CEO, I noticed that my "destination" for student learning improved. As I got to know them and how to utilize my leadership, I had a better understanding of how to read the blueprint for what I was trying to build. With my finished product better understood, I could improve my architectural design so that I had the correct materials and systems that would enhance growth and learning. With a sharper vision of where I was going, I had a better sense of direction so I could improve the student learning experience. I began to understand that teaching was far more than just giving students content and data to remember for the exam. I needed them to know and understand data, but more importantly, how to apply the data learned so it was not just forgotten 3 days later. Destination and direction are essential for each teacher to grasp. Keep them at the forefront of daily planning so they are at the forefront of the student learning experience while you build your masterpiece as the CEO architect.

每个 CEO 都需要知道目的地和方向，但他们还必须具有有效完成旅程所需的领导技能。简而言之，一个好的 CEO 要学会如何与学生建立联系和沟通。这有助于增强方向性的曲折迂回。我作为老师的最佳技能不是我对书本内容的熟练掌握，而是我理解中学生思想和个性的能力。因为我可以在他们的社交和情感层面上与他们建立联系，所以我也能够通过创造性和引人入胜的方向性活动成功地将他们送达目的地。成功的老师与学生保持联系；正如成功的 CEO 与他们所领导的人建立联系那样。

Every CEO needs to know the destination and direction, but they must also have the leadership skills necessary to effectively complete the journey. Simply stated, a good CEO learns how to connect and communicate with students. This serves to enhance the directional twists and turns. My best skill as a teacher was not my masterful command over the content, but rather my ability to understand the minds and personalities of middle school students. Because I could connect and relate to them at their social and emotional level, I was also able to be successful in delivering them to the destination through creative and engaging directional activities. Successful teachers connect with their students; just like successful CEOs connect with those they lead.

这时，你可能怀疑自己是不是领导者，因为你感觉自己并不像什么CEO。我讲领导者仅仅定义为能影响他人的人。领导者不一定非得拥有多么高的头衔。领导者不一定是指职务。它只是指能够影响他人的人。有效的领导者不仅要树立清晰的愿景，而且要让他们带领的人"认可"。当他们认可时，他们将跟随你到达愿景中所述的目的地。在领导的带领下，你一路历经所有的方向性曲折将他们最终引向愿景。

At this point, you may doubt that you are a leader because you do not feel like a CEO. My definition of a leader is simply one who influences others. A leader does not necessarily have to have the supreme title. Leadership is not necessarily a job title. It just refers to anyone who influences others. Effective leaders not only cast a clear vision, but also get those they lead to "buy in". When they buy in, they will follow you to the destination set out in the vision. You lead them toward the vision through all the directional twists and turns taken under your guidance as a leader.

我的大部分"CEO"教育来自我当教练的时候。我在教学生涯中，我花了很多年的时间教授篮球、足球和网球。在体育运动中，任何一支球队的目标都是获得最高程度的认可。然而，随着赛季的开始，每次练习和比赛都成了朝着目的地迈进的方向性步骤。知道如何使团队到达目的地包括许多因素，这些因素可能会导致整体的成功或失败。伟大的教练也是伟大的建筑师。他们看到了愿景，但也知道如何领导团队一步一步积累，逐步实现团队的目标。

Much of my "CEO" education came when I was a coach. I spent many years of my teaching career coaching basketball, soccer, and tennis. In sports, the destination of any team is to earn the highest level of recognition attainable. However, as the season begins, each practice and game played becomes a single directional step towards the destination. Knowing how to get a team to the destination includes many factors that can contribute to overall success or failure. Great coaches are great architects. They see the vision, but also know how to lead the team with the incremental steps needed to move the team towards reaching its goal.

带领团队获胜的教练会告诉你，成功不仅仅在于教练的计划，甚至也不在于球员的执行力。还必须对参与者进行强有力的管理（领导指引）。获胜的球队经常会说，球队就是一个家庭或者是紧密联系的一群人，他们能够为球队的利益而不顾自我。像老师一样，教练也需要了解团队中球员的个性、技能和情感。教练必须获得球员的认可，这样一来他们在朝着建筑师的愿景前进时才会建立牢固的纽带。优秀的教练和优秀的老师通过了解他们所领导的每个人，对他们的球员／学生进行投入。优秀的教练和老师了解让一群人朝着集体和个人目标努力的心理。

Winning coaches will tell you that success is not just about the coach's plan or even the player's execution. There also must be a strong management (leadership guidance) of the players. Winning teams will often comment that the team is a family or deeply connected group of individuals who were able to put personal ego aside for the good of the team. Like a teacher, a coach also needs to understand the personalities, skills, and emotions of the players on their team. The coach must get player buy in, so they create a strong bond together as they move towards the vision cast by the architect. Great coaches and great teachers invest in their players/student by knowing everyone they lead. Great coaches and teachers understand the psychology of getting a group of individuals to strive towards a collective and personal goal.

经常有人问我："我怎样才能成为一名出色的老师？"其实并没有一种模板可以让教师、领导者或引导者轻易应对任何情况并突然成为一名出色的领导者。让我惊讶的是，尽管我在中国进行了大量的领导力培训，从没有两个人走的是相同的道路。尽管他们存在相似之处，但是每个团队和情况都是独一无二而且截然不同的。团队会发展出相似的"团队规范"和行为，但是由于每个团队的动态始终是独一无二的，因此每次培训都给人不同的感觉。不变的要素只是我培训内容中安排的那些核心活动。我的目的地永远是固定的，尽管根据情况我的方向可能会略有变化。但是，令每次培训课程独一无二的最大原因是每个参加者的个性。

I am often asked, "How can I be a great teacher?" There is no template for a teacher, leader, or facilitator to simply apply to any situation and suddenly become a great leader. I am still amazed that, given the large number of leadership trainings I have done in China, no two have gone the same way. Even though there are similarities, each group and situation are uniquely different and distinct. Groups develop similar "group norms" and behaviors, but because the group dynamic is always unique, each training feels distinct. The elements that remain fixed would be activities that are at the core of my training content. My destination is always fixed, though my direction may change slightly based on circumstances. But the biggest reason that each training session is unique comes in the individuality of each person that attends.

我的最终目标是让老师们看到并感受到他们如何共同朝着我想要的目的地前进。尽管每次培训都只有短短的两天时间，作为"建筑师"，我设计了方向性活动，但在这样做的过程中，我了解了团队成员的独特个性。我必须根据这些个性进行领导。我必须处理它们带来的优势和劣势。有些人参与愿意强，并经常参与到培训中来，而另一些人则对我的领导能力提出了更大的挑战。请记住，正如出色的教练所做的那样，你必须管理团队中的每个人，以便他们可以共同取得成就。

My end goal is to have teachers SEE and FEEL how the group moves together towards my desired destination. Although each session is only two short days together, as the architect, I design the directional activities, but in doing so, I get to know the unique personalities of those in the group. It is these personalities that I must lead. I must manage the strengths and weaknesses that they bring to the process. Some participate willingly and frequently, while others present a bigger challenge to my leadership skills in getting them to buy in. Remember, like a great coach, you must manage the individuals on the team so that they can achieve something together as a group.

每个个体以及团队的集体成长过程被称为团队成长过程。每当一个团队聚在一起时，变化就会发生。作为这一过程中有意识的建筑师，我设计了以人为本的活动，以此向目的地前进。我不能简单地背诵固定的脚本，因为它不能帮我建立起我想要实现的个人联系。我很高兴看到培训会的开展并接受在团队成长过程中引导方向性过程的挑战。有些参与者能比其他人更先看到团队成长的发生，我可以从这些参与者的表情中看出这一点。他们的眼睛闪烁出光芒，笑容变得更灿烂，并且他们在此过程中的参与度已提升到了更高的水平。他们现在进入了认可阶段，并亲眼目睹了团队成长过程。

The process of growth in everyone, as well as in the collective group, is called the Group Growth Process. Anytime a group comes together, change is going to occur. As the intentional architect of this process, I design people-centered activities to achieve movement towards my destination. I cannot simply recite a fixed script because it does not make for the personal connection that I am trying to achieve. It is so much fun for me to see the workshop unfold and to accept the challenge of facilitating the directional process through this Group Growth Process. I can literally see the expression on the faces of participants who begin to see it ahead of the others. Their eyes light up, a bigger smile takes over and their level of engagement in the process moves to a more heightened place. They now are at the point of buy-in and have seen and felt the Group Growth Process for themselves.

要明白，无论你是否采取任何措施，团队成长过程都会发生。成长是不可避免的。但是，为了确保团队的成长是积极的并朝着你预期的方向发展，你必须对流程进行管理。这就是引导的艺术。你知道目的地在哪里。你可以设计方向性活动，并通过影响力来管理参与者的个性。这就是领导。

Understand that the Group Growth Process is going to happen whether you do something about it or not. Growth is inevitable. However, to ensure that the growth is positive and moving towards the direction you intend, you must manage the process. This is the art of facilitation. You know the destination. You design the directional activities, and you manage the personalities through your influence. This is leadership.

在西方教育中，"教育'全面发展的'孩子"（情感、身体、精神、智力）是挂在嘴边的口头禅。对老师的期望除了教育整个班级（指班上所有的孩子）之外，他们也必须教育每个孩子。教育每个孩子需要不同的学习技巧，以适应每个学习者的学习风格和挑战。这真是个挑战啊！试图使所有团队成员向目的地迈进的领导者需要一定的一致性和统一性。但是，当我们在指导过程中开展富有创造力和吸引力的活动时，学习的个性和体验对于每个学习者而言都是独一无二的。教师需要了解他们的班级，以及班级中每个人各不相同的学习风格。

"Teaching the 'whole' child" (emotional, physical, spiritual, intellectual) is a strong mantra in western education. In addition to a teacher being expected to teach the whole class (referring to all the children in the class), it is also essential that they teach each individual child, as well. Teaching each child requires differentiated learning techniques to meet the learning styles and challenges within each learner. What a challenge! A leader attempting to get all the group members headed towards their destination requires some conformity and uniformity. But, when we enact creative and engaging activities in the direction process, individuality in learning and experience is unique to each learner. The teacher needs to know the class, as well as the different learning style in each personality within the class.

例如，行动型学习者和听觉型学习者在理论上都朝着老师确定的方向前进。尽管属于同一班级的成员（即，属于相同的团队成长过程），但每个人对每个方向性活动的参与和反应都将是独一无二的。这就是使教学和领导如此令人惊叹同时又充满挑战的原因！老师可以谨慎地指导班级朝着一个明确的方向发展，但也必须精心管理所有学生的个性（学习风格）。优秀的老师会不断反思和评估学生的学习过程，就像我不断评估培训参与者的参与程度一样。它成为老师和学生之间未经事先编排的舞蹈，并与更大的团队融为一体，当它起作用时，便是一种纯粹的美。

For example, the kinesthetic learner and the auditory processing learner are theoretically heading in the same direction established by the teacher. Although members of the same class (ie. the same Group Growth Process), each individual's engagement and response to each directional activity will be uniquely different. That is what makes teaching and leading so amazing and so challenging at the same time! Teachers can carefully steer the class in a clear direction but must also delicately manage all the individual personalities (learning styles). Great teachers constantly reflect on, and assess, the learning processes of their students, just like I constantly assess the level of engagement with my training participants. It becomes an un-choreographed dance between teacher and student, mixed in with the larger group, and when it works, it is a thing of sheer beauty.

我的每个培训研讨会都是相似的，但又各有独特之处。 同样，每个班级的学生都是相似的，但同时又是独特的。一位出色的领导者，就像一位出色的教练，必须进行管理和投入，认识每个人，以便最大程度地发挥团队的潜力。就像伟大的体育运动员有成为优秀得分选手或打进全明星的目标一样，学生也有个人要实现的目标。一位了解学生的老师会了解并重视学生的个人目标，并会努力帮助他们实现目标。但是老师也要管理那些个人的追求，并设法使他们理解，他们是更大的队的一部分，他们也必须努力发挥其潜力。 伟大的领导者也是伟大的引导者。他们管理和培育每个人与众不同的特征：我们所有人都具有的情感、身体、精神和智力需求。这样一来，每个人都会感到自己得到了重视和满足，能够实现自己的个人目标，但是他们也将感受到与更大的团队的集体目标的联系和责任。这也满足了人类成为家庭／团队成员的愿望。 发生这种情况时，团队成长过程会不断发展，并揭示出帮助他们引领成功的引导者的才能和技能。

Each of my training seminars is similar, but they are also uniquely different. So, too, is each class of students similar, but uniquely different. A great leader, like a great coach, must manage and invest in getting to know each individual so he/she can maximize the potential of the group. Just like great sports players have goals to be great scorers or All-Stars, so too, students have individual goals to achieve. A teacher who knows the students, understands and values those personal goals and will work hard to help them be achieved. But the teacher also manages those individual pursuits and tries to get them to also understand that they are part of a larger group that also must strive to reach its potential. Great leaders are great facilitators. They manage and nurture the characteristics that make people distinctly human: the emotional, physical, spiritual, and intellectual needs that we all have. In doing so, everyone will feel valued and fulfilled, and able to achieve their personal goals, but they will also feel connected and responsible for the collective goals of the larger group. This also feeds the human desire to be part of a family/team. When this occurs, the Group Growth Process evolves and reveals the talent and skill of the facilitator who helped lead them towards success.

如果你正在阅读本书但不是老师，那也没关系。 目的地和方向也适用于企业领导或人生的诸多不同领域。也许你是大型或小型公司的 CEO，或者小型员工团队的经理。无论如何，缺乏明确的目标（有时在业务中被称为"愿景"），领导者很少会成功。如果你不知道要让你的公司或你管理的公司走向何方，你又怎么把他们送到目的地呢？在业务过程中，目的地描绘的是 CEO 想把公司带向何方的远景，方向则是在考虑愿景的情况下做出的日常运营决策。好的领导者清楚目的地，然后与他们领导的人一起工作，以帮助大家实现这些目标。 商业和教育在领导能力上颇有相似之处。

If you are reading this but are not a teacher, it's ok. Destination and direction are also applicable to business leadership or many different areas of life. Maybe you are the CEO of a big or small company, or the manager of a small team of workers. Regardless, without a clear destination (sometimes termed in business as "vision") those who lead can rarely be successful. If you do not know where you want your company, or those you manage, to go, how can you possibly get them there? In business, destination is the vision that delineates where the CEO wants to take the company, and direction is the day-to-day operational decisions made with the vision in mind. Good leaders know the destination, and then work with those they lead to help them achieve those goals or objectives. Both business and education have parallels in leadership.

你也可以从育儿的角度研究这个问题。结婚后，两个具有独特个性特征以及个人目标的人合并成为一个组合。这也是团队成长过程的一个例子。这两个人将根据他们的沟通和协作方式而成长和变化。不久之后，他们可能会在团队中添一个孩子。在这一点上，具有独特需求和需求的另一个独特个体进入了这个团队。管理所有这些需求和个性肯定需要统一的领导！这种情况下，目的地是幸福而充实的家庭生活。方向则是父母为达到目的地而设计和进行的所有事情。在家庭中，要使团队成长过程变得快乐和成功，领导者必须管理好个人的个性和梦想。平衡个人目标和实现团体整体利益的野心是父母领导力中的挑战之一。

You may also examine this from the perspective of parenting. Once married, two individuals with unique personality characteristics, as well as individual goals, merge to form a unit. This, too, is a sample of the Group Growth Process. These two individuals will grow and change based on how they communicate and collaborate. A short time later, they may add a child to their group. At this point, another unique personality, with unique demands and needs, enters the mix. Managing all these needs and personalities requires unified leadership for sure! The destination is a happy and fulfilled family life. The direction is all the things that parents design and do to move towards that destination. In the family, for the Group Growth Process to be happy and successful, the leader(s) must manage the individual personalities and dreams. Balancing personal goals and ambition for the overall good of the group is one of the challenges in parental leadership.

总结
Summary

引导学生探索和理解是教育的本质。正是在指导的过程中，教师的创造力可以（并且应该）使学习环境充满乐趣。正是在独特的方向性曲折中，学习者被导向目的地。领导者是团队成长过程中有意识的"建筑师"，他们影响并管理着独特的个体，但这样做的重点是团队的团结。尽管目的地和方向受领导者的影响，但参与者的个体独特性对参与者的成败起着至关重要的作用。这也是引导艺术所面临的挑战。

Leading students on a path of discovery and understanding is the essence of teaching. It is in the process of direction that teacher creativity can (and should) make the learning environment engaging and fun. It is in the unique directional twists and turns that the learner is guided towards the destination. The leader, the intentional architect of the Group Growth Process, influences and manages the unique individuals, but does so with a focus on the unity of the group. Whereas the destination and direction are under the leaders' control of influence, it is the participants who play a crucial role in the success or failure of the group because of their uniqueness as individuals. This is where the art of facilitation is challenged.

打磨引导技能，要提高目的地和方向的清晰度，这需要大量的尝试、错误和实验。认识到团队成长过程势必会发生，你最好成为这一过程中有意识的建筑师，以尝试为个人和整个团队达成所需的目标。

Sharpening both destination and direction requires lots of trial, error and experimentation as facilitation skills are built. Recognizing that the Group Growth Process will happen, it is better to be the intentional architect of the process to try to obtain your desired destination goal for the individuals and the group as a whole.

教学远远不只是传达考试中应用的事实性内容而已。教师也是领导者，他们不仅要分享知识内容，而且可以以有意义和令人难忘的方式影响他们所领导的那些人。

Teaching is far more than just communicating factual content to be given back on an examination. Teachers are leaders who can not only share content knowledge, but also influence those they lead in a meaningful and memorable way.

教学生面对失败——建立情商
Teaching Students to Fail – Building EQ

Image credit: Wanderlust Worker

9 岁的时候，我勇敢地走上棒球场，为自己的家乡而战。我很骄傲地穿着我的金莺队队服。我深感自豪，因为那是我最喜欢的美国职棒大联盟球队，而且碰巧我的球队被选为金莺队。对我来说，我觉得这套制服使我成为了像李.梅或马克.贝兰格这样的球员（该队著名的职业球员）。当我走进击球位进行挥棒练习时，我比任何 9 岁的球员都充满了大联盟般的信心。我看着对方的投手，心中对他不得不向我投球而感到抱歉，因为我打算将球击得很远。我觉得在我打出全垒打之后，他会让他的球队失望，这可能会让他感到难过。我信心十足，几乎没有考虑到失败即将降临。当投手向我发起挑战时，关键时刻到了。他在三次投球中发挥出了最佳水平。经过 3 次挥棒，我证明了自己是个速战速决的人。

I stepped up to bat as a brave 9-year old playing baseball for my hometown team. I was proudly wearing my Orioles team uniform. Proud because that was my favorite Major League Baseball team, and it just so happened that my team was chosen to be the Orioles. For me, I felt as if this uniform transformed me into a player like Lee May or Mark Belanger (famous professional players for that team). As I stepped into the batter's box to take

133

my practice swings, I was full of all the major league confidence any 9-year old could have. I looked out at the opposing pitcher and felt sorry he had to pitch to me because I planned to hit the ball very far. I thought he might feel bad that he let his team down after I hit a homerun. With confidence sky high, I approached this at bat with little consideration of possible failure. The moment of truth approached as the pitcher challenged me. For three pitches he threw his best stuff. With 3 swings I proved to be one very quick out.

刚刚发生了什么？我心里这样想。我几乎眨眼的功夫都没有，我挥舞了3次球棒，每次都没打中。这可不是我心里想的那种击球方式啊。但是，它转瞬之间便成为了现实。我失败了，而不是他！我走回休息区，因为让我的团队失望而垂头丧气。当我陷入赛后思考时，我觉得当时那几棒没打好，但从那以后，肯定会有所改善。

What just happened? I thought. I barely had time to blink and I swung the bat 3 times, missing each pitch. That wasn't the way this at bat had played out in my mind. However, it quickly became the reality. I failed, not him! I walked back to the dugout hanging my head wondering, knowing I let my team down. As my postgame thoughts took over, I figured it was just a bad at bat and surely things would improve from that point forward.

一局接一局，一场又一场比赛，同样的结局像噩梦般反复出现。然后有一天，奇迹发生了！我走进击球位（基于我以前的击球失败率，我当时的绝对自信值为零）。我盯着道奇队的投手，他是联盟中最好的9岁投手之一，显得势不可挡。他看起来更像一个半大的男人，甚至没准当天他是开车去参加比赛的！他发挥了强大的发球能力，投出了自己最好的快球。在球飞到本垒板的那一瞬间，我几乎看不到以音速朝我飞来的那一团模糊的白色。我闭上了眼睛，准备好迎接最猛烈的冲击。幸运的是，以他的投球速度，我甚至没有时间把球棍从我的肩膀上移开。那一球投得又高又准。太高了，它击中了我的击球头盔。令我惊讶的是，我还活着，并听到裁判授予我进入一垒的机会！我接受了邀请，并且在那一年的四个赛季中第一次成为了球队的跑垒员。

Inning after inning, game after game, the same result played out like a recurring nightmare. Then one day, a miracle happened! I stepped into the batter's box (this time with absolutely zero confidence based on my previous proven failure at hitting). I stared at the imposing and mighty Dodger's pitcher. He was one of the best 9-year old pitchers in the league. He was more like a man-child and probably even drove himself to the game that day! He took his powerful windup and unleashed his best fast ball. In the mere split-second that the ball took to reach me at the plate, I could barely get a glimpse of the white blur coming towards me at the speed of sound. I closed my eyes and was prepared to take the biggest swing I could muster up. Fortunately for me, with the speed at which he threw, I did not have time to even move the bat off my shoulder. The pitch was high and inside. So high that it hit off my batting helmet. To my stunning surprise, I was still alive to hear the umpire award me a free pass to first base! I took the invitation and for the first time all year, I became a base runner for my team.

你读的时候可能一直在期待奇迹，期待这是我第一次打出全垒打，双打，三打或至少单打的球。我也可以肯定的是，你可能会认为这个故事的寓意是关于通过失败的毅力，有一天，如果坚持下去，成功就会到来。这是一个很好的建议，对于许多人来说，这是一个英勇的动力，可以防止他们放弃梦想。但是，在我的情况下，我在小联盟社区棒球运动中的失败的结果是我父亲给了我很有益的忠告，"儿子，也许你应该换一项运动？"

You may have been expecting the miracle that, for the first time, I had hit the ball for a homerun, double, triple or at least a single. I am also certain you might think the moral of this story is about perseverance through failure, and that, one day, if you stick with it, success will arrive. That is good advice, and it is a valiant motivator for many, preventing them from giving up on their dream. However, in my scenario, my failure in little league community baseball led to my dad giving me some great words of advice, "Son, maybe you should pick another sport?"

父母总是说："你下决心做的任何事都可以做到！"或者，"如果你足够努力，也许有一天你将成为美国总统。"或者，"不要因失败而失望。只要继续努力，好事就会发生。"这些话语都意味着鼓励，但其中根本没有蕴含太多现实或真理。

How many times does a parent say, "You can be anything you set your mind to!" Or, "If you work hard enough, maybe one day you will be President of the United States." Or, "Don't let failure slow you down. Just keep working hard and good things will happen." Those words and phrases are all meant to be encouraging but are not filled with much reality or truth at all.

我最近看到了一则有趣的新闻报道，该则新闻记录了5年前五名9岁的学生的视频。在最初的采访中，每一个孩子都对他们的美好未来表现出很高的信心。每个人都对自己在高中及以后所能取得的成就满怀"自信"。一个说要成为职业舞蹈家，另一个说要从事执法工作，还有一个说要成为职业运动员。他们的笑容和他们自己预言的未来一样灿烂。然后，在他们高中那年，这五个学生又被采访了。采访时向他们展示了五年前的视频，视频中他们脸上的表情十分清晰。当被问及五年后这个孩子现在在哪里时，每个人似乎都说着那个曾经高度自信的孩子，现在却不知道在承受着什么压力。他们说，他们在高年级时感受到的压力使他们对未来的计划没有了把握。

I recently saw an interesting news report that video-recorded five 9-year old students 5 years ago. In that initial interview, each of the five children demonstrated high levels of confidence in their bright future. Each spoke with "major league" confidence about the great things they would accomplish in high school and beyond. One was going to be a professional dancer, the other would work in law enforcement and still another would be a professional athlete. Their smiles were as big and bright as the future they predicted for themselves. Then, in their senior year of high school those same five students were interviewed again. They were shown their video from five years earlier and the look on their faces was revealing. When asked where is that child now five years later? Each spoke as if elements of that once over-confident child now had no idea what pressures they were to encounter. They revealed that the pressures they feel now in their senior year have left them insecure about their future plans.

压力不只是学业挑战，而是更大的人生挑战。社会压力是巨大的，自第一次面试以来，这种压力使他们最初的信心出现下滑。随着想成为舞者的学生意识到别人比她更有才华，她的职业目标发生了变化。前途无量的职业运动员被从他的高中队中除名，这似乎立即扼杀了他成为最佳运动员的梦想。在过去的 5 年中，他们经历了失败，而应对失败成为改变人生的力量，而这种力量曾经是充满信心的希望和梦想。

The pressure was less about the academic challenge but more about the challenge of dealing with life. Social pressure was significant, and it chipped away at their initial confidence since the first interview. Career goals had shifted as the dancer realized others were far more talented than she. The hopeful professional athlete was cut from his high school team, which seemed to instantly kill his dream of being an athlete at the highest level. Over the past 5 years of life, failure was introduced and dealing with that failure became a life-changing force that altered once confident hopes and dreams.

我是五个孩子的父亲，我知道当我自己的孩子失败时，我都满怀善意给出建议，让孩子们坚持下去或者继续努力。我不希望他们因失败而放弃。我想成为一个不断的鼓励者，以便他们理解毅力可以带来良好的结果。但也许这完全就是一条错误的信息。只要人们下决心去做某件事，他们就能完成任何事情或实现任何梦想，真是这样吗？我们如何教导孩子们有关失败的知识，将影响他们未来的希望和梦想。教育就包括着很多失败，老师和家长需要注意失败发生时我们所传达给孩子们的信息。

I am a father of five, and I know when my own children have failed, I have given each the well-meaning advice to stick with it or to keep working hard. I did not want failure to cause them to give up. I wanted to be a constant encourager, so that they would understand that perseverance could bring about good results. But maybe that message is the wrong message altogether. Is it true that if someone just puts their mind to do it, they can accomplish anything or be anything they dream to be? How we teach children about failure will impact their future hopes and dreams. Education includes a lot of failure, and teachers and parents need to be mindful of the message we give when failure happens.

回顾一下我那失败的棒球试验，父亲给我的信息是："儿子，也许你应该换一项运动"，这就是很好的建议。他本可以告诉我再坚持一两年，在某些情况下，成熟和更多的经验可能确实会有所回报。但是，在这种情况下，他的话对我来说给了我自由！我并没有因为父亲知道我明显缺乏能力而丧失信心。相反，父亲提出的换一项运动的建议使我开始学习足球和篮球，这最终成为我生命中两项重要的运动。我将自己在球场上与队友和教练共度的时光视为我梦寐以求的的最佳人生经历和职业培训。通过运动，我学会了如何应对失败。

Looking back at my failed baseball experiment, the message my dad gave me, "Son, maybe you should try another sport" was excellent advice. He could have told me to stick with it another year or two, and in some cases, maturity and additional experience could possibly pay off. But, in this case, his words were freedom to me! I wasn't crushed that my father did not have confidence in my obvious lack of ability. On the contrary, the suggestion from my dad to seek another sport led me to pick up soccer and basketball, which ended up being two significant sports in my life. I credit my time on the court and the field with teammates and coaches as the best life experience and professional job training I could have asked for. Through sports, I learned how to handle failure.

篮球运动员迈克尔. 乔丹是有史以来最著名的职业运动员之一。我曾读到他的一句名言，让我印象深刻，他在其中透露了他对失败的反应。他提到一个事实，在他杰出的职业生涯中，他有9,000多次投球没进。有23次他的教练和团队指望他再次投篮，从而有机会打成平局或赢得比赛。在他所经历的每一次信任中，迈克尔. 乔丹都失败了。在超过300场比赛中，他和队友都没能打败对手。这也是300个迈克尔. 乔丹的失败。（公平地说，我相信他的队友也发挥了作用。）然而，通过所有这些失败，他认为失败的机会是他最终成功的关键！我们可以从失败中学到很多东西，尤其是如果我们知道如何正确处理它，就更是这样。

One of the most famous professional athletes of all time was Michael Jordan, a basketball player. I was impressed when I came across a quote attributed to him where he revealed his reaction to failure. He relates the fact that in his illustrious career, he missed over 9,000 shots. Twenty-three times his coach and team looked to him to make a last second shot with a chance to tie or win the game. In each of those times of trust placed in him, Michael Jordan failed. More than 300 times, he and his teammates failed to defeat the opponent. These were also 300 Michael Jordan failures. (To be fair, I'm sure his teammates played a role as well.) Yet, through all these failures, he attributes the opportunity to fail as the key to why he succeeded! There are many lessons we can learn through failure, especially if we know how to deal with it properly.

当我们害怕失败时，我们就从自己、孩子和学生那里偷走了机会。

它阻止我们获得有价值的观点和人生经验。大多数学生不知道如何处理失败。与此同时，大多数父母都不希望自己的孩子在失败发生时感到不适。他们经常指手画脚，试图把责任推卸到别人身上。我们不知道如何应对失败，因此，我们不知道如何教育我们的孩子应对失败。

When we fear failure, we are stealing opportunity from ourselves, from our children and from our students. It prevents us from gaining valuable perspective and life lessons. Most students do not know how to deal with failure. Compound that with the fact that most parents who do not want their child to experience discomfort when failure does happen. They often point fingers and look to deflect the cause to make it someone else's fault. We do not know how to deal with failure and, consequently, we do not know how to teach our children about failure.

当我反思我人生中最有价值的课程时，我发现许多课程之前都有过影响巨大的失败。积极的课程可能不会在失败后马上出现，但它们似乎奇怪存在于那些失败的时刻。我不会单纯为了学会如何坚持而去经历失败。但我明白失败乃成长的机会。我仍然可能不喜欢或无法享受自己的失败，但如果我的成长心态是强大的，我可以更容易地坚持下去，并尝试从中找寻我可以学到的课程。

As I reflect on the most valuable lessons in my life, I find many are preceded by rather impactful failures. The positive lessons may not come immediately after, but they seem to come strangely close to a time of failure. I do not set out to fail simply so I can learn how to persevere. But I have learned that failure is an opportunity for growth. I still may not like or enjoy my failure, but if my growth mindset is strong, I can more easily persevere and try to look for the lessons I can learn.

教育中有很多失败。全球教育面临的一个最艰难的困境是，很大一部分往往是结果导向。分数往往被用来衡量学习。分数和平均绩点成为了判断一个学习者成功或失败的标志。糟糕的成绩不仅反映了学生的表现，也令人担忧地暗示了老师的失败。在大多数国家，老师要为学生取得的成绩承担巨大的压力和责任。如果学生成绩不够好，许多老师都要承担责任。学生、老师和学校都害怕失败。

There is a lot of failure in education. One of the hardest dilemmas of global education is that so much of it tends to be results-driven. Grades tend to be used to measure whether learning is taking place. Grades and G.P.A. (Grade Point Average) become the identifier of an individual learner's success or failure. Poor grades do not just reflect the learner's accomplishments, or lack thereof, but alarmingly, they may suggest the teacher failed, too. In most countries, there is tremendous pressure and responsibility placed on teachers for the grades earned by the students. Many teachers are held accountable if students do not score well enough. Students, teachers, and schools are afraid of failure.

为什么我们如此害怕失败？失败可不可以是一件好事？我们能从失败中吸取有价值的教训吗？是的！我不是说我们都能成为迈克尔.乔丹，但我确实认为我们都能从我们的失误中吸取教训，就像伟大的迈克尔.乔丹做到的那样。乔丹学会了如何处理失败，他做得比大多数人都好，把失败变成了动力。

Why are we so afraid of failure? Can failure be a good thing? Can we learn valuable lessons through failure? YES! I am not suggesting we can all be Michael Jordan, but I do think we can all learn lessons from our missteps, as did the great Michael Jordan. MJ learned how to handle failure, better than most, by turning his failures into his motivation.

我们能改善自己对失败的看法吗？是的。我相信，情感的成熟和高情商能让我们重新审视失败。因为我们可以清楚地识别我们的感觉，管理我们的情绪，保持心理和情感上的完整，这样一来，我们便给自己更大的机会从挫折中受益。

Can we improve our personal perspective on failure? Yes. I believe that emotional maturity and a high EQ allow us to rewire our perspective on failure. Because we can clearly identify our feelings, manage our emotions, and remain mentally and emotionally intact, we give ourselves a greater opportunity to benefit from our setbacks.

让学生为失败做好准备
Equipping Students to Fail

记住，我们恐惧的不应该是失败本身，我们应该恐惧的是永远不经历失败，因为我们可以在失败中学习。我们应该让学生做好失败的准备。失败的机会中蕴含着成长和学习，而不仅仅是失败的结果本身。

Remember, our fear should not be of failure itself, but rather never having to experience failure, because in failure can be learning. We should be equipping our students to fail. There is growth and learning in the opportunity, not just in the outcome.

教育文化淹没在竞争和成功之中。地方教育局总是想要宣传他们有最好的地方学校，这对广大家庭和学生极富吸引力。学校想成为最好的学校，希望自己被公认为本市最好的学校。校长们希望和学校一起被认为是最好的，这给他们带来名声和发展。老师希望被认为是最优秀的老师，这样他们可以提高他们的地位和工资。父母希望他们的孩子成为最好的学生，将来能进入最好的大学，过上最好的生活。学生们疯狂地努力成为班上的第一名，以使周遭的每个人都开心。这种循环或追求让我想到了一句谚语"狗在追自己的尾巴"。须知狗转得再快，也追不上自己的尾巴。

The education culture is drenched in competition and success. The local education bureaus want to promote that they have the best regional schools, and this attracts families and students. Schools want to be the best schools, so they can be recognized as the best in the city. Principals want to be recognized as best along with the school, which brings them notoriety and advancement. Teachers want to be considered the best teachers, so they can elevate their status and salaries. Parents want their students to be the best students, so they can get into the best universities and have the best life. Students frantically work to be number one in their class to make everyone else happy. This cycle or pursuit makes me think of the proverbial saying, "The dog is chasing its own tail". As fast as the dog may spin, it can never catch up to its own tail.

学校、家长和学生的部分追求是令人敬畏的。当然，我们都应该尽我们最大的努力去实现目标和梦想。但我担心的是，当前人们的关注点没有给失败留出空间。在这种模式下，成功是唯一的选择。一个60人的班里能有几个第一名？一个城市能有多少所顶尖的学校？所有的焦点都集中在第一名的成功上，那么剩下的竞争者的失败呢？他们对失败做好准备了吗？他们知道如何管理自己的失败吗？这种失败是有帮助的、有成效的，还是只是破坏性的、令人灰心丧气的？

Part of the pursuit by schools, parents and students is awesome. Sure, we should all work to our fullest potential to achieve goals and reach dreams. But my fear is that the current focus has no room for failure. In this model, success is the only option. How many number ones can there be in a class of 60 students? How many top schools can there be in any one city? With all the focus on the success of the top one, what about the failure of the remaining competitors? Are they prepared for failure? Do they know how to manage their failure? Can this failure be helpful and productive or simply devastating and disheartening?

我记得有人告诉我，"如果你没能取得成功，至少你成功地尽了最大的努力。"通过失败可以实现个人成长，甚至学到有价值的东西。失败的结果不一定是唯一的标识符或学到的教训。用成长的心态来吸收失败是有可能的，这样才能吸取教训，继续实现转变。了解失败的一个好方法就是研究那些经历了失败的人。

I remember someone telling me, "If you fail to succeed, at least you didn't fail to give it your best effort." There can be personal growth, and even valuable learning, through failure. The results of failure do not have to be the only identifier or lesson to be learned. It is possible to absorb the failure with an attitude of growth mindset so that lessons can be learned, and transformation continued. One great way to learn about failure is to study those who have failed.

美国最伟大的发明家之一是托马斯.阿尔瓦.爱迪生。爱迪生被认为是美国最伟大的发明家和商人之一，他在发电、大众通讯、录音和电影等领域发明了许多装置。在所有这些装置中，也许白炽灯泡是最有意义的。发明家当然了解失败。他的一些著名的关于失败的名言阐明了成长心态如何帮助我们在失败发生时管理自己的人生。"生活中的许多失败体现在人们放弃的时候并没有意识到他们离成功其实有多近。""我没有失败，我只是找到了一万种行不通的方法。"

One of America's great inventors was Thomas Alva Edison. Considered one of the greatest American inventors and businessman, Edison developed many devices in fields such as electric power generation, mass communication, sound recording, and motion pictures. Of all these devices, maybe his work on the incandescent light bulb was most significant. An inventor certainly knows failure. Some of his notable quotes about failure shed light on how a growth mindset can help us manage life when failure happens. "Many of life's failures are people who did not realize how close they were to success when they gave up." "I haven't failed. I just found 10,000 ways that won't work."

多么美好的失败视角啊。我们中有多少人在尝试了 9, 000 次、500 次甚至仅仅 3 次之后就放弃了？学生的课堂生活几乎连一次失败都容不下，更不用说多次失败了！我们需要借助失败来学习。当我把试卷发回去的时候，大多数学生只是看看自己的成绩，抱怨或欢呼，然后把它收起来。最好的学生则会检查他们的试卷，看看哪里出了错，甚至纠正这些错误来巩固他们的学习。失败的机会可以是值得学习的宝贵经验，也可以是毁灭性的，有时甚至是惊天动地的事件。

What a beautiful perspective on failure. How many of us would have given up after 9,000, 500, or even 3 attempts? So much about a student's life in the classroom barely gives room for 1 failure, let alone multiple failures! We need failure to help us learn. When I used to hand test papers back, most students simply looked at their grade, moaned or cheered, and then put it away. The best students looked through their test papers to see where the mistakes were made and even corrected those mistakes to solidify their learning. The opportunity to fail can be a valuable experience from which to learn or, it can be a devastating, and at times earth-shattering, eventuality.

运动员了解如何失败，因为他们失败的机会太多了。在任何体育比赛中，都有输赢之分。最好的教练和球员会从失败中回顾比赛录像，并试图分析他们可以做得更好的地方。然后他们将这些改变纳入他们未来的比赛计划中。传奇的大学篮球教练约翰.伍登曾告诉他的球队："失败是成功的后门。"他明白，当你赢了的时候，你很少会想办法去提高自己。获胜的前提是你每件事都做对了，结果你赢了，而另一个队输了。然而，胜利可能导致自满，并导致一种扭曲的观点，即胜利便等于完美。

Athletes know how to fail because they have so many opportunities to fail. In any athletic contest, there is a winner and a loser. The best coaches and players review the game film from a loss and try to dissect where they could have done better. They then build those changes into their future game plans. The legendary college basketball coach John Wooden would tell his team,

"Failure is the backdoor to success." He knew that when you win, you rarely look for ways to improve. Winning assumes you did everything correctly and, as a result, you won and the other team lost. However, winning can lead to complacency, and to the warped perspective that the victory equates to perfection.

许多学生害怕在教育中冒险，因为在结果导向的教育中，从糟糕的成绩挫折中恢复的空间很狭小。由于大家的分数中只有一小部分将学生划分为"最高分"，任何微小的风险都可能导致平均绩点的下降，从而导致班级排名的下降。学生们不愿冒险去追求好奇心或挑战某种假设，因为他们担心冒险的代价不值得。这是一种耻辱。生活中的伟大发明之所以能够实现，是因为人们的好奇心达到了顶峰，人们愿意承担风险。根据"数据"，对结果进行评估，好奇心可能会加深，并承担额外的风险。失败并不会让学习停止。它只是塑造和完善着学习的过程。

So many students are afraid of taking risks in education because in results-driven education, there is little room to recover from a poor grade setback. With just a fraction of a grade separating students for the "top spots", any slight risk could cause a drop in grade point average and therefore a drop in the class ranking. Students are hesitant to take a risk to pursue curiosity or challenge an assumption, for fear the risk is not worth the result. That is a shame. Great inventions in life were only achieved because curiosity was piqued, and risks were taken. Based on the "data", results were evaluated, curiosity was likely deepened, and additional risks were taken. Failure did not stop the learning. It simply shaped and refined it.

作为教育者，我们应该让学生体验参与式学习。我们不应该简单地把答案背下来，然后在考试时再现他们。那不是教育！相反，我们必须促进一种氛围，在这种氛围中，课堂上的冒险是健康的。我们希望他们挑战假设、质疑内容、验证他们的理论，以确保他们在学习。然后，我们

146

可以对他们和他们的学习进行公平的评估。评估之后，我们可以帮助他们应对学习中的成功和失败，通过建设性的评估达到更深层次的理解。

As educators, we should want students to experience engaged learning. We should not simply give them the answers to memorize and give back on an exam. That is not education! Rather, we must promote an atmosphere where it is healthy to take risks in the classroom. We want them to challenge assumptions, question content, and test their theories to ensure that they are learning. Then, we can assess them and evaluate their learning fairly. After the assessment, we can help them process the success and failure of their learning to reach even deeper depths of understanding through constructive evaluation.

学校、班级和学生之间总是会有竞争。无论如何，最优秀的学生将被视为最优秀的学生，但这就意味着大多数学生都是失败者的假设。这不是我们应该传递的信息。事实上，要成功，你不是非得成为第一。成功有很多层次。要鼓励学生别害怕失败，因为在失败中，学习也是可以发生的。我们应该教导学生永不失败就意味着永不尝试。这显然是一种不现实的人生观和生活方式。生活将充满失败，未来的失败可以带来未来的成功。失败可以提供不同视角和学习。然而，学校、校长、教师、学生和家长的态度目前并不承认失败的好处。无论如何，我们必须改变对失败的看法，这样人们才能对这种不可避免的、往往是有益的情况抱以一种更为健康的态度。

There will always be competition in schools, classes and among students. No matter what, the top students will be heralded as the best, but that leaves the assumption that the majority are failures. That is not the message to send. In fact, you don't have to be number one to be successful. There are many levels of success. Encourage students to not fear failure because in failure, learning can happen. We should teach students that to never fail is to never try. This is obviously an unrealistic outlook and approach on their life.

Life will be full of failures and future failures can produce future success. Failure can provide perspective and learning. However, the attitudes of schools, principals, teachers, students, and parents are not currently acknowledging the virtues of failure. Somehow, we have to change the narrative about failure, so people can adopt a healthier attitude toward this inevitable, and often beneficial, circumstance.

我们如何让学生做好失败的准备？
How Can We Prepare Our Students to Fail?

做好心态上的准备——教导学生每一次失败的经验都是一次丰富的学习机会。失败提供了胜利不能提供的视角。只有当我们亲身体验某件事时，我们才能对它有一个真切的看法。我不知道膝盖手术后的恢复会是什么样子，直到我自己经历了这一切。一个人不可能知道经历癌症治疗是什么感觉，除非他目睹或近距离感受。大多数人不愿意忍受消极的经历，但是生活中需要的心态和情商只能通过经历来培养。当失败发生时，预设的心态不仅是生存的重要工具，也是个人成长的重要工具。失败本身并不一定反映出一个人的身份。它只是成长过程的一部分。为失败做准备的方式是拥抱这样一种心态：从不经历失败实则会剥夺我们深入和真实的个人成长机会。

Prepare the Mindset - Teach students that each new experience of failure is a rich opportunity to learn. Failure provides perspective that winning does not. We can only gain a true perspective of something when we experience it for ourselves. I did not know what recovery from knee surgery would be like until I went through it on my own. One cannot know what it feels like to go through cancer treatment unless it has been seen or felt close up. Most people do not want to endure a negative experience, but the mindset and emotional intelligence needed in life is only developed through experience. A pre-determined MINDSET, when failure happens, is an important tool for not only survival, but for personal growth as well. The failure, itself, does not have to reflect the personal identity. It is just part of the growth process. Preparation for failure takes the form of accepting the mindset that to never experience failure robs us from the opportunity for deep and authentic personal growth.

预先确定反应。"心态"是我们想要的态度。而反应则是所采取的行动。它支持"行胜于言"的说法。一家业内领先的移动电话公司最近为商店抢劫实施了一项"虚拟现实模拟培训"。尽管企业高管们知道这种情况可能比较少见，但他们选择了积极的虚拟现实培训，而不是静态的 PPT 培训。最后，他们花了很多钱聘请了一家虚拟现实公司来创造多种生动的现实场景，这样员工们就能更好地准备好做出训练有素的反应。他们知道，如果事情真的发生了，在它发生之前演练一种反应会让人们做出更好的反应。这也是消防队员、警察和军事人员花费大量时间进行演习训练的原因。他们希望这种反应是预先计划好的肌肉反应，而不是毫无计划的情绪反应。人类可以预先思考和演练一个反应，这样一来，当失败发生时，他们便可以依靠他们的训练来减轻冲击和改善反应。教师可以帮助学生设想和演练各种冒险带来的不愿看到的结果。实践可以为难以避免的不幸事件提供虚拟现实训练。

Pre-determine the response. "Mindset" is the attitude we want to have. The response is the action taken. It supports the saying that "Actions speak louder than words". One major cell phone company recently implemented a "virtual reality simulation training" for store holdups. Even though corporate executives know these may be rare events, they opted for active virtual reality training instead of a static PPT training. They ended up spending a lot of money hiring a virtual reality firm to create multiple vivid reality scenarios so that employees felt better prepared to give a trained response. They know that practicing a response before it happens creates a better human reaction, should the event take place. This is the same reason firefighters, police officers, and military personnel spend so much time in drill training. They want the response to be a pre-planned muscle-response, not an unplanned emotional response. Humans can pre-meditate and rehearse a response, so that when failure happens, they can rely on their training to ease the shock and improve the response and reaction. Teachers can help students visualize and rehearse various scenarios where the risk-taking brings about undesired results. The practice can provide virtual reality training for the inevitable unfortunate occurrence.

建立应对机制——做好**万一**失败的准备是很重要的，但是做好失败**发生时**的准备更好，因为生活中难免会有挑战。机制则是应用的工具。当失败发生时，我们需要"求助"一个应对机制。在危机时刻，许多人求助于他们喜欢的机制工具——推卸责任或编造借口。像大多数人一样，我对此感到内疚！尽管我很努力，但我对失败的第一反应往往是寻找让我失望的人或事。通常，经过一些思考，我找到时间更诚实地评估实际情况，然后我便可以接受那可能是我自己的错，也可能不是我自己的错。

Develop A Coping Mechanism - It is important to Be prepared **IF** failure happens, but it is even better to be prepared for **WHEN** it happens, because life is inevitably challenging. A mechanism is a tool to apply. We need a "go to" coping mechanism when failure happens. In times of crisis, many people reach for their favored mechanism tool - cast blame or create an excuse. Like most, I am guilty of that! As hard as I try, my first response to failure is often to look for who or what I can blame for letting me down. Usually, after some reflection, I find time to evaluate the situation with more honesty, and I can, then, accept what may or may not have been my fault.

许多人没有应对机制，因此，当失败发生时，他们会进入情绪恐慌模式或在压力下走向崩溃。拥有优秀情商的人在遭遇失败时能建立起良好的应对机制。像迈克尔.乔丹这样的人并不比其他人更享受失败。只不过当失败发生时，他们运用了更强的应对机制。像他一样，我比任何人都想要失败！善于失败意味着我知道如何接受它，并比别人更好地处理它。我的机制必须很强大。

Many people have no coping mechanism and therefore, when failure happens, they go into an emotional panic mode or simply crumble under the pressure. Individuals with exceptional emotional intelligence are those who develop excellent coping mechanisms when failure finds them. People like Michael Jordan don't enjoy failure more than anyone else. They simply apply stronger coping mechanisms to the situation when failure happens. Like him, I want to fail better than anyone else! Being good at failure means that I know how to accept it and handle it better than others. My mechanisms must be strong.

开发健康的手段来处理失败是很重要的。有些人会向比自己聪明的人请教，以此帮助他们处理事件和情绪。老师和家长通常是提供建议和观点的好资源。有些人把阅读作为一种处理失败的工具，而另一些人则把写日记作为一种健康的方式来处理他们的失败。还有一些人则会进行一些极具攻击性的活动来"发泄"和反思。关键是找到一种工具来采取行动，被称为健康而富有成效的反应的行动。许多人会发展出一些破坏性的工具，如责备、药物治疗或抑郁。健康的工具是建设性而非破坏性的。

It is important to develop healthy tools for dealing with failure. Some turn to counsel with someone wiser than they to help process events and emotions. Teachers and parents are often great resources for advice and perspective. Some turn to reading as a tool to process, while others turn to writing in a journal as a healthy way to deal with their lack of success. Still others turn to highly aggressive activity to "burn off steam" and reflect. The key is to find a tool to put into action that is known as a healthy and productive response. Many people develop destructive tools such as blame, medication, or depression. Healthy tools are constructive, not destructive.

分析应对方式——精神上做好准备，然后积极应对是很重要的，但是需要不断评估这些"手段"的有效性。这就像一场赛后新闻发布会，教练必须在球队输球之后进行复盘。教练进入新闻发布室时，知道他／她将回答记者关于发生了什么以及为什么球队失败等方面的问题。教练将会对比赛指令、球员执行、比赛策略和决策进行分析。分析情况并形成对逆境的应对方式有助于确定所采用的应对手段是健康的还是不健康的。

Analyze the Response - Mentally preparing, and then actively responding, are important, but these "tools" need to be constantly evaluated for effectiveness. This is like a post-game press conference that a coach must deal with after a team loss. The coach enters the press room knowing he/she will field questions from the reporters as to what happened and why the team failed. The coach is expected to give an analysis for play calling, player execution, game strategy and decisions. Analyzing the situation and formulating a response to adversity help one determine whether the coping tools applied are healthy or unhealthy.

健康的分析练习需要对所有情况和个人反应进行清晰的回顾。这是有可能独立做到的，在导师的指导和客观性的帮助下做这件事也是很有帮助的。进行分析的时间会有所不同，但重要的是它要发生。以层层深入的方式，找出难题，寻求真理。反应的有效性、反作用和结果将变得愈加清晰。这将导致更好的自我理解和反应手段的强化。

A healthy analytical exercise requires a clear-minded review of all circumstances and personal reactions. It is possible to do this independently, or it may be helpful to do it with the guidance and objectivity of a mentor or someone who gives good counsel. The timing of when this analysis takes place will vary, but what is important is that it happens. Peel back the layers, ask the difficult questions, and seek the truth.   The effectiveness of the response, reaction, and results will become clear.   This will lead to greater self-understanding and the sharpening of the response tools.

寻找最佳疗法——失败可能会带来创伤，但不一定会使人衰弱。失败往往会带来不安全感和尴尬。当这种情况发生时，一些人倾向于躲到一个私人的、通常是黑暗的地方，而不是寻求有助于恢复信心和治愈的治疗。我们都时不时地需要疗愈，有些人的需求更甚于其他人！

Seek the Best Therapy - Failure can be traumatic, but it does not have to be debilitating.   Failure often produces insecurity and embarrassment. When this happens, some tend to retreat into a private and often dark place, instead of seeking the therapy that will help restore confidence and provide healing. We all need therapy from time to time, and some of us more than others!

要选择高效的疗法。许多人寻求不同形式的治疗方案。有些人向知己寻求建议，而有些人则选择求助该领域的专家。有些人想获得保证和肯定，而另一些人则希望获得诚实的客观性。寻求治疗是重要的，知道需要治疗的水平也同样重要。当我们犯错时，一个有害的倾向是向那些使我们感觉更好的人寻求肯定。在这种时刻，我们不需要判断或建议，而是在寻求支持和肯定，以减轻伤害的感觉。虽然我们在绝望的时候都需要安慰，但任何一种治疗都只有在以温和的诚实的方式揭示真相时才具有价值。有益的治疗应该"实事求是"，而非仅仅告诉我们想听的话。

Choose productive therapy.   Many seek therapeutic solutions in different forms.   Some seek the advice of confidants, while some choose experts in the field.   Some want reassurance and affirmation, while others want honest objectivity.   The act of seeking therapy is important and knowing the level of therapy needed is equally important.   One detrimental tendency, when a mistake is made, is to seek affirmation from those who make us feel better.

In this moment, we don't want judgment or advice. We are looking for support and affirmation to mitigate hurt feelings. Though we all need comfort in our times of despair, therapy of any kind is only valuable when there is a revelation of truth offered with a gentle dose of honesty. Helpful therapy should "tell it like it is" and not just tell us what we want to hear.

教师和家长可以是很好的治疗选择，前提是他们可以先倾听，然后给出建议。一个好的治疗师会专注地倾听，不仅仔细衡量患者的解释或话语，而且要管理他们自己的情绪，这样他们才能在回应时保持客观性。当一个治疗师得知你的失败时，若他开始哭泣或大笑，你便会对他失去信心。一个好的治疗师须保持情感上的抽离，这样他们可以在没有情感依赖的情况下给出分析和建议。学生们常常觉得没有人听他们说话。许多父母都不会倾听，他们只是自作主张地给出建议。太多的老师也不倾听，他们只是告诉他们的学生要"加倍努力"。如果你的课堂是一个人们可以安心失败的地方，那么你的学生可能也会觉得你是一个有同情心而且公平的人，这样一来，他们便会在需要好的治疗时向你寻求帮助。

Teachers and parents can be great therapy options, provided they can listen first and advise second. A good therapist listens intently, carefully measuring not only the individual's explanation or words, but also managing their own emotions so that they can remain objective in their response. One would lose confidence in a therapist who started crying or laughing when they learn of your failure. A good therapist remains emotionally disconnected so that they can be analytical and advise without emotional attachment. Students often feel they have no one to listen to them. Many parents do not listen. They simply give unsolicited advice. Too many teachers do not listen. They just tell their students to "work harder." If your classroom is a safe place to fail, then your students may also feel that you are an empathetic and fair person for them to seek out when good therapy is needed.

重新设定方向——最终，如果人们从中学到了东西，也能做出改变，那么，失败相对而言是无关紧要的。不要让失败获得永久居留权。坦承失败、感受和原因，然后重新设定你的方向。生活充满了方向性的重置，我们要不断地调整以适应眼前的环境。

Reset the Course - Ultimately, failure is relatively inconsequential if learning occurs, and changes can be made. Don't let failure take up permanent residency. Acknowledge the failure, the feeling, the causes, and then reset your course for a new direction. Life is full of directional resets, as we constantly adjust to the circumstances presented to us.

让我们想象一个水手，他研究天气、风、潮汐和水图，以确定最佳和最安全的航行路线。然后，经过分析，他确定了最好的航线。他把他的仪器调校到正确的位置，只有在所有这些设置和关键步骤都完成之后，他才会走开。即使在所有这些预防措施都做好之后，有时水手也会根据情况的变化而做出调整。简单地根据第一组数据"保持航向"可能会使船只陷入一场猛烈的风暴。

Consider the sailor who studies the weather, wind, tide and water charts to ascertain the best and safest course of travel. Then, after analysis, he decides the best course. He sets his instruments to the correct alignment and will only then depart on the trip, once all those settings and crucial steps have been completed. Even after all these preparatory precautions, there are times when the sailor makes adjustments based on the changing conditions. To simply "stay the course" based on the first set of data could lead the boat into a fierce storm.

在绘制海洋航线时，航海仪器要根据新的数据进行调整。这些调整常常意味着为了支持新的计划而放弃原来的计划。失败不在于计划的重新调整，而在于缺乏在需要时进行调整／改变的敏感性。有了正确的心态，从失败中学习，从而揭示新的信息，这样我们就可以重新规划我们的方向。重新绘制我们的航向算不上失败，但**不**学习使用新数据进行必要的调整则潜藏着巨大的失败。

　　In plotting a course in the ocean, adjustments to the navigational instruments are made based on new data. These adjustments often dictate the abandonment of the original plan to support the new one. The failure is not in the realignment of the plan, but rather in the failure to not have the sensibility to adapt/change when needed. With the right mindset, learning through failure reveals new data so we can re-chart our direction. There is no failure in re-charting our direction, but there is significant potential failure in NOT learning to use new data to make needed adjustments.

　　考虑风险 DNA——我相信，对失败的恐惧与对风险的承受能力密切相关。有些人似乎反感风险带来的暴露感，而另一些人则完全被风险所削弱。最近，我看了国家地理频道的纪录片《徒手攀岩》，该片讲述了极限登山者亚历克斯.霍诺德的故事。他试图徒手攀登北美最令人恐惧的花岗岩面——酋长岩。值得注意的是，对于一个徒手攀岩者来说，失败就意味着死亡。他们在攀登岩面时不使用绳索或安全措施。如果霍诺德失败了，他就会死。

　　Consider the Risk DNA - I believe the fear of failure is closely connected to the tolerance for risk. There are those individuals who seem to be slightly averse to the feeling of exposure that risk can offer, while others are completely debilitated by it. I recently watched the National Geographic documentary entitled, *"Free Solo",* featuring extreme mountain climber Alex Honnold, who attempts to free climb the most feared granite face in North America - El Capitan. It is important to note that for a free-climber, failure means death. Free-climbers climb rock faces without the use of ropes or safety measures. If Honnold fails, he dies.

　　我不是个攀岩者，因为我恐高。在整部电影中，当我试图理解霍诺德是如何应对摔倒的恐惧，以及如何保持克服这种恐惧所需的精神毅力时，我本人被恐惧所笼罩。就像乔丹比大多数人更能应对失败一样，霍诺德也比大多数人更能应对恐惧。他承认有时恐惧是很强烈的，他坚称自己并没有求死之心或想要早点结束生命的愿望。然而，霍诺德似乎有一种特殊的能力，能将常见的恐惧和失败的感觉转化为强烈的专注和决心。他减轻了自己的恐惧，提升了自己的专注和动力。大多数人则恰恰相反。通常情况下，恐惧使人丧失行动能力，使他们无法行动或至少无法清醒地思考，而对霍诺德而言，恐惧只是一种被他掌控的、可识别的、受人尊敬的力量。因此，他并没有忽视恐惧，只是比普通人更好地控制了它。

I am not a climber because I am fearful of heights. Throughout the movie, I was gripped with fear as I tried to understand how Honnold dealt with the fear of falling and sustained the mental stamina required to manage that fear. Like Jordan, who can handle failure better than most, Honnold is able to manage his fear better than most. He acknowledges times when fear is intense and he insists that he does not have a personal death wish or desire to exit life early. However, it seems that Honnold has a special ability to channel and focus common feelings of fear and failure into intense focus and determination. He mitigates his fear to accentuate his focus and drive. Most people are the opposite. Typically, fear incapacitates people and renders them unable to act or at least think clearly, whereas for Honnold, it is simply a recognizable and respected force to be contained and controlled by him. As a result, his fear is not ignored. It is just better controlled than it is for the average person.

大量关于大脑的新研究似乎揭示了强有力的证据，表明风险承受力与选择无关，而更多地与基因编码有关。遗传学家告诉我们，DRD4（被称为"新奇基因"）附着在 11 号染色体上，它决定了你是一个风险承受者还是一个风险规避者。根据泰勒.特沃伦（风险学创始人，他称自己为内向者撰写有关成为伟大领导者的科学和策略的文章）的说法，一个人的风险承受能力实际上是一种写在遗传密码里的性格特征。

Plenty of new studies on the brain seem to reveal strong evidence that risk tolerance is less about choice and more about genetic coding. Geneticists tell us that DRD4 (referred to as the "novelty gene") is attached to Chromosome 11, and that it holds the key as to whether or not you are a risk taker or risk avoider. According to Tyler Tervooren (founder of Riskology - who claims he writes for introverts about the science and strategies for becoming a great leader) an individual's risk tolerance is, in fact, a personality trait written in the genetic code.

特拉华大学的研究人员研究了出生时被分开的同卵双胞胎。他们很好奇，想知道被分开的双胞胎是否因为各自的基因而表现出彼此的特征，或者他们的环境是否影响了他们的基因编码。研究表明，被分开的双胞胎表现得更像他们的亲生父母，而不是他们的环境父母。这似乎证实了预设遗传编码的说法。

Researchers at the University of Delaware studied identical twins that were separated at birth. They were curious to see if the separated twins showed characteristics of the each other because of their genes, or if their environments shaped them regardless of their genetic coding. The study revealed that the separated twins acted like their biological parents more than their environmental parents. This seems to affirm the case for the predetermined genetic code.

是什么让一些人能够冒险而另一些人则不能呢？是什么让企业家们敢于冒险？他们在生物学上就是被这样设计的吗？企业家似乎能看到机会，在普通人认为不值得冒险和恐惧的地方采取行动。在研究了 550 位企业家后，他们意识到企业家并不认为自己是冒险家。大多数企业家认为自己是风险厌恶者，而非冒险者。特沃伦认为，企业家往往依赖于博学的无知，而不是经过周密计算的风险管理。这并不是说他们更愿意承担风险，而是他们比其他人更愿意承担风险，他们只是能够以不同的方式看待风险。

What makes some able to take risks and others unable? What makes entrepreneurs risk takers? Are they biologically designed to do so? It seems as if entrepreneurs see opportunity and can act where the average person sees the fear and the risk not worth taking. After studying 550 entrepreneurs, they realized that entrepreneurs do not self-identify as risk takers. Most entrepreneurs identify themselves as risk averse rather than risk takers. Tervooren thinks that entrepreneurs are often dependent on learned ignorance, rather than calculated risk management. It is not that they are more open to taking a risk, but rather more than anyone else, they are just able to view the risk differently.

我有很多朋友是企业家，也有很多朋友不是。我想我明白特沃伦表达的意思了。我的一些企业家朋友把机会视为高风险的东西，然后避开它们，而另一些人则把机会视为挑战，并倾向于直面它们。成功的企业家之所以出类拔萃，不是因为他们没有看到其他人所看到的危险，而是因为他们只是以不同的方式应对或管理了这些恐惧。看不到的东西你是无法逃避的！

I have friends who are entrepreneurs and I have many who are not. I think I see what Tervooren is saying. Some of my entrepreneurial friends see an opportunity as a high level of risk and then avoid it, while others see opportunity and gravitate towards it for the challenge. Successful entrepreneurs excel, not because they fail to see the hazards that others do, but because they simply appease or manage those fears differently. You can't run away from that which you cannot see!

好消息是，虽然你的遗传密码可能控制着你的风险承受力，但可能有一些方法可以提高你承担更多风险的能力。研究人员认为，你可以通过一些集中的练习，简单地训练你的大脑绕过杏仁核（大脑中用来远离危险的部分）。如果你能避开大脑决策的这一部分，你就能创造一个旁路机制，让你开始看到机会，而不是只感知风险。

The good news is that although your genetic code may claim control over your risk tolerance, there may be some ways to improve your ability to take more risks. Researchers believe that you can simply train your brain to bypass the amygdala (part of the brain designed to keep you away from danger) with some concentrated practice. If you could avoid that part of the decision-making brain, you could create a bypass mechanism, which could then allow you to begin seeing the opportunity more than sensing the risk.

我可能永远不会跳伞。我为什么要跳出一架机况完美的飞机？我永远不会带着安全绳爬酋长岩，当然没有安全绳就更不会爬了——这似乎是必死无疑的。我不会体验自由落体，也不会考虑蹦极——这两种运动对我来说都相当危险。为什么我不能像看待其他类型的"冒险"行为一样看待这些活动呢？很明显，有些人看待它们的风险（或恐惧）程度与我不同。我恐高。我想我对高度的厌恶在很大程度上被 11 号染色体上的东西注定了。然而，我身边的人告诉我，我是个冒险家。

I probably will never sky dive. Why would I jump out of a perfectly good plane? I will never climb El Capitan with ropes and certainly not without ropes - that seems like guaranteed death. I will not free fall, nor will I consider bungee jumping - both seem dangerous to me. Why is it that I cannot view these activities in the same way as I do other types of "risky" behavior? Clearly some do not view them with the same level of risk (or fear) that I do. I am afraid of heights. I think my aversion to heights is locked into chromosome #11 in a big way. However, there are those close to me who tell me I am a risk taker.

这可能有助于解释为什么有些学生在学校缺乏自信，不敢在课堂上举手，不敢尝试担任领导职务，或不敢参加运动队。也许他们的基因编码将竞选学生干部职位和从一架完美的飞机上跳下来画上了等号！也许站在同事面前发表演讲就像你的脚踝上绑着一根巨大的弹簧绳，然后从桥上被甩下去一样让你害怕。也许 11 号染色体对于每个人的影响是不同的，而且是独特的、难以抗拒的。一种人看到风险，另一种人看到机会。一种人害怕失败，另一种人则看到可能性。一种人在恐惧中退缩，而另一种人则似乎信心倍增。它可能不是胆量、天赋或勇气。它可能只是遗传编码使然。

This may help to explain why some students lack the self-confidence in school to raise their hands in class, try out for leadership positions, or try out for a sports team. Maybe their genetic coding equates running for a student leadership position to jumping out of a perfectly good airplane! Maybe standing in front of peers to give a speech is viewed with the same fear as having an over-sized and super-charged rubber band tied around your ankles and being thrown off a bridge! Maybe the #11 chromosome has a different impact on each person in a unique and compelling way. Where one sees risk, the other sees opportunity. Where one fears failure, the other sees possibilities. Where one retreats in fear, the other surges with seemingly unending confidence. It might not be bravery, talent, or courage. It might just be living out the genetic code.

教师与学生建立个人关系是很重要的，这样他们可以更好地帮助学生管理和理解失败的恐惧。在理想情况下，父母也应该参与到这项任务中来，但由于许多父母忙于工作，孩子们常常被抛在一旁，需要自己去发现这一点。基因编码在我们对恐惧和失败的个人看法中起到了作用。帮助学生了解自己将帮助他们更好地驾驭人生，塑造他们面对恐惧和失败的方式。

It is important for teachers to build a personal relationship with students so that they can better help students manage and understand fear of failure. Ideally, parents should also participate in this task, but with many parents who are too busy with work life, children are often left to discover this for themselves. Genetic coding contributes to our personal perspective of fear and fear of failure. Helping students learn about themselves will help them better navigate life and shape their approach to fear and failure.

总结
Summary

人们对失败和恐惧的态度及反应在年轻时就已经形成了。遗传编码似乎在风险承受或风险规避方面起到了作用。教师和家长对学生的成长有着不可否认的影响，因此，他们必须认识到自己的责任和使命，从而真正地教授更多的东西，而不仅仅是学科知识。真正的教育要把学业内容和人生管理结合起来。细心的良师益友必须细心地指导他们的学生。要做到这一点，他们必须非常了解学生。

Attitudes and reactions to failure and fear are established at a young age. The genetic code seems to contribute to risk tolerance or risk aversion. Teachers and parents have undeniable influence on the growth of students and, consequently, must recognize their responsibility and mission to truly teach more than just subject content. Real education combines academic content with life management. Attentive mentors, who understand, love, and care, must carefully guide their students. To do that, they must know them well.

迈克尔.乔丹因为不够好而被高中篮球队除名。然而，他的教练很小心地帮助迈克尔克服了这次失败，并将其转化为一种鼓舞。四年后，他帮助北卡罗来纳大学赢得了大学篮球赛全国冠军。迈克尔.乔丹并没有打算失败。事实上，他对失败恨之入骨。然而，他学会了比大多数人更好地处理失败。通过失败，乔丹提高了他的专注力，约束了他的行动，重新下定决心，培养毅力并形成观点。他拥抱失败的机会，不是因为他喜欢失败，而是因为他可以从中吸取教训。你的课堂里的失败文化是这样的吗？

Michael Jordan was cut from his high school basketball team because he wasn't good enough. However, his coach was careful to help Michael manage that failure, which he turned into inspiration. Four years later, he helped the University of North Carolina win the College Basketball National Championship. Michael Jordan did not set out to fail. In fact, he hated failure with every fiber of his being. However, he learned to handle failure better than most. Through failure, Jordan was able to sharpen his focus, discipline his actions, reset his determination, develop his perseverance and shape his perspective. He embraced the opportunity to fail, not because he loved failure, but for the lessons that could be learned. Is this the culture of failure in your classroom?

没有人想要失败，但是从失败中获得的经验和教训可能是毁灭性的，也可能是影响深远的，这取决于一个人管理失败的能力。我们不应该害怕失败，而应该害怕丢失失败可以提供给我们的机会。有了正确的心态、态度、指导和反应，所有人都能学到人生课程并形成未来的经验。有了决心和努力，学生们就能学会接受失败的教训，虽然这常常让人不舒服，但却是有必要的。有了耐心、爱心和同理心，老师和家长需要提高警惕，并且意识到教育学生如何正确处理失败的必要性。

No one wants to fail, but the experience and learning that can come through failure can be either devastating or impactful, depending on one's ability to manage it. We should not fear failure, but we should fear not having the opportunity that failure can provide. With the proper mindset, attitude, guidance, and response, all humans can learn life lessons and shape future experiences. With determination and hard work, students can learn to embrace the often uncomfortable, but necessary, lessons of failure. With patience, love, and empathy, teachers and parents need to be vigilant and aware of the need for teaching students how to properly fail.

学校需要智商，人生需要情商
IQ for School – But EQ for Life

Image credit: Greater Zurich Area

年幼的孩子演示了情绪智力发展的最佳图景。把一组 2 岁和 3 岁的孩子放在同一个房间里，把玩具数量放得比孩子的数量少，你就会发现谁的情商得到了增强，而谁的情商还有待提高。他们的互动似乎是天生的反应，而不是深思熟虑之后的选择。我们都知道学校的任务是提高学生的智商，但是谁来负责学生的情商呢？其中哪一个对人生的"成功"更为重要呢？

Young children provide the best picture of what emotional intelligence (EI) development looks like. Put a group of 2 and 3-year old children in a room together with fewer toys than there are children and you will see who has, or who needs increased EQ (Emotional Quotient) enhancements. Their interactions appear to be innate reactions, as opposed to thoughtful choices. We all know schools are charged with increasing the learner IQ, but who is responsible for the student EQ? Which will be more crucial to "success" in life?

摘自 2013 年 12 月 28 日的文章《智商是遗传的吗?》作者 IQ-Brain：
"智商是先天决定的还是后天环境造就的?长期以来，科学家们一直对智

商的起源以及智商是遗传的还是环境刺激的结果很感兴趣。事实上，如果智商能解释为环境因素(即养育，而非天性使然)，那么这便验证了全球数以百万计的父母的做法，他们相信他们为孩子投入的所有时间，精力和金钱，以及由此创造的环境刺激将使他们的孩子获得更高的智商，而更好的教育和智慧将帮助他们的孩子在这个充满竞争的世界表现得更好。"

According to the December 28, 2013 article, "IS IQ GENETIC?" by IQ-Brain: *"Is IQ genetically pre-determined or is IQ formed and acquired by the environment? Scientists have long been intrigued by the origins of IQ, and whether IQ is genetically inherited or whether a high IQ is the result of a stimulating environment. If IQ is, in fact, explained by environmental factors (i.e. nurture rather than nature) then this provides validation to millions of parents, globally, who would like to believe that all the time, effort, and money that they are investing in creating stimulating environments for their children will pay off with higher IQs, and that greater education and smarts will help their children to do better in a competitive world."*

然而，如果智商被发现是遗传决定的，那么这就对许多学校赖以生存的高压、以结果为导向的学习环境的有效性提出了质疑。可能有一部分学生在这种环境中茁壮成长，因为他们的智商早已被内置，只是在学习中受到了激发。对其他人来说，他们在努力挖掘自身潜力时，被迫感到缺乏安全感和能力。父母和老师要求他们加倍努力地学习。然而，如果智商存在于基因编码之中，又能有多少变异和改变的可能呢？虽然通过数据得出的结论表明智商主要是由基因编码决定的，但情商则是由经验开发和塑造的。哪个对一个人未来的人生有最大的贡献呢？

However, if IQ is found to be genetic, then this calls into question the usefulness of high pressure, results-driven learning environments in which many schools thrive. There may be some segment of students who thrive in this setting because their IQ is already built in and is simply stimulated. For the others, they are forced to feel insecure and less than capable as they try to work towards their potential. Parents and teachers demand they work harder. However, if IQ is in the genetic coding, how much variation and change is possible? Whereas it seems conclusive through data that suggest IQ is primarily determined through genetic coding, EQ is developed and shaped by experiences. Which will make the greatest contribution to one's future life?

在 2016 年世界经济论坛的一篇文章《机器人能做你的工作吗？》中，创始人克劳斯. 施瓦布重申，需要采取"紧急和有针对性的行动"，建立一支具备未来所需技能的劳动力队伍。人们可能很快就会认为，在这个人工智能创新的时代，"应对未来的技能"可能会集中在高技术和先进的计算机或工程技能上。显然，这些技能是有需求的，并将继续保持需求。然而，哈佛大学副教授大卫. 戴明强调，分享和谈判等技能也将至关重要！"现代的工作场所中，人们在不同的角色和项目之间转换，非常类似于幼儿园，我们在那里学到社会技能，比如同情和合作。"事实证明，应对未来技能是我们在学前班就学到了的！具有讽刺意味的是，这些认识不是通过读书或听讲座形成的，而是通过早期简单的以经验为基础的游戏而形成的。据估计，通过玩耍（10-20 次重复）形成联系的速度要比其他学习方式快 400 倍。我们可以从观察孩子行为中学到很多东西，有证据表明，如果你提供有趣的游戏体验，学生的情商会迅速提高。

In a 2016 World Economic Forum article, *"Can a Robot do your job?"*, founder Klaus Schwab iterated that there is an "urgent and targeted action" needed to build a workforce equipped with future-proof skills. One might be quick to assume that, in this AI (Artificial Intelligence) age of innovation, "future proof skills" might be centered on highly technical and advanced computer or engineering skills. Clearly these skills are in demand and will continue to be so. However, associate professor at Harvard University, David Deming, highlights that skills such as sharing and negotiation, will be crucial! "The modern workplace, where people move between different roles and projects, closely resembles pre-school classrooms, where we learn social skills such as empathy and cooperation." It turns out that future-proof skills are those we learned at the pre-school age! Ironically, those realizations were formed not through book reading or attending a lecture, but through simple experience-based play at the earliest age. It is estimated that connections are formed faster through play (10-20 repetitions) versus 400 repetitions for other types of learning. We have much to learn from simply watching children, but evidence suggests that if you provide fun, play experience, a student's EQ increases very rapidly.

EQ（情商）或 EI（情绪智力）可以简单地归结为理解两个实体——自我和他人。情商是识别、理解和管理自己情绪的能力，也是识别、理解和影响他人情绪的能力。高情商要求的不仅仅是专注和自我认知。同样重要的是要有能力看到别人的内在品质。高情商的人通常具有以下特征：与他人合作融洽、理解团队的概念（他人第一，自我第二）、有表达同理心的能力。同理心的定义是准确地感知他人感受或表达的情感。还是那样，最纯粹的观察情商发展的形式是观察一群幼儿玩耍和互动。你将能从中观察到那些已经在构建情商的人以及那些对其提出挑战的人。观察是确定情商存在的最好方法。任何学龄前孩子的老师都会告诉你，他们大部分学生行为的重新定向或 SEL（社会情感学习）都基于孩子如何对待他人。这就是情商训练。

EQ (emotional quotient) or EI (Emotional Intelligence) may be broken down to simply understanding two entities - self and others. EQ is the ability to recognize, understand, and manage your emotions, but to also recognize, understand and influence the emotions of others. High EQ requires more than just focus and recognition of self. It is equally important to have the ability to see the intrinsic qualities in others. Characteristics of those with high EQ typically include working well with others, understanding the concept of team (others first, self-second) and having the ability to express empathy. The definition of empathy is accurately perceiving the emotions felt or expressed by others. Again, the purest observable form of blooming EQ is to watch a group of toddlers play and interact. In doing so, you will be able to observe those who are already building EQ and those for whom it is a challenge. Observation is the best way to determine the presence of EQ. Any preschool teacher will tell you that much of their student behavior redirection, or SEL (Social Emotional Learning), centers on how children treat others. This is EQ training.

可能智商的最好定义是在专门测试智力的标准化评估中获得的评估分数。简而言之，智商是对所学信息的认知推理和回忆，是将这些知识应用于技能的能力。智商较高的人可以抽象地思考，并且可以进行逻辑或技术上的联系，以简化归纳。智商高的人具有学习复杂信息、进行整理的能力，然后他们可以回忆并将其应用于现实生活中。

IQ might be best defined as an evaluated score received from standardized assessments designed to specifically test intelligence. Simply put, IQ is the cognitive reasoning and recall of information learned, and the ability to apply that knowledge to skill sets. People with higher IQ's can think in the abstract and supposedly make logical or technical connections to make generalizations easier. Those with high IQ possess the ability to learn complex information, sort it out, and can then recall and apply that knowledge to real life situations.

许多人认为智商中位数为 100（偏差约为 15）。有多种智商测试表格可用于建立智商分数。韦克斯勒成人智力量表和斯坦福—比奈测验等热门测验显示，平均分数介于 90 到 109 之间。在这些相同的测试中，落在 110 和 119 之间的分数被认为是较高的平均 IQ 分数。80 到 89 之间的分数则被归入低平均水平。

Many believe the IQ median score is 100 (with a deviation of about 15). There are various IQ test forms used to establish an IQ score. Popular tests such as Wechsler Adult Intelligence Scale and the Stanford-Binet test, reveal that the average scores fall between a range 90 and 109. On these same tests, scores that fall between 110 and 119 are considered high average IQ scores. Scores between 80 and 89 are classified as low average.

晶态智力是指人类运用和利用知识、技能和经验的能力。晶态智力依赖于从长期存储中检索到的信息。它就像人一生中获得知识的主要存储库一样。人们相信，随着经验的积累，晶态智力会随着时间的推移而改善，从而进一步促进知识的增长。这里所传达的简单信息是充分生活，以尝试积累尽可能多的经验。你会因此变得更聪明！晶态智力扩展了我们的知识存储，但也被认为在 70 岁左右或没有使用时就会开始下降。还是那句话，要积极活跃地充实你的大脑，因为"如果不使用它，你就会失去它。"保持好奇心并继续学习新事物，以使你的晶态智力变得敏锐并积极投入。

Crystallized intelligence refers to the human ability to apply and utilize knowledge, skills, and experience. Crystallized intelligence relies on information retrieved from long-term memory storage. It is like the main storage vault of knowledge obtained and acquired throughout an individual's lifetime. Crystallized intelligence is believed to improve over time, as experience is added, and would therefore contribute further to the growth of one's knowledge. The simple message here is to live life fully in an attempt to add as much experience as possible. You will be smarter because of it! Crystallized intelligence expands our knowledge storage, but it is also thought to begin declining at about age 70 or without usage. Again, live an active and full life to engage your brain because, "if you don't use it, you lose it." Stay curious and continue learning new things to keep your crystallized intelligence sharp and actively engaged.

流体智力很容易被认为是个人利用理性解决新遇到的问题或情况的

能力。流体智力高的人可以轻松应对新问题或新情况，并创建合乎逻辑的解决方案。它需要归纳和演绎推理，逻辑思维过程以及数学、科学和/或对技术数据的回忆。流体智力也被定义为一个人的天生学习能力。流体智力是一个人脚踏实地思考、处理信息并做出适当反应的能力。

Fluid intelligence may be easily thought of as an individual's capability to utilize reason to solve newly encountered problems or situations. A person with a high fluid intelligence can comfortably approach new problems or situations and create logical solutions to use in their response and reaction. It requires both inductive and deductive reasoning, a logical thought process, and the recall of mathematical, scientific, and/or technical data. Fluid intelligence is also defined as a person's innate ability to learn. Fluid intelligence is a person's ability to think on his/her feet, process information, and come up with an appropriate response.

流体智力是一个人从以往的经验中得出的道理，合乎逻辑地处理新情况和解决问题的能力。流体智力不是通过书籍或记忆学来的，而是通过识别模式和空间关系来习得的。它使用已学到的知识和技能来解决任何以前获得的知识之外的新问题（非常适合填写空白的测试问题或确定单词量，例如词汇测试题）。

Fluid intelligence is a person's ability to logically deal with new situations and solve problems using reason drawn from previous experiences. Fluid intelligence is not learned through books or memorization, but rather from identifying patterns and spatial relationships. It uses learned knowledge and skills to resolve new problems outside of any previously acquired knowledge (great for fill-in-the blank test questions or defining words such as vocabulary tests).

我在许多以学生考试成绩为中心的学校里，看到的是对事实记忆的狭隘关注，而对"经验"或课堂知识应用的忽视。重复学习是有价值的，但是学生也非常需要体验可以挑战流体智力的新场景。看重事实性知识的课堂常常忽视过程对产品的价值。如果学生在考试中得分不高，则会被认为没有进行有效的学习。许多专家认为，过分强调测试结果的学校会向学生传递错误的信息，因为这种策略赞成获得晶态智力，而这往往是以牺牲流体智力为代价的。也许学校可以更好地平衡对流体学习和晶态学习的重视程度。我认为这将鼓励教师改变他们的教学风格和方法，以便学生能够不断地适应和全面锻炼他们的智商。

What I see in many schools where the focus is on student testing results is a narrow focus on factual memorization and less about "experiences" or application of knowledge in the classroom. There is value to repetition in learning, but students also have a significant need to experience new scenarios in which they can challenge their fluid intelligence. The factual classroom often disregards the value of process over the product. If the student does not score well on a test, the assumption is that the student has not learned effectively. Many experts believe that schools which over-emphasize testing results send the wrong message to students, because this strategy endorses gaining crystallized intelligence, often at the expense of fluid intelligence. Perhaps schools could do a better job of balancing their emphasis on fluid versus crystallized learning. I think this would encourage teachers to vary their teaching styles and methods, so that the learners would be able to continually adapt and exercise their full IQ.

研究发现，尽管基因在决定智力方面确实发挥了作用，但环境因素也是很关键的。数据表明，提高平均智商得分的因素还可能包括教师素质、学习环境、学生的健康和营养水平、社会经济状况、测试偏见以及学生群体的少数群体状况等。智商测试也无法解决诸如学生对整个世界的好奇程度等考量指标。教育环境不能简单地迫使每个学生进入"学习模板／模型"并试图疯狂地产出高智商的"克隆人"。促进因素非常重要，而且它们无法均等控制或轻易得出。因此，那些只讲一种基本方法而不理会差异化的教学方式的学校就将它们所服务的大量学生排除在外了。他们没有教育每个孩子，而是只教一种智力风格，并最终无视其他风格。

Research has found that while genes do play a role in determining intelligence, environmental factors are also key contributors. Data indicates that factors that enhance the average IQ scores may also include teacher quality, learning environment, the health and nutrition of the student, socioeconomic status, and testing bias, as well as the minority status of the student population. IQ tests also fail to address considerations like how curious the student is about the world in general. The education environment cannot simply force each student into a "learning template/mold" and attempt to frantically produce high-IQ clones. The contributing factors are significant and cannot be equally controlled or easily reasoned away. As such, those schools that simply teach one basic way and disregard differentiated teaching and learning styles exclude a significant population of the students they serve. Instead of teaching each individual child, they teach to one intellectual style of child and ultimately disregard the others.

麻省理工学院的神经科学家与哈佛大学和布朗大学的教育研究人员合作，在2013年的一项研究中得出结论，学业成绩优异的学生不一定能改善流体智力。有趣的是，在标准化考试成绩中获得最高成绩的学生在流体智力方面并未有同等表现。实际上，那些在晶态智力测试中得分较高的学校也并位看到学生在流体智力技能——记忆容量和回忆能力、信息处理速度以及解决抽象问题的能力——测试中的表现有所提高。"看起来好像并没有像你希望的那样轻易获得这些技能（流体智力），只是通过大量学习和成为一名好学生罢了。"约翰.加布里列（麻省理工学院的神经科学家和脑与认知科学教授）说道。

Massachusetts Institute of Technology neuroscientists, working with education researchers at Harvard University and Brown University, concluded in a 2013 study that students at academically high-performing schools did not necessarily have improved fluid intelligence. Interestingly, students who had the highest gains on standardized test scores did not show equal gains in their fluid intelligence. In fact, those schools which recorded higher scores on crystallized intelligence tests failed to show an increase in student performance on tests of fluid intelligence skills: memory capacity and recall, speed of information processing, and the ability to solve abstract problems. *"It doesn't seem like you get these skills (Fluid Intelligence) for free in the way that you might hope, just by doing a lot of studying and being a good student*," says John Gabrieli (neuroscientist and professor of brain and cognitive sciences at MIT).

弗吉尼亚大学心理学教授丹尼尔. 威灵厄姆（不属于上述研究团队的成员）说：“我们通常主要关注在校成绩，但潜在的机制也很重要。”这为教育过程提供了支持，而不仅仅是针对产品或最终结果的教育。在全球范围内，学校花费大量时间专注于提高晶态智力，但却牺牲了流体智力。威灵厄姆希望最近和将来的发现将鼓励教育者和决策者重新考虑当前的“最佳教育实践”，以设计一种可以增强学习者广泛认知技能的教育模式。这类研究表明，学生的流体认知能力确实会影响他们的整体学习成绩，并为他们人生中的成功做出更大的贡献。 但是，以结果为导向的教育很少能提出这样的主张。

Daniel Willingham, a professor of psychology at the University of Virginia (who was not part of above-mentioned research team) said, *"We're usually primarily concerned with outcomes in schools, but the underlying mechanisms are also important.*" This gives support to the *process* of education, not just the product or end results-focused education. Globally, schools spend much of the time and focus on improving crystallized abilities, but at the sacrifice of fluid intelligence. Willingham hopes recent and future findings will encourage educators and policymakers to reconsider current "best practices" to emphasize designing an education model that enhances a broad range of cognitive skills for learners. Studies like this reinforce that students' fluid cognitive skills do influence their overall academic performance and contribute more to their life success. However, results-driven education rarely can make this same claim.

在这一点上，我要对克里斯托弗.伯格兰德（《运动员之道》的作者）在大脑方面的研究工作表示赞扬。我鼓励你在《今日心理学》中查找其 2013 年的文章，你可以在下列链接找到：他总结了我在成长型教育期间对个体智商的个人看法，在这方面做得比其他人都好。

At this point I want to credit Christopher Bergland (author of *The Athlete's Way*) for his research work on the brain. I encourage you to seek out his 2013 article in "PSCHOLOGY TODAY" which you can find below. Better than anyone else, he summarized what I personally felt about my own IQ during my formative education years.

https://www.psychologytoday.com/us/blog/the-athletes-way/201312/too-much-crystallized-thinking-lowers-fluid-intelligence

我高中学习成绩顶多算中等。我知道自己并不傻，但是在某些学科领域，我就是感到自己学不进去。我从小就知道自己的个性，可以轻松地结交和管理朋友。我很受欢迎，人们喜欢我，认为我很有趣，很多人很高兴有我陪伴。我一直很喜欢周围有朋友，这一点一直保持至今。同样，我知道那些不喜欢我的个性风格的人。我很容易理解他们提出的社交暗示，即我不成熟且令人讨厌（对此我不会表示一丁点不同意）。同样的不成熟行为使我被踢出了西班牙语班和乐队。（我对两位老师深表歉意。）本来应该把美术课加进去，但是我的美术老师去了我父亲的教堂，我想她很可怜我是传教士的儿子。我以全班排名第 25 的成绩结束了高中生涯。听起来好像不错，但如果知道我所在的班级一共就 29 名学生的话，这就让人很痛苦了！

My high school academic performance was mediocre at best. I knew I wasn't dumb, but in certain subject areas, I felt out of my league. I knew at an early age that I had a personality, and it was easy for me to both make and manage friends. I was well liked, popular, considered funny and many people were happy to share in my company. I always liked having friends around me, and that remains constant to this day. Likewise, I was aware of those who did not prefer my personality style. I could easily read the social cue that was cast by them that I was immature and annoying (and I would not disagree with them one bit). That same immature behavior got me kicked out of Spanish class and Band. (My apologies to both teachers.) Art class would have been added to that list, but my art teacher went to my dad's church, and I think she took pity on my being the preacher's son. I ended my high school career ranked 25th in my class. That may sound good, but knowing my class was comprised of a total of 29 students puts that into a painful perspective!

像 SAT 这样的标准化测试结果似乎为我平庸的学业表现提供了证明。老实说，我不记得我的确切分数，但是肯定比平均分数低。这些结果使我感到好像"善于书本知识"与我无关。幸运的是，我的舒适区域是体育运动方面。我擅长任何与体育有关的事情。不是说我是"最好的"，而是我有能力，因此很有信心。我可以快速学会技能，有高水平的表现，更重要的是，我觉得体育似乎是我排名顺数第四，而不是倒数第四的领域。我在运动场上获得的成功帮助我发展了影响力技能，包括领导能力、决心、时间管理、接受指导、阅读社交线索、沟通、解决问题等诸多技能。有些同学的科学或数学得分为最优，而在体育领域我却是全班排名最高的。最终，体育将成为一种使我收获成功和成就感的职业。我选择了 20 年的职业生涯，教体育课以及担任运动教练。

My lackluster academics were seemingly supported by my standardized test results such as the SAT. I honestly do not recall my exact score, but it was certainly less than average. These results made me feel as if "book smarts" was not my thing. Fortunately, my comfort zone was in the area of athletics. I excelled in anything that involved sports. Not that I was "the best", but I was competent and therefore confident. I could learn skills quickly, perform at a high level, and more importantly, I felt as if sports were a place where I was ranked 4th from the top, as opposed to 4th from the bottom. The success I experienced in the sports arena helped me develop my impact skills that included leadership skills, determination, time-management, accepting instruction, reading social cues, communication, problem-solving, and many more such skills. Whereas some classmates scored straight A's in Science or Math, in the area of sports, I was near the top of my class. Eventually, sports would become a vocation that made me feel successful and fulfilled. I chose to teach PE and coach sports for a 20-year career.

在教室里的时候，我目睹事实性知识被灌进学生的大脑，等待考试时使用。我发现所学的书本知识与未来生活所需的信息之间没有任何联系。但是，经验方面的流体智力启发了我，最终使我对更大的晶态智力产生了兴趣。我很幸运，因为我就职的小型私立学校对我很有耐心，许多学校是没有的。通常给我这样的学生的信息是："你不够好"，直到你获得更高的成绩。

While in the classroom, I saw the facts that were being crammed into my brain as simply facts to be recalled for a test to take. I saw no connection between the book facts being learned and the information I would need in future life. However, the fluid intelligence of experience was inspiring to me, and it drove me to an eventual interest in greater crystallized intelligence. I was fortunate in that my small private school was patient, but many schools are not. Too often, the message to students like me is that "you are not good enough" until you get higher grades.

在一位有影响力的老师（感谢唐.马丁代尔）的指导下，我确定自己的情商比智商高，正是我的情商驱动了我在人生中获得成功。当然，他鼓励我努力学习和工作，但是有限潜力的链条给我的动力比投入更多时间研究无聊且不切实际的信息要多。他让我知道，尽管我的学习成绩很差，但我已经足够好了。 因为他帮助我在某些领域收获了成功的感觉，所以我得以够提高自己的晶态智力。

One influential teacher (thank you Don Martindale) guided me to a self-assurance that my EQ was higher than my IQ, and that it would be my EQ that would drive my success in life. Of course, he encouraged me to study and work harder, but the chains of limited potential provided me with far more motivation than investing more hours into studying data that I found boring and impractical. He let me know that despite my weak academic performance, I was good enough already. Because he helped me feel successful in some areas, I was able to improve my crystallized intelligence too.

经过努力和可能的恩典，我不仅成功地从大学毕业，而且连研究生学习也平安度过了。我非常感谢他（和其他人）对我的情商进行的大量投入，这在我的一生中一直培养并保持着我的好奇心和企业家精神。如今，我挑战自我，去体验对我的智商和情商都有帮助的新事物。其中蕴含着教育的力量：通过激励，帮助学生发挥他们的潜力，而不是让他们灰心丧气，仅仅根据他们的学业成绩而让他们向命运低头。要让学生知道他们已经足够好了。他们可能只是在过程中与其他人不在同一个地方。不要让他们的学业成绩成为他们是谁或成为什么样的人的唯一标识符。要提高他们的情商，使他们信心满满。

With effort and probably some grace, I managed to not only graduate from a university, but then survived graduate school as well. How grateful I am that he (and others) invested heavily in my EQ, which has nurtured and sustained my curiosity and entrepreneurial spirit throughout my life. Nowadays, I challenge myself to experience new things that will contribute to my IQ as well as my EQ. Therein lies the power of education: to help students reach their potential through empowerment, not by discouraging them and relegating them to a destiny based solely on their academic results. Let students know they are good enough already. They may simply be at a different place in the process than others. Do not let their academic results be the sole identifier of who they are or what they will become. Sharpen their EQ so the confidence may lead them to a place of fulfillment and confidence.

现在有新证据证明 SEL（社会情感学习）技能是可以教授和衡量的。SEL 能促进积极发展、帮助减少有问题的行为，同时提高学生的学业成绩、社交技能以及身心健康。 这些是更有可能预测学术、生活和职业成就的特征，也是在全球教育中需要更好地平衡的素质。SEL 的实施取决于老师，但是我们需要政策和决策者摆脱自己的方式，并允许开展真正有意义的学习。

New evidence now confirms that SEL (Social Emotional Learning) skills can be taught and measured. SEL promotes positive development and helps reduce problematic behaviors while improving students' academic performance, social skills, and mental and physical health. These are the characteristics that are more likely to predict academic, life, and career success. These are the qualities that need to be better balanced in global education. The implementation of SEL rests with the teachers, but we need policy and decision makers to get out of their own way and allow true meaningful learning to take place.

金伯莉. A. 舒纳德—赖克尔在她的《社会、情感学习与教师》一文中分享了弗吉尼亚大学的帕特里夏. 詹宁斯和宾夕法尼亚州立大学的马克. 格林伯格的研究人员的发现。 *"师生关系的质量，学生和课堂的管理以及有效的社交和情感学习计划的实施，都可以调节课堂和学生的学习成果。"* 具有良好师生关系的课堂可促进学生的深度学习：与老师和同龄人相处融洽的孩子们更乐于应对具有挑战性的材料并坚持艰苦的学习任

179

务。相反，当教师对教学中的社交和情感要求管理不善时，学生则表现出较低的学业表现和任务行为。显然，我们需要通过帮助教师建立自己的社交情感能力，来优化教师的课堂表现以及他们在学生中促进 SEL 的能力。"

In her article, ***Social and Emotional Learning and Teachers***, Kimberly A. Schonert-Reichl shares findings from researchers Patricia Jennings of the University of Virginia and Mark Greenberg of Pennsylvania State University. *"The quality of teacher-student relationships, student and classroom management, and effective social and emotional learning program implementation all mediate classroom and student outcomes."* *Classrooms with warm teacher-child relationships promote deep learning among students: children who feel comfortable with their teachers and peers are more willing to grapple with challenging material and persist at difficult learning tasks. Conversely, when teachers poorly manage the social and emotional demands of teaching, students demonstrate lower performance and on-task behavior. Clearly, we need to optimize teachers' classroom performance and their ability to promote SEL in their students by helping them build their own social-emotional competence."*

做出改变人生决定的学校行政人员、校长、教育局和任何其他高等教育官员应首先接受 SEL 支持培训。也许那时他们会接受教育改革并优化教师的影响力。太多的官员，要么离开教室太久了，要么根本没上过课，他们正在迫使老师和学生陷入高压倦怠的状态。才华横溢的教师成为决策者们无知的牺牲品，这些决策者们决定将学生获得较高的考试成绩作为"赞美"，展示在他们的领子上。这些荣誉是以有才能的老师和学生的牺牲为代价的。真正学习和享受人生的职业和机会被用作实现个人认可（职位爬升）的典当品。

School administrators, principals, headmasters, education bureaus and any other higher education officials who make life-altering decisions should be the first ones to receive SEL support training. Maybe then they would embrace education reform and optimize the impact teachers can have. Too many officials, who either have been out of the classroom too long or never in it at all, are driving both teachers and students to high-pressure burnout. Talented teachers fall prey to the ignorance of policy makers who have decided that achieving high student test scores should be used as "pins of praise" to be placed on their lapels. These honors come at the expense of talented teachers and students. Careers and opportunities for true learning and life enjoyment are used as pawns for personal recognition.

与许多老师的交谈中，他们坦率地透露，尽管他们同意教导学生情商，但那是不可能的，因为雇用他们的人首先需要优异的考试结果。实际上，许多人发现自己陷入了与同一所学校中其他老师的竞争，因为他们希望能够声称自己的学生是最好的，从而获得升职。学生的最大兴趣应该始终放在教育的中心。很遗憾地说，在学习的某些方面，甚至找遍等式都找不到它的踪迹！

I have spoken to many teachers who frankly reveal that, as much as they agree with teaching their students EQ, it is impossible because those who employ them demand strong test results first. In fact, many find themselves competing against other teachers in the same school, as they hope to be able to claim their students are the best, thereby earning themselves a promotion. The student's best interest should always be at the center of education. I am sorry to say that, in some places of learning, it doesn't even seem to be found anywhere in the equation!

向学生施压以使其适应相同的学习成绩模型是一个危险且错位的概念。它恶化了教育的哲学概念，后者是建立在管理生活和维护社会所需要的知识和经验的基础上的。不幸的是，许多国家正在培养一群智商高的人，他们的大脑充满了知识、事实和算法，但是其中许多人缺乏关于如何在现实生活中使用或吸收其知识的常识。当然，他们可以记住和吸收很多信息，甚至可以回忆起来，但是这样做有什么好处呢？他们缺乏合作、团队协作和沟通等面向未来的技能，这使他们无法接受全面的教育，并无法在工作场所和人生中取得成功。

Pressuring students to fit in to the same academic performance mold is a dangerous and misaligned concept. It deteriorates the philosophical concept of education, which is to build a base of knowledge and experience that will be needed for the management of life and the maintenance of society. Unfortunately, many countries are producing a segment of HIGH IQ individuals who have a brain full of knowledge, facts, and algorithms, but many of these people lack common sense regarding how to use or assimilate their knowledge in a real-life concept. Granted, they can memorize and absorb lots of information, and maybe even recall it, but for what benefit? They lack the future-proof skills of cooperation, teamwork, and communication, which round out a complete education and lead to success in the workplace and in life.

我知道，对于不符合高学业成绩标准的学生，许多文化和社会对他们并不总是表示公开支持或夸耀。我最近拜访了中国山东省的一所学校。到目前为止，我可能已经拜访了中国60所学校，但这是我有幸拜访的第一所"职业"学校。在参观期间的某一时刻，我停下了脚步，告诉副校长，墙上挂着的学生和老师的照片令我震惊，因为照片中的所有人都在笑！她问我是什么意思？我告诉她，在中国（和美国）有如此多的学校，学生们承受着巨大的学习压力。在那些学校里，我很少见到像在她的学校那样微笑的学生。这是说得通的，因为她的学生不必参加高考。对于她的学生来说，他们不会为可怕的期末考试而心生惧怕，他们为此感到高兴。他们确实承受着家庭和社会的耻辱，也许不像传统教育体系那样"聪明"，但我相信职业学校的学生非常聪明和勇敢。他们可能是冒险者，他们将在各种领域中从事有价值的工作，也将是冒险创业的人。他们可能并不是读书的料，但他们非常聪明。许多人的情商也很高。

I know many cultures and societies do not always openly support or boast about their population of students who do not fit in the standard "academic" mold of high academic performers. I recently visited a school in Shandong Province, China. At this point, I have probably visited more than 60 schools throughout China, but this was the first "vocational" school I had the pleasure of touring. At one point on the tour, I stopped and mentioned to the Vice Principal how noticeable it was to me that the photos of the students and the teachers posted on the walls were striking because all were smiling! She asked me what I meant? I shared with her that so many schools throughout China (and the US) have students who are under tremendous academic pressure to perform. In those schools, I rarely see as many smiling students as I did at her school. It makes sense because her students will not take the Gaokao examination. For her students, they do not feel the fear of the dreaded final examination, and as a result, they seem quite happy because of it. They do bear the family and social stigma of maybe not being as "smart" as those in the traditional educational system, but I believe the vocational students are quite bright and bold. They will likely be the risk takers who will work valuable jobs in all sorts of business areas and will also be those taking the risk to launch a business. They may not be book smart, but they are very intelligent; many with high EQ's as well.

在教育全面发展的孩子时，我们必须认识到每个学生独特的学习风格和兴趣。教师经常坚持要求所有学生必须对数学和科学有很高的理解，认为只有那样才能过上成功的生活。为什么？我经营着几家公司，我的数学技能十分有限，但我适应得很好，仍然获得了成功。我的商务学位不是从学校或大学获得的，而是来自生活这所学校。当我陷入困境并且需要更高的知识水平时，无论是自己学习还是回忆，我都只会将其推荐给我的会计师。我现在从事的各种工作与我接受的正规科学教育几乎都没有关系。为什么我要花时间学习周期表，或者混合一些老师们试图说是至关重要的化合物呢？我倒希望我的理科老师教给我完美的配方，让我能煮出完美的咖啡来。那对我的日常生活要有用得多，而且利润颇丰！生活中的基本技能是基础更广泛的实践技能，比测试学生的大多数事实性知识要重要得多。

In teaching the whole child, we must recognize the unique learning style and interests of each student. Teachers often insist that all students must have a high level of Math and Science understanding for success in life. Why? I run several businesses, and I have learned to adapt my limited Math skills and still be successful. My business degree was not from a school or university, but from the school of life. When I am stumped and need a higher level of knowledge than I can either learn on my own or recall, I simply refer it to my accountant. The various jobs that I do now have little, if anything at all, to do with the formal Science education I received. Why did I spend time learning the periodic table chart, or mixing certain compounds that my teacher tried to convince me was so crucial? I wish my Science teacher had taught me the perfect compound combination so I could make the perfect cup of coffee. That would have been far more useful to my everyday life, and quite lucrative as well! Essential skills in life are more broad-based practical skills that are far more significant than most of the facts that students are being tested on.

当老师和学生了解学习的成果收益时，在老师和学生之间建立联系就更加具有意义。当我知道新知识将是生活中必不可少的实用知识时，我总是能学得更加专心和满怀兴趣。我认为学生也是一样。如果他们知道学习的原因，以及学习方法能如何惠及他们的现实生活，他们将变得更加积极主动。这就是企业主从经验中学习的原因，因为一旦他们发现自己不了解的知识，便会尝试去学习，以便为下一次做好准备。

Making a connection between teacher and student is so much more meaningful when the teacher and student understand the outcome benefit for learning. I am always more attentive and interested in new knowledge when I know it is going to be essential and practical learning. I think students are the same way. If they know the reason for their learning, and how it will benefit their real life, the more motivated and attentive they will be. It is why business owners learn from experience, because once they learn what they don't know, they then try to learn it for the next time.

总结
Summary

成功与学生建立牢固联系的老师们将走上正确的道路，提供超越考试成绩的真正教育收益。很少有学校会放弃将考试作为对学生进行排名和评估的一种手段，但是真正的社交情感学习不仅可以培养同理心，而且可以教人如何处理压力。

Teachers who successfully build strong connections with their students are on the right path to providing true educational benefits that extend beyond the examination results. Very few schools will ever abandon exams as a means for ranking and assessing students, but true social emotional learning teaches not only empathy, but also how to manage the stress.

真诚地教育整个班级、教育全面发展的孩子以及每个孩子，这些都是老师面临的最大挑战。对于大多数人来说，本能似乎是自然的，但是他们发现自己所处的"系统"宣扬的是不同的信息。对于许多一片好意的老师来说，在这样的环境中进行教学意味着达到一种艰难的平衡。

Making a sincere effort to teach the whole class, the whole child, and each individual child is the single greatest challenge facing teachers. For most, the instinct seems natural, but the "system" they find themselves in preaches a different message. It is a difficult balance for many well-meaning, well-intended teachers to teach in these environments.

根据研究，我们的智商可能是受到基因编码左右的，可能无法改变，但是研究表明，新的经验以及不断追求好奇心会对整体智商产生积极影响。排在倒数第 4 位的学生的流体智力可能的确是中等偏下的水平。但是，同一位学习者也可能非常有动力并且非常努力，而这可能导致晶态智力的提高。好奇心真的是无可替代的东西，因为它会导致积极的努力。

According to research, our IQ may be genetically coded and may be unable to change, but research is suggesting that new experiences, and the continued pursuit of curiosity, can positively impact overall IQ. It is likely that the student ranked 4th from the bottom may indeed have low to moderate fluid intelligence. However, that same learner may also be extremely motivated and hardworking, which can lead to an increase in crystallized IQ. There really is no substitute for curiosity that leads to motivated hard work.

发挥最大潜力是一个值得追求的目标。为什么有些人似乎"充分利用了自己的智慧"，而另一些人却似乎永远无法发挥自己的潜力？我感到自己在生活中取得了成功。我有一个美满的家庭，儿孙满堂。我并不总是过着经济宽裕的生活，但我的状况比许多人要好。我已经创业，从事令人满足且充实的职业，曾在中国各地广泛开展教师培训，并有许多有趣而宝贵的生活经历。我认为，由于我在自身性格优缺点的基生活和学习，因此提高了我的智商。我并不是将成功定义为物质财富的积累，而是定义为一个人将所做的事情视为对自己和他人有意义的事情。根据我的标准化测试结果，我觉得自己已经超额完成了。我不确定根据自己的生活经历，我对"感觉"进行了多少遗传编码或提升。但我确实知道的一件事是，有一位老师曾让我觉得我自己已经足够好了，我对新奇事物的追求都要归功于他的同理心，这些新事物激发了我的智商和情商的发展。

Reaching maximum potential is a worthy pursuit. Why do some individuals seem to "make the most of their intelligence" and others seem to never reach their potential? I feel successful in life. I have a beautiful family of children and grandchildren. I haven't always lived a financially comfortable life, but I feel better off than many. I have started businesses, worked a satisfying and fulfilling career as teacher, traveled extensively in China training teachers, and have had many other intriguing and valuable life-experiences. I think I have sharpened my IQ as a result of living and learning within my personality strengths and weaknesses. I do not define success as an accumulation of material goods, but rather as doing things that I feel are meaningful to self and to others. Based on my standardized test results, I feel that I have over-achieved. I am not sure how much of what I "feel" was genetically coded or elevated based on my life experiences. But one thing I do know is that a teacher made me feel that I was good enough already, and I credit his empathy to my pursuit of new curiosities that inspired my IQ and EQ development.

当然，智商对学校很重要，对生活而言，情商则绝对是至关重要的。我个人认为，我的成功有85%来自情商，而15%与智商有关。我认为我的运动和生活经历提高了我的流体智力和好奇心，进而激发了我晶态智力。我认为毅力、艰苦的工作和较高的情商使我得以在这个星球上有目的和有意义地存在。我感谢那些曾让我相信自己已经足够好的老师们，他们耐心地使我对看得见的优势领域充满信心，而不是专注于我明显的智商劣势领域。当我的学业成绩很容易使我陷入不安时，他们的指导唤起了我的自尊和自信。也许我已经超额完成了，或者也许我只是按照我的计划去实现了自己的遗传编码。无论如何，我要感谢那些耐心而慈悲的人，他们奉献自己，让我成为了后来的我。永远不要低估你在领导生涯中能对至少一名学生（可能更多）产生的影响。

Sure, IQ is important for school and absolutely EQ is essential for life. I personally feel 85% of my success is a result of my EQ and 15% is related to my IQ. I think my athletic & life experiences have sharpened my fluid IQ and my curiosity, which in turn, inspired my crystallized IQ. I think grit, hard work, and a high EQ combined to give me a purposeful and meaningful existence on this planet. I am grateful to the teachers who helped me believe I was good enough already and then patiently empowered me with confidence in visible areas of strength, instead of focusing on my clear IQ areas of weakness. Their guidance kept my self-esteem and self-confidence alive when my academic results could have easily driven me into insecurity. Maybe I have over-achieved or maybe I have simply lived out my genetic code as I was designed to do. Whatever is the case, I am grateful for those who patiently and lovingly gave of themselves to make me who I am. Never underestimate the influence you can have on at least one student, probably more, over the course of your leadership career.

信息点：与老师和同学相处融洽的孩子，更愿意面对有挑战性的材料，并坚持完成困难的学习任务。

Point of Information: Children who feel comfortable with their teachers and peers are more willing to grapple with challenging material and persist at difficult learning tasks.

- 肯德拉. 切里，流体智力 vs. 晶态智力，更新日期2019 年 3 月 15 日。

  Kendra Cherry, Fluid Intelligence vs. Crystallized Intelligence, Updated March 15, 2019. (https://www.verywellmind.com/kendra-cherry-2794702)

- 肯德拉. 切里，平均智商意味着或者暗示着什么，更新日期2019 年 3 月 13 日。

  Kendra Cherry, What an Average IQ Means and Indicates, Updated March 13, 2019. (https://www.verywellmind.com/kendra-cherry-2794702)

- EQ vs. IQ, Diffen.com.Diffen LLC, n.d. 2019 年 4 月 13 日。
  "EQ vs IQ." *Diffen.com.* Diffen LLC, n.d. Web. 13 Apr 2019.
  (https://www.diffen.com/difference/EQ_vs_IQ)

- 克里斯多弗.伯格兰，《运动员之道：汗水和生物学祝福》
  Christopher Bergland, *The Athlete's Way: Sweat and the Biology of Bliss* (www.theathletesway.com)

- 克里斯多弗.伯格兰，体育活动能够提高流体智力吗？，《今日心理学》，2013 年 12 月 13 日。
  Christopher Bergland, Can Physical Activities Improve Fluid Intelligence?, *Psychology Today*, December 13, 2013

- 金伯莉.A.舒纳德—赖克尔，《社会、情感学习和老师》，VOL. 27/NO.1/2017 年春。
  Kimberly A. Schonert-Reichl, *Social and Emotional Learning and Teachers*, VOL. 27 / NO. 1 / SPRING 2017.

预备，开火，瞄准
Ready, Fire, Aim

Image credit: CX Simplicity

作为"美国内战"课题的狂热爱好者，我研究了士兵们在美国内战的激烈战斗中射击子弹的过程和步骤。士兵的步枪重约 7 至 10 磅。再加上携带的其他装备，很明显，一个典型的士兵很容易在负重 45-50 磅的情况下为了活命而"奔跑"。如果敌人在你开枪前想先对你开枪的话，背着这么重的装备尤其是个问题。使用当今的武器，熟练的士兵可能会在 1 分钟的时间内打中 4 个目标球。而那时候当士兵朝向敌人或远离敌人的方向移动时，很容易花费更长时间。然后，考虑到装填和射击过程所需的多个步骤，要说士兵在一分钟内可以实际击发 2 或 3 发子弹是现实的。如果给敌人配上一把可以每分钟射击 12-16 发子弹的连发步枪（斯宾塞连发步枪）将是多么不公平啊！在生活中，有时候我感觉自己就是那位内战士兵，尽我所能地用老式步枪"射击"，而敌人却似乎拥有无穷无尽的装弹能力和射击能力，以及出色的枪法！

As a civil war enthusiast, I have studied the process and procedure it took for soldiers to get a rifle shot off during the hectic battles of the American Civil War. A soldier's rifle could weigh anywhere from 7 – 10 pounds. Couple that with the other gear carried, and it becomes apparent that a typical solider could easily be "running" for his life, burdened with 45-50 pounds of gear. Carrying that much weight is particularly problematic when being chased or shot at by those who would prefer to shoot you before you shoot them. With the weapons of the day, a skilled solider could possibly get 4 aimed shots off in a 1-minute timespan. That time proficiency would easily be lengthened as that soldier moves towards or away from the enemy. Then, factor in the multiple steps required in the loading and firing process, and it is not unrealistic to say a soldier may realistically get 2 or 3 shots off in one minute. How unfair it would be to introduce a repeating rifle (Spencer Repeating Rifle) to the enemy who could now shoot 12-16 shots per minute! There are times in life when I feel as if I am that civil war soldier trying my best to "get shots off" with the old rifle, while the enemy seems to have endless reload and firing capabilities to go with their excellent marksmanship!

常见的枪法训练命令可能是"预备，瞄准，开火！"当他觉得瞄准了的时候，听话的士兵会稳定自己、瞄准并自信地扣下扳机。但是，在业务和领导过程中，我经常发现自己使用的是"预备，开火，瞄准"，而不是"预备，瞄准，开火"。我想说的是，在我停下脚步，稳定自己并朝着既定目标迈进之前，我的业务和个人计划始终将"目标"放在明确的位置，但完全不是这么回事。这到底是我在竞争中处于十字准线的反应，还是由于缺乏规划和设计呢？可能两者兼而有之吧！

Common marksmanship training commands would likely follow with "ready, aim, fire!" The obedient solider steadies himself, takes aim, and confidently squeezes the trigger when he feels the shot is a good one. However, in business and in leadership, I often find myself using "ready, fire, aim", as opposed to "ready, aim, fire". I would like to say that my business and personal plans always have the "target" in clear site before I stop, steady myself, and fire towards the intended goal, but that simply isn't true. Is this a reactionary response because I am in the crosshairs of competition, or is it due to lack of planning and design? Probably a combination of both!

在担任中学老师的那些年里，我感到自己经常还没瞄准就开火了，我借助学生们的反应来帮助自己瞄准。许多课堂活动的想法起初只是一个简单的点子，而没有经过深思熟虑。在这种时候，我"扣动了扳机"，以了解学生的反应。看到反应之后，我调整目标，并以比最初的尝试更高的精确度调整或重新定位目标。我觉得我最初的目标对最终的成功并不重要，反而是先开火并对子弹行进或着陆的位置进行衡量更加重要。有时候，我命中的点离靶心很远，但有的时候，我打得比想象的要准得多。

In my years spent as a middle school teacher, I felt I was constantly firing without clear aim, and I let the reaction of my students help improve my aim based on their response. Many classroom activity ideas started out as a short thought or idea without deep planning. In these times, I "pulled the trigger" to see what the student response and reaction would be. Once I saw the reaction, I adjusted my aim and refined or repositioned my target with a greater degree of accuracy than what I achieved in my original effort. I felt as though my initial aim was not as significant to the eventual success as was simply firing and getting an immediate gauge as to where the bullet traveled or landed. Sometimes, I was way off, and other times, I was far more accurate than I had imagined.

我不建议对所有事物都使用这种"命中或脱靶"的方法，但我确实认为它具有一定的价值。也许我认同"行动胜过无所作为"的口头禅，或者是你通过说的话或做的事"要么影响要么感染"他人的想法，但是我发现这就是我的风格，而且"预备，开火，瞄准"对我而言比这组词的常规顺序更加好用。作为一名老师，我想冒险，尝试一些我认为可能会吸引或启发我学生的想法。一旦我尝试并评估了学生的反应，就可以修正或停止。这两种反应似乎都很有价值，因为反馈表明会揭示成功或失败。如果我正在投资，并且继续观察资产下跌的价值，那么我有两种选择——等它回升或停止投资。

I do not recommend this "hit or miss" method for everything, but I do think there is some value to it. Maybe I am fixated on the mantra that "action always beats inaction", or the idea that you either "affect or infect" people by what you say or do, but I have found that this is my style, and that "ready, fire, aim" works better for me than does the more common order of the phrase. As a teacher, I wanted to take risks and try ideas that I thought might appeal or inspire my students. Once I tried and evaluated the reaction of students, I could either revise or discontinue. Either response seemed valuable because feedback revealed success or failure. If I am investing, and I continue to watch the value of an asset drop, I have two choices - wait it out or discontinue the investment.

总结
Summary

教育倾向于预备，瞄准，开火。 教育喜欢清晰的目标，精心计划和明确的预定标靶。但是，教育中的许多"士兵"更喜欢现成的目标。我认识的许多老师都是最灵活的那种人。 他们可以快速适应和调整，因为许多老师每天都在这样做。但是，对于许多人来说，这种灵活性是一种挣扎，因为他们的性格类型要求控制和秩序。

Education tends to be ready, aim, fire. Education likes clear goals, careful planning, and clear intended targets. However, many of the "soldiers" in education prefer ready, fire, aim. Many teachers are among the most flexible people I know. They can adapt and adjust quickly because many teachers do that on a daily basis. However, there are many for whom this flexibility is a struggle because their personality types demand control and order.

学生经常缺乏灵活性，因为老师或体制缺乏灵活性。 一致性这种构造使教学工作变得容易开展。但是在某些情况下，有些学习者被整合和秩序所吞噬，他们天生的好奇心遭到了削弱，因为这被视为无赖的表现。

Students often lack flexibility because the teacher or the system also lacks flexibility. Conformity, as a construct, makes teaching easy. But in some instances, there are learners who are swallowed up in the conformity and order, and their natural curiosity is diminished because it is seen as rogue.

要成为在每个独特的学生中寻找优点和缺点的老师。尝试去满足每个学生的需求，同时管理整个班级的需求。这是巨大的教学挑战。 许多人也认为他们应该"教育整个（全面发展）孩子"，但却没有得到这样做的支持。课程决定教学流程，考试时间表也决定教学流程。结果是弱小的"士兵"们试图顺应预备、瞄准、开火的顺序，但实际上，他们太害羞了，根本无法扳动扳机。缺乏自信使他们感到忧虑和不安，这几乎确保了他们即使选择开火也无法命中目标。

Be the teacher who looks for the strengths and weaknesses in each unique learner. Try to meet the needs of each student, while you also manage the needs of the entire class. This is the great teaching challenge. Many believe they should "teach the whole child" but are not given the support to do so. The curriculum dictates progress and the examination schedule dictates process. The results are weak "soldiers" who try to conform to ready, aim, fire, but in reality, they are too shy to pull the trigger at all. Lack of self-confidence has rendered them apprehensive and insecure, which almost ensures that they will not hit the target, even if they do choose to fire.

应该鼓励师生们冒险。拥有"扣动扳机"的信心会产生显著而未知的结果。整合更易于管理和操纵，但结果往往只照顾倒了很小的一部分，而忽略了自由思考、有好奇心的学生。教师应树立创造力和灵活性的榜样。教师应该承认自己的学习目标，但也不要害怕在脱靶时对目标进行调整。灵活性可以激发好奇心，而这将继续激发学习的热情。

Teachers and students should be encouraged to take risks. Having the confidence to "pull the trigger" can produce remarkable and unknown results. Conformity is easier to manage and maneuver, but the results are too often directed to a very small percentage, while ignoring the freethinking, curious learner. Teachers should model creativity and flexibility. Teachers should acknowledge their intended targets for learning, but also not be afraid to adjust the target when the shot fired misses the intended target. Flexibility can breed curiosity, which will continue to inspire learning.

你打算什么时候挑战自己？
When Are You Going to Challenge Yourself?

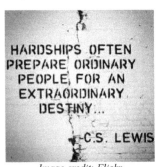

Image credit: Flickr

　　我认为体育运动之所以如此吸引人我的原因之一就是它们带来的挑战。对于许多运动员来说，尝试学习或掌握一项技能可以满足他们接受挑战的无限需求。这一挑战为竞争者提供了一个"试试看能不能"的机会，也为一小部分人提供"证明我能"的机会。

　　I think one of the reasons sports were so appealing and even inviting for me was the challenge they provided. For many athletes, trying to learn or master a skill fills an insatiable need to accept a challenge. This challenge presents an opportunity for the competitor to "see if I can" or, for a smaller number, "prove that I can".

　　也许我对运动挑战的渴望是学业挣扎的结果，这些挣扎使我在传统的学习环境中感觉"缺乏装备"，但是在体育领域，我感觉自己比大多数人都要精通。对于运动员来说，练习是为实际比赛进行准备所需的时间。在实践中，我们完善比赛策略，发展自律，演练时间管理，加强团队沟通，并听取教练的指导。实际比赛是对练习期间是否进行学习的即时反馈评估。这种学习流程是实用的，因此对我来说很有意义。我发现体育运动是我乐于接受的挑战。我不怕失败。实际上，在这种情况下，我只怕自己不去冒险。

Maybe my thirst for the athletic challenge was a result of some academic struggles that made me feel ill-equipped in the traditional learning environment, but in the sports realm, I felt better equipped than most. For athletes, practice was time taken for actual game preparation. In practice, we perfected our game strategy, developed self-discipline, rehearsed time-management, enhanced team communication, and listened to coach's instruction. The actual game competition became the instant feedback assessment as to whether or not learning took place during the practice. That flow of learning was practical and therefore made sense to me. I found sports to be a challenge that I loved to accept. I did not fear failure. In fact, in this case, I feared not taking the risk.

是什么让你不敢思考当前的挑战是否值得呢？你是否害怕失败的可能性，还是害怕连在挑战中失败的机会都没有？为什么有些人将挑战视为可怕的障碍，而另一些人却仅仅将其视为人生道路上的减速带呢？这些问题的答案可以对我们最深层感情提出挑战。

What holds you back from seeing if the current challenge is one worth taking? Do you fear the possibility of failure or do you fear never having the opportunity to fail at a challenge? Why do some people view a challenge as a fearful obstacle, yet others see it as a mere speed bump in the road of life? Answers to these questions are those that can challenge our deepest feelings.

父母可能负责孩子的最初遗传连接，而老师则似乎对于重塑学生对挑战的看法有很大作用。回顾我的求学时代，我发现有些老师比其他老师更能够提出有助于塑造我观点的挑战。最好的老师说服了我，尽管过程将十分艰难，但结果将是对我有益的，值得我去奋斗。这些老师让我相信教育过程更多的是关于整个过程中的成长，而不仅仅是考试的结果。

他们告诉我成长存在于过程中，而不仅仅存在于最终的产品中。

Whereas parents may be responsible for the initial genetic wiring of children, teachers seem to have a lot to do with the re-wiring of the student's mind regarding their perspective on a challenge. Looking back on my education, I found some teachers were more able than others to present the challenge in a way that helped shape my perspective. The best teachers convinced me that although the process will be difficult, the result and benefit would be beneficial and worth my struggle. These teachers made me believe the education process was more about growth through the process than it was about the results of the examination. They taught me that growth was in the process, not just in the product.

我记得曾教过八年级学生有关历史研究论文写作的过程。我们曾花费几个星期的时间开展这项工作，在痛苦的研究写作过程中，有条不紊地逐步加强学生的学习。对于大多数学生来说，这是他们首次尝试完成此类项目。我告诉他们，我从以前的学生那里听到最多的话是"感谢你让我写出 8 年级的研究论文！"尽管他们在读八年级的时候感到痛苦，但他们发现挑战的结果在他们进入高中之后被证明是非常值得的。

I remember teaching my 8th graders about the history research paper writing process. We would devote several weeks of class time to this endeavor, methodically stepping and scaffolding student learning through the painful research writing process. For most, this was their first attempt at completing such a project. I would tell them that one of the things I heard most from former students was "thank you for making me do the 8th grade research paper!" As painful as the process was when they were 8th graders, they found the result of that challenge to be well worth it when they arrived in high school.

如果教师能够说服学生知识或技能的实用性，那么学生就可以看到为了长期获益而承受暂时痛苦的价值。这可能是学校有些科目对我无用的原因，因为我不敢相信我在将来的生活中会随时需要用到这些知识。例如，在我追求体育和历史学位时，记忆元素周期表似乎是一项完全没用的任务（请不要通过电子邮件向我表达你的反对意见，试图说服我接受相反的观点）。同样，有些数学概念被吹捧为对考试至关重要，但由于我不知道它们对生活有何用处，学习过程也十分折磨。结果是我的大脑拒绝吸收它们。学习材料的挑战并没有使我有兴趣接受这一挑战。这到底是因为材料本身、挑战提出的方式还是我与老师提出挑战的"脱节"导致的呢？

If teachers can convince students of the usefulness and application of the knowledge or skill, then students can see the value in enduring the temporary pain for the sake of long-term gain. It may be the reason why some subjects in school felt useless to me, because I could not believe I was ever going to need that knowledge at any point in my future life. For example, memorizing the periodic table seemed like a completely useless task (please do not email me with your disagreement trying to convince me otherwise) in my pursuit of a Physical Education and History degree. Likewise, there were Math concepts that were touted as crucial for the test, but sheer torture to learn because I had no idea how they would be crucial for life. As a result, my brain refused to absorb them. The challenge of learning that material did not present itself as a challenge I was interested in accepting. Was it the material, the way the challenge was presented, or was it my "disconnect" with the teacher's presentation of the challenge?

老师和领导者是否可以帮助塑造学生及他们所领导的人的态度，让他们拥抱任务呢？有没有办法说服学习者，告诉他们现在要求他们进行的努力对以后的生活或学习是极具价值的？如果教师和领导者可以将过程的好处与最终结果的必要性联系起来，则可以变得更加有效。如果老师可以说服学生，现在他们难以忍受的这个过程将会带来不小的好处，那么这就是有可能做到的。

Can teachers and leaders help shape the attitude of students and those they lead in such a way that the task can be embraced? Is it possible to convince the learner that the required effort will be later viewed as invaluable to life or future learning? Teachers and leaders can be far more effective if they can connect the process benefits to the necessity of the end result. If a teacher can convince the student that the displeasure of enduring the process now will pay dividends down the road, then it may be possible.

有时候，我们可以清楚地看到自己经历的痛苦最终是值得的。我自身的例子是当我在演唱会表演中在舞台上撕裂了自己的ACL（膝盖前交叉韧带）。在我们最后的告别演唱会的结尾演唱了3首歌。我希望这场表演给我们自己和观众都留下深刻印象，我无疑实现了我的愿望。我们总是将最后4或5首歌曲安排为我们组合中最劲爆的歌曲。作为主唱，我认为我的工作是尝试唱出正确的音符，但更重要的是，使观众疯狂，这样他们才能在音乐会结束时感受到乐队的能量，并通过雷鸣般的掌声表达他们的认可。

There are times when we can clearly see the pain endured to be worth it in the end. My physical example of this is when I tore my ACL (anterior cruciate ligament in the knee) live on stage during a concert performance. My band was 3 songs from the end of what was to be our final farewell concert. I wanted the show to be memorable to us and to the audience, and I certainly got my wish. We always saved the last 4 or 5 songs to be among the strongest and most lively songs in our set. As the lead singer, I saw my job as to try to hit the right notes, but more importantly, to work the audience into a frenzy so that they would feel the energy of the band at the end of the concert and hopefully acknowledge us with affectionate applause.

我的嗓音是我的乐器，而我在舞台上的动作和能量是我与观众联系的真正方式。对我而言，与他们的联系非常紧密，因为我的能量是直接的，并且是对他们能量的回馈。我试图在每次表演中都带来高能量，但是有时候观众却没有同样的反馈。在那些节目中，我的精力在前几首歌之后就下降了。我记得自己好像是唯一享受我们所做的工作的人。但是，当观众精力充沛时，我的精力也会提升，我的肾上腺素会飙升，飙高音或记住所有歌词并不像我所展示的精力那么重要。

Whereas my voice was my instrument, my movement and energy on stage were my real modes of connection to those who watched. The connection to them was intense for me because my energy was direct, and it was a reciprocal feed to their energy. I tried to bring high energy during every performance, but there were times when the crowd didn't have it. In those shows, my energy dropped after the first few songs. I remember feeling as if I were the only one enjoying our work. However, when the audience energy was high, mine would increase as well, my adrenaline would spike, and singing on pitch or remembering all the lyrics were not as important as the energy I displayed.

在最后的一场演出中，能量非常高，与观众之间的联系被点燃了！用很多叮叮当当的音符、大的吉他和弦结束歌曲并弹奏最终的乐器音符是非常有趣的事情。为了结束这首特别的歌曲，乐队一直专注于我的滑稽动作，直到我给他们发出大结局的信号。那一刻到来了。为了发出信号，我跳到空中，将拳头伸过头顶。和往常一样，他们完全按照我的提示结束！但是当我着陆时，我的右 ACL 韧带过度伸展并在膝盖内断成碎片。我倒在地上，感受到剧烈的疼痛。不确定到底发生了什么，我跳下台，想知道为什么我站不起来。可以想象，那短暂的停顿几乎把整个房间里的空气和能量都吸走了，因为观众不知道刚才发生了什么。有些人以为我们已经完成了，并开始喝彩鼓掌让我们再来一个。我们决定演完最后的曲目，我一条腿跳来跳去，试图重新找回我们之前拥有的能量。

In this one final show, the energy was at a very high level and the audience connection was right on! Ending the songs with lots of clanging symbols, big guitar chords and holding out the final instrumental notes was so much fun. To end this particular song, the band was focused on my movement antics until I gave them the signal for the big ending. The moment came. To initiate the signal, I jumped high into the air with fist stretched up high over my head. As usual, they ended perfectly on my cue! But as I landed, my right ACL ligament hyperextended and shredded into pieces inside my knee. I collapsed to the floor, feeling the intense pain. Unsure of what had just happened, I hobbled off the stage wondering why I could not stand up. As you can imagine, the short break pretty much sucked the air and energy out of the room because the audience had no idea what had happened. Some thought we were done and were applauding for an encore. We decided to finish the final songs with me hopping on one leg trying to regain the energy we once had.

即将进行的手术使我的腿在 6 周内无法动弹，而前 3 周是不能负重的。医生告诉我，破坏疤痕组织会很痛苦，但必须确保充分愈合并恢复所有活动能力。他是对的。这是该过程中最痛苦的部分。但是这种痛苦是可以忍受的，因为我有清晰的目标，那就是膝盖完全恢复，让我对它有完全的信心并回归积极的生活方式。他无需说服我我想继续做我以前喜欢的所有事情。作为我的"老师"，他帮助我重新进行了思考，明白了康复的痛苦最终是值得的，因为我最终会在无需挂背带或带着恐惧的情况下恢复全部活动能力。

The impending surgery had my leg immobilized for 6 weeks and the first 3 were non-weight bearing. The doctor told me that breaking up the scar tissue would be painful but necessary to ensure full healing and to resume the full range of activities. He was right. It was the most painful part of the process. But that pain felt bearable because my desire to resume an active lifestyle with full confidence in my knee was my clear goal. He didn't have to convince me that I wanted to continue to do all the things that I previously enjoyed. As my "teacher", he helped rewire my thinking to know that the pains of rehabilitation would be worth it in the end when I could resume full activities without a brace or fear.

接受这一考验中遇到的挑战需要正确的心态。关于我们如何看待挑战的一些参数可能已预先植入我们的 DNA 中，但是老师、父母和领导者可以帮助我们重新思考，以便我们虽然可以将挑战视为痛苦的过程，但却明白它将带来积极的成长与变化。所有领导者（老师也是领导者）都必须谨慎对待并计算如何向学生或团队提出挑战。摆出清晰的视野，同时列出可能会遇到的经历和感受，这可能很困难，但有助于塑造他们的思维方式。如果将其视为愈合和恢复过程的一部分，则可以忍受恢复过程中伴随的疼痛。

Accepting the challenges encountered in this ordeal required the proper mindset. It is possible that some parameters regarding how we view the challenges are precast in our DNA, but teachers, parents, and leaders can help re-wire our thinking so that we can view challenges as a painful, process but one that will bring about positive growth and change. All leaders (and teachers are leaders) need to be cautious and calculated in how challenges are presented to students or teams. Casting a clear vision, while laying out the likely experiences and emotions that will be encountered, may be difficult but beneficial to helping shape their mindset. Pain in recovery can be endured when it is seen as part of the healing and restoration process.

如果人们可以理解，在将来的人生经历或工作中，双语能力将是必不可少的救命技能，那么持久的语言学习之苦是可以被认为是值得经历的。如果我们能够说服学生他们有一天可能需要掌握化学特性知识来制造药物，那么学习元素周期表甚至可能就会很有价值。要指出的是，领导者和教师可以铸就清晰的愿景，但愿景铸就并不是全部。领导者是否可以抛弃愿景，在情感和心理上为追随者做好准备，以使准备好面对那终将对他们有益，目前却痛苦的学习过程？那些被领导的人是否可以因为相信结果带给他们的好处而接受过程中的痛苦和不适呢？没有远见的领导者当然无法有效领导，但是不能准确传达痛苦过程中有价值的信息以及结果信息的领导者也无法有效领导。

The pain of enduring language learning can be seen as worthwhile preparation if it is understood that one day, in an immersion experience or job, the bilingual abilities will be life-saving or essential. Learning the periodic table may even be valuable, if we can convince those who may one day need to have that chemical property knowledge to make medicine. The point to be made is that leaders and teachers can cast a clear vision, but vision casting is not the whole story. Can the leader cast the vision, but also emotionally and mentally prepare the follower for the painful learning process that will benefit them personally? Can those being led embrace the pain and discomfort of the process because they believe the result will be good for them? Leaders without vision certainly cannot be effective, but neither can leaders who cannot accurately communicate the message that there is value in the painful process, as much as in the result.

许多人有"遗愿清单"，里面列举的是他们在生命中想完成的挑战。"遗愿清单"是他们在"踢桶"之前想要做的一组体验或要做的事情。（"踢桶"是英语惯用语，委婉语，意为"去世"。）遗愿清单可能包含极端挑战（例如蹦极跳，跳伞或驾驶飞机）或造访某些特定的地点（阿尔卑斯山，长城或艾菲尔铁塔）。坦白说，我们所有人都应该有一个遗愿清单，因为它代表了我们设定的终生目标。达成目标时，清单可以为我们提供动力、决心以及满足感和成就感。我们将为实现我们认为值得努力和牺牲的目标而更加努力。

Many people have a "bucket list" of challenges they intend or desire to complete in life. A 'bucket list' is a set of experiences or things they want to do before they "kick the bucket". (To **kick the bucket** is an English **idiomatic**

expression, considered a euphemistic slang term meaning "to die".) A bucket list may contain an extreme challenge (such as bungee jumping, sky diving, or flying an airplane) or a visit to some desired location (the Alps, the Great Wall, or the Eiffel Tower). Truthfully, we should all have a bucket list because it represents lifetime goals we set with great intention. A bucket list can provide us with motivation, determination, and a feeling of satisfaction and accomplishment when the objectives are achieved. We will work harder for the goals that we determine are worth the effort and sacrifice.

总结
Summary

你打算什么时候挑战自己？人们很容易陷入常规。我们以一定程度的一致性开展工作，这可能会带来舒适感，但也会让你感到自满。曾经被视为我们"知道如何做好自己的工作"的事物迅速变成了我们以难以摆脱的例行工作。为此，我们需要重新思考并集中精力，并开始制定一项计划，该计划将为自己提出挑战，以新的紧迫感和重要性重新努力工作。

When are you going to challenge yourself? It is easy to fall into the rut-routine. We go about our work with a level of consistency that may yield comfort but can also give way to complacency. What was once seen as us "knowing how to do our job well" quickly morphs into us performing our job in a rut routine that is difficult to steer out of. To do so we need to renew our minds and focus and begin to enact a plan that will challenge ourselves to work back towards taking our job with a renewed sense of urgency and significance.

偏离常规需要付出努力和耐心。保持自满要容易得多，因为它比起打破常规所需的精力少得多。我的建议是从微小而可衡量的事情做起，但也不要害怕大胆的梦想。

Steering out of the rut will require effort and endurance. It is far easier to stay complacent which requires far less energy than breaking the routine does. My advice is to start small and measurable but do not be afraid to dream big and bold.

尝试任何事情时，起初几次不要指望立即收获大的变化。可能需要一些时间才能将变化融入你所从事工作的文化中以及班级或团队的文化中。所有相关人员都需要时间进行调整和做出反应。重要的是，你要尽力而为。

When trying anything for the first few times, do not expect massive change right away. It may take some time to build the change into the culture of what you have been doing and the class or group has been experiencing. All involved need time to adjust and react. The important thing is that you try and make the sincere effort.

选择你认为可以实现的一两个关键事项，这将对你的领导方式和你领导的人带来不同。如果是老师，并且你觉得自己的课程呆板，那就花点时间每周做 1 堂课，一堂 M&M 重点课（令人难忘且有意义的课）。这节课将具有更深层次的学生参与度，其设计与之前的课程都不同。评估这一节课，然后在下周考虑第二节课。当你养成新习惯时，这种节奏就可能会持续下去。

Pick one or two key things that you think you could implement that would make a difference in how you lead and to who you lead. If a teacher, and you feel like you are in the rut routine with your lessons, spend time making 1 lesson per week a M & M focus lesson (Memorable & Meaningful). This lesson has a deeper level of student engagement and is designed differently than your previous lessons. Evaluate this one lesson and then consider a second lesson the following week. This pace may be something able to sustain as you build in your new habits.

如果你真诚地希望与你的学生或团队建立更深的联系，那么请承诺做出改变并对结果进行回应。变革总是困难的，但是过程和结果对自己和他人都是有益的。 随着你越来越多地实践变化，挑战变得愈加容易，变化的目标也变得愈加大胆。突然之间，你会发现自己已经脱离常规，走上了一条新的道路，充满活力，并准备好应对你的"遗愿清单"中的其他挑战。

If it is your sincere desire to build a deeper connection with your students or a group, then commit to change and respond to the results. Change is always difficult, but the process and results are rewarding to self and to others. As you practice change more and more, the challenge becomes easier and the goals for change become more even more bold. Suddenly you will find yourself out of the rut routine and on a new path, feeling energized and ready to tackle other such challenges in your bucket list.

结论
Conclusion

Image credit: Best Sayings Quotes

生活的画布开始都是空白的，等待着被称为经验的艺术家添加大而明亮的色块以逐渐形成图像。随着我们的生活不断向前，这幅画从未处于完好无损的状态，痛苦和令人愉悦的时刻不断添加到画面中。有时我们能控制艺术家，而其他时候则不能。除了经验丰富的艺术家之外，我们还从许多帮助我们绘图的人那里收获宝贵的贡献。个体的每次互动都会留下一个印记，联系越紧密，这些颜色在画布上的显示就越多。通过经验和个人相遇可以使人感受到人生的丰富性。

The canvas of life starts out blank and colorless waiting for the artist known as experience to begin adding both bold and bright colors to slowly form an image. The picture is never quite finished as we live and continue to add to the painting with both painful and pleasurable moments. Sometimes we control the artist and other times we do not. In addition to the experience artist we also find valuable contributions from the many people who help in building our picture. Each personal interaction leaves a mark and the more intimate the connection the more those colors appear on the canvas. The richness of life is felt through experience and personal encounters.

我非常感谢人生中的许多或好或坏的经历。 有许多经历是我所追求的，而有些经历我希望它们从未发生，但无论如何，我仍然必须全神贯注。不管是丰富的经验还是较小的经验，我都逐渐尝试去体会每种经验对我人生的贡献。这些经验的最终影响帮助塑造了我对教育和领导能力的看法。在经历失败和成功的时间里，我的观点被雕刻和塑造出来，形成了我目前的思想和观念。如果我以正确的心态看待每种体验，那么它们都能够对我有所贡献。

I am so grateful for the many good and bad experiences in my life. Many of the experiences I have sought after and others I wished had not happened, but all had to be absorbed nonetheless. Whether the experience was profound or minor in comparison, I have grown to try to appreciate the contribution each experience has had in my life. It is the culminating impact of these experiences that have helped shape my thoughts on both education and leadership. Through times of both failure and success my view is chiseled and shaped and forms my immediate thoughts and ideas. Each experience can have something to add if I view it with the right mindset.

为这幅人生画面做出深刻贡献的另一个群体是我生命中的人们。我画布上显眼的第一道颜料来自我亲密的家人。从家中五个孩子之一的人成长到到拥有自己的五个孩子的人，每种关系对我都有着重要的意义，而且永远都无法取代。老实说，我对生命中的人的重视程度超过了对经验教训的重视。由于大多数经验无论如何都会有人参与，因此在为我的画布上涂颜色时，人际关系的画笔似乎要浓墨重彩得多。感谢我的大家庭为我的人生画面提供了深层次的基调。

The other profound contribution to this life painting has been the people in my life. The obvious first paint on my canvas came from those in my intimate circle of family. From being a child in a family of five children to having my own family of five children, each relationship has something significant to offer and never replaced. To be truthful, I value the people in my life more than I do the lesson of experience. Since most experiences have people included anyway, relationships seem to have a much thicker paintbrush when applying color to my canvas. Thank you to my big family for providing a deep color base to my life painting.

　我有很多朋友，他们也做出了很多贡献。只是谈朋友对我的影响就可以写一整个章节，但我只想简单地说，与朋友在一起的生活更加丰富多彩和充满活力。对我来说，我知道我需要身边的人。有些人可能会与较少的朋友融洽相处，但我却需要靠朋友活下来。我希望我为他们的生活做出的贡献与他们对我的贡献一样。感谢朋友们，正是我们的互动塑造了我这些书页中分享的想法。愿你们在我慢慢长大后依然对我保持耐心！

　　I have a lot of friends who have added greatly as well. I think I could write a whole chapter just on the impact friends has had on me, but I will simply state that life is far more colorful and vibrant with friends. For me, I know I need people close to me. Some people may fair well with fewer friends, but I survive on many friends. I hope I contribute to their life as much as they contribute to mine. Thank you friends, it is our interactions that have shaped ideas shared within these pages. May you continue to show patience for me as I slowly grow up!

　　从广义上讲，但重要性丝毫不减的，许多为我的画面做出贡献的是伟大的老师领袖。如果不是他们相信我，我怀疑我自己都难以相信我自己。也许我的 DNA 决定了我会成为谁，但我相信我的命运受到那些努力塑造我的人的极大影响。许多无私的老师来到我的身边，这帮助我找到了我的强项，增强了我的长处，知道了我的弱点，并且知道了面对人生挑战的益处。我不能说我一直都享受这个挑战中的痛苦，但是我听到他们内心深处的声音，说到了最后，这一切都是值得的。他们没有让学习成绩简单地变成我的自我价值感。他们鼓励我努力，但又以某种方式使我相信，我的学业成就只是人生图画不断变化过程的一小部分而已。学生的自我价值远远超出他们所取得的考试成绩，并且在此过程中的成长远重于结果本身。感谢老师们，你们的艺术贡献深刻地塑造了我的图画。

On a broad level, but not necessarily in a diminished role, has been the many great teacher leaders who have contributed to my painting. Had it not been for their belief in me, I doubt that I would have believed in myself. Maybe my DNA was wired to pre-determine whom I would become, but I believe my destiny was heavily influenced by those who worked so hard to shape me. Many selfless teachers poured into me which helped me find my sweet spot, enhance my strengths, know my weaknesses, and know the benefits of accepting a challenge in life. I can't say I always love the pain in the process, but I hear their voices inside my head saying this, too, will be worth it in the end. They did not let my academic results simply become my sense of self-worth or value. They encouraged me to work hard but somehow helped me believe that my academic results were just a small and temporary part of the changing landscape of the picture being painted. A student's self-worth is far greater than the grade earned, and the growth found in the process is greater than the outcome itself. Thank you to the teachers. My picture was profoundly shaped by your artistic contributions.

在一些非常好的经历和一些非常好的人启发下，我写了这本书。在过去的十年中，我有幸去了很多次中国。故事开始的时间距今太长了，但是我们只能说是一件事导致了另一件事，而一种关系又导向了另一件事，总之最终的结果是，我在旅途中收获了很棒的人生经历，遇见了无数伟大的人。我最初的目的只是参观我的国际营员生活的地方，最后却变成了在一个令人惊叹的国家／地区培训老师和营地负责人的机会。现在，我每年都要来回几次培训中国的老师，了解他们的团队成长过程，以及如何在师生之间建立更个人化的课堂。为什么？因为我的图画正是这些类型的人和经历描绘出来的。

I was inspired to write this book because of a some really great experiences and a some really great people. I have been fortunate to make many trips to China over the past 10 years. The story of how this started is far too long but let's just say one thing led to another and one relationship invited another and the end result is that I have had great life experience and met nothing but great people on these trips. What turned out to initially be a visit to see where my international campers lived has turned into the opportunity to train teachers and camp leaders in an amazing country. Now, I travel a back and forth a few times each year training Chinese teachers about the Group Growth Process and how to have a more personally connected classroom between teacher and students. Why? Because it has been these types of people and experiences that paint the picture.

我的希望是激励人们无私奉献，我就曾受到这样的对待，让学生知道自己的价值远远超出他们所取得的成绩。他们以某种方式说服了我，尽管上学是一种经历，但这并不是我唯一可以学习的经历。与我要过的人生相比，我在学校的时间非常短暂。我相信人们在我身上进行了一些重要的投入，并且在学校中曾发生了一些非常重要的领导机会。我认为我的教练和我从事体育运动的经验与我曾经拥有的任何基础经验同等重要。感谢的老师们，特别是唐.马丁代尔的耐心和坚持。 你的贡献为你的笔刷提供了大量鲜艳的色彩。

My hope is to inspire someone to do for a student what was selflessly done for me- reach out and let them know they have value far beyond their grade earned. They somehow convinced me that even though school was an experience to be had, it would not be the only experience I would learn from. My time spent in school was brief in comparison to the education I would get living life. I believe there were some significant investments made in me by people and some very important leadership opportunities that happened in school. I consider my coaches and my experience playing sports as to be as vital as any foundational experience I ever had. Thank you to the many teachers, in in particular one- Don Martindale- for the patience and persistence. Your contributions provided massive strokes of bright colors with your brush.

与家人、朋友、老师和领导相处，信任、认识并希望帮助你成为一个更好的人。拥抱生活为人生图画增添的色彩。有时，颜色是柔和，有意添加进去的，但有时候又似乎是一种飞溅的颜料，使你在每次刷动时都喘不过气来。请吸收它，从中学习，并尝试将其视为正在进行中但尚未完成的艺术品的一部分。

Surround yourself with good family, friends, teachers, and leaders who you trust, and who you know want to help make you a better person. Embrace the color that life adds to the painting. Sometimes the color is added softly and with great intention and other times it seems as if it is a splatter paint that leaves you gasping at each flick of the brush. Absorb it, learn from it and try to appreciate it as being part of an ongoing, yet unfinished work of art.

团队成长过程涉及经验和人员。二者紧密相连，不可分割。当被安排在领导者的位置（例如老师）时，请意识到你班上的学生就像我一样。排在倒数第四位，请努力为学生带来价值。相反，你应该认识到，作为有影响力的人生领导者，你有能力通过在图画中添加色彩来改变某人的人生轨迹。他们的回报可能不是立竿见影的，或者可能是当该学生将来写书时才会出现，但是尽管如此，还是请你无私地倾注吧，当你展示握住他们人生图画的画笔时，请为他们画上鲜艳的色调，那将在他们的一生中成为主色调。教师为每个学生的生活增添色彩，这种色彩比任何给定的知识都能持续更长的时间。这才是真正的教育。

The Group Growth Process involves both experience and people. They are intimately connected and unable to be separated. When placed in a position of leadership, such as a teacher is, please realize that in your class is a student just like me. Ranked fourth from the bottom and struggling to feel value as a student. Make sure you do not overlook that student or mistakenly make him/her feel as if they may have nothing of value to contribute in the future. Instead, recognize that as an influential life leader you have the power to change the course of someone's life by adding your color touches to their painting. They payback may not be immediate, or it may come when that student writes a book in the future but nonetheless, pour selflessly into them so they feel loved and valued for that temporary time that you hold the paintbrush in your hands and hopefully apply bright and happy colors that dominate the picture for that time in their life. Teachers apply color to the life of each student which will last longer than any content knowledge given. This is true teaching.

额外材料
Bonus Material

Facilitating the
Group Growth Process
引导团队成长过程

成为有意识的"建筑师"，为团队设定方向和目标
Become the intentional architect
of the direction and destination of your group

Image credit: Ray Chong

215

联系活动
Connection Activities

这个额外部分旨在通过为引导者配备一些简单的游戏和活动来提高他们的能力，他们可以利用这些游戏和活动来塑造通往目标目的地的过程。这些活动可能并不总是能将你的团队带到所需的**目的地**，但是它们至少可以帮助你按照希望的**方向**带领你的团队。

This bonus section is designed to empower facilitators by equipping them with some simple games and activities, which they can utilize to shape the process of moving towards an intended destination. The activities may not always take your group to the desired d**estination,** but they can at least help guide the group in the **direction** you want them to go.

了解团队成长过程
Understanding the Group Growth Process

每当一群人第一次（或头几次）聚在一起时，成长过程就会启动。这种成长不仅发生在当下的个体中，而且还发生在整个群体中。编写本手册的目的是为引导者配备工具，使他们能够带领团队朝预期的方向前进。这样可以确保更有效地实现你的目标或团队目标。

Anytime a group of individuals comes together for the first time (or first few times), a growth process is initiated. The growth occurs not only in the individuals present, but also in the group as a whole. This booklet is written to equip the facilitator with tools that empower the facilitator to move the group in the intended direction. This ensures that your objective or destination for the group can be more effectively achieved.

重要的是要了解，无论是否存在有意的设计，团队的成长过程都会发生。作为领导者，努力成为过程中有意识的建筑师，以便实现想要的结果。

It is important to understand that the group growth process is going to happen with or without your intentional design. As a leader, strive to be the intentional architect of the design process so you can achieve your desired results.

有许多因素可能会阻碍团队的方向和成长。这些因素包括：目的、团队规模、社区的感觉、引导者的经验、引导者与团队共处时间的长短，甚至包括团队成员的个性等。良好的领导能力和团队管理的关键是要认识到这一过程中的力量，并意识到通过利用它，引导者／领导者是可以指导和激发团队成长过程的建筑师。

There are many factors that may impede the direction and growth of a group. These include: purpose, group size, the feeling of the community, the experience of the facilitator, the length of time the facilitator must work with the group, and even the personalities of those within the group. A key to good leadership and group management is to recognize the power in this process and to realize that by harnessing it, the facilitator/leader is the architect that can guide and inspire the group growth process.

许多人发现团队的成长经历很尴尬，社交上也让人不舒服。社交上充满自信和外向的参与者最终承担了大部分的社交风险，而害羞和内向的人则感到这种社交实验令他们很痛苦。强有力的引导者可以识别团队中的个性，了解社会规范的形成，并设计活动以帮助引导团队朝着预期的方向前进。这便是引导的艺术。通过利用有目的性、参与性和趣味性的活动，团队成长过程的有效性可以牢牢掌握在引导者的手中，而不会是偶发事件。

Many people find the group growth experience to be awkward and socially uncomfortable. Participants who are socially confident and outgoing end up taking most of the social risks, while the shy and reserved find this type of social experiment painful. The strong facilitator can recognize the personalities in the group, see the social norms forming, and design activities to help guide the direction of the group towards the intended destination. This is the art of facilitation. By utilizing purposeful, engaging, and fun activities, the effectiveness of the group growth process can be firmly in the hands of the facilitator and not left to chance.

方向与目的地
Direction vs. Destination

Image credit: Lundbeck.com

了解你希望团队到达的目的地至关重要，这样你才能知道前进的方向。

It is crucial to know where you want the group to end up so you can know the direction to take.

为了这些目的，"团队"这个词用于表示出于某个目的或目标而聚集在一起的人的集合。无论是一次聚会还是重复聚会，大多数团队都会有开会的目的。它可能是一班聚集学习的学生，或者是为设计学习目的而进行交流的教师或系部。也可能是一群在工作场所聚集在一起训练的同事。无论何种情况，"团队"都因目的地（结果或目的）而结合在一起。

For these purposes, the term "group" is used to refer to the collection of individuals brought together for a purpose or objective. Whether it is for a one-time gathering or for repeated gatherings, most groups will have an objective or purpose for meeting. It may be a class of students gathering to learn, or a faculty or department of teachers who communicate together for the purpose of designing the learning. It could also be a group of colleagues in the workplace who gather to train. Whatever the occasion, the "group" has come together with a destination (result or purpose) in mind.

作为引导者，你将充当建筑师，设计团队成长过程的方式。你的领导角色至关重要，它将决定过程的成败。如果你控制过度，团队可能会拒绝你的指导。而如果你太被动，你可能会失去对团队中更强大的领导者的控制。有效的引导需要自信、领导经验、具有吸引力的性格、清晰的视野以及阅读和操纵各种个性特征的能力。一旦成功，引导者将提高团队的动态效率，并在整个过程中为团队的成功做出贡献。

As a facilitator, you serve as the architect who will design how the group growth process will unfold. Your leadership role is crucial and can make or break the process. If you are too controlling, the group may resist your guidance. If you are too passive, you may lose control to stronger leaders within the group. Effective facilitation requires self-confidence, leadership experience, an engaging personality, the ability to cast a clear vision and the ability to read and manipulate various personality characteristics. When successful, the facilitator increases the efficiency of the group dynamic and contributes to the success of the group throughout the process.

> "你不能在一夜之间更改目的地，但你可以在一夜之间改变方向。"
> — 吉姆. 罗恩
> "You cannot change your destination overnight,
> but you can change your direction overnight." – Jim Rohn

成为好引导者的五个简单要点
Five Simple Keys to Being a Good Facilitator

除了死之外，人们最害怕的就是公开演讲！我说的不是在一大群人面前讲话，我说的是那些连在 15、10 甚至 5 个人面前讲话都成问题的人。要成为一名良好的引导者，必须在各种规模的团队面前表现自如。引导者需要意识到，每个团队的引导机会中都有一个表演要素。为了提高效率，引导者必须表现得很自在，并与一群参与者一起工作。对于那些感到恐惧的人，我有个好消息。这种引导的信心和技巧是可以通过练习来培养的！对于已经熟悉此过程的人员，你已经清除了团队引导的第一大障碍。

Second to dying, people are most afraid of public speaking! I am not just talking about speaking in front of large crowds. I'm talking about those who feel incapacitated to speak in front of only 15, 10 or even just 5 people. To be a good facilitator, one must be comfortable in front of groups of various sizes. Facilitators need to realize that there is an element of performance in each group facilitation opportunity. To be effective, the facilitator must appear comfortable speaking and working with a group of participants. For those who find this fearful, there is good news. This facilitation confidence and skill can be developed through practice! For those already comfortable with the process, you have cleared the first hurdle in group facilitation.

*1. **拥抱表现**——获得在他人面前站立或讲话的经验。为了舒展自己，请先写一些预先准备好的内容（最好是你感兴趣的话题），然后简单地阅读你已准备的内容。这可能在学生和教职员工面前进行，或者你可能是加入读书俱乐部这样的安全场所，让你可以在一个团队中表达自己。这是第一个障碍。如果你不能在别人面前表现出自信，那么你可能会很难带领或引导一个团队实现预定的目标。*

*1, **Embrace the performance** - Gain experience standing or speaking* *in front of others. To stretch yourself, start with something pre-written (preferably a topic you are interested in) and simply read what you have prepared. This could be in front of students, faculty, or maybe you join a book club as a safe place to express yourself in a small group. This is the first hurdle. If you cannot gain confidence performing in front of others, you will likely struggle to lead or facilitate a group towards an intended goal.*

2. 设计你的过程——理想情况下，每个团队或会议都应有明确的目的。 作为引导者，你要确保知道原因。了解会议目的可以帮助你设计预期成果的活动。引导者可能会被派到一个功能失调的团队中，或带领一个成员互不相识的团队。了解你带领的团队的目的地，以便精心设计指导过程。

2. Design your process - *Ideally, each group or meeting should have a defined purpose for gathering. As a facilitator, you want to make sure you know the reason for the gathering. Knowing the purpose for meeting helps you design the activities for the intended outcome. A facilitator may be brought into a dysfunctional group or lead a group where members may not know each other. Know your group destination so you can carefully design the process of direction.*

3. 超额准备，以便超额完成——成为一个很好的引导者需要经验和实践。作为引导者，你应该具有良好的语言和表达能力。你应该具有吸引人的个性，以赢得团队的关注和信心。熟悉你手上的资料，使自己显得知识渊博且能够自如地传递内容。在设计团队时间时，请多做准备，以便超额完成。这也使你可以在整个过程中解读你的团队，并在必要时更轻松地进行改变。

3. Over prepare so you over deliver - *Being a good facilitator takes experience and practice. As facilitator, you are expected to use good language and presentation skills. You should have an appealing personality to gain the* *attention and confidence of the group. Know your material so that you appear knowledgeable and comfortable delivering the content. As you design your group time, over-prepare so you can over-deliver. This will also allow you to read the group throughout the process, and it will allow you to make changes more easily when needed.*

4. 成为将要发生的团队成长过程的一部分——*经验丰富的引导者通常对团队可能会最终到达的目的地很了解，但是由于团队成员的个性，最终目标的路径（方向）总是各不相同的。敬业的引导者会为他引导的团队准备替代活动。团队成员将显示不同的个性。会有一些人只是坐着，听着，然后按照你的要求去做。其他人会坐着，不听，实际上也不会按照你的要求去做。你可能会遇到领导者性格，有人甚至可能试图（有意或无意）劫持你的团队，或至少控制引导者的时间和精力。引导者不仅是流程的建筑师，而且还是贡献者。你如何"利用"你的个性来进行引导非常重要。你应该足够警惕，以适应房间中的各种个性，并在需要引导时足够灵活以帮助引导团队。有时，当需要这种视角时，引导者只需要坐下来观察。*

4. Be part of the Group Growth Process that will take place - *An experienced facilitator usually has a good idea where the group will likely end up, but the path (direction) to the end goal is always different because of the personalities of those in the group. Engaged facilitators are prepared to propose alternate activities as they read the pulse of the group. Group members will display different personalities. There will be those who simply sit, listen, and do what you ask them to do. Others will sit, not listen, and really not do what they are being asked to do. You may encounter leader personalities who may even try to (knowingly or unknowingly) hijack the group, or at least dominate the time and attention of the facilitator. The facilitator is not just the architect of the process, but also a contributing member. How you "use" your personality to facilitate is very important. You* *should be alert enough to embrace the various personalities in the room and flexible enough to help steer the group, when it needs to be steered. Sometimes, a facilitator just needs to sit back and observe, when that perspective is needed.*

5. 平易近人——许多小组成员会因为性格或不安全感有关的多种原因而害怕与引导者建立联系。也有其他人会积极接触引导者来占用你的时间和注意力。作为引导者，你必须平易近人。一个好的引导者将在活动中、休息时间或会议前后与参与者积极互动。这对于你与正在共处的人建立联系是非常宝贵的时间。平易近人包括具有良好的社交能力，例如：进行眼神交流、微笑、展示出聆听的能力、以适当的身体触摸（握手，拥抱，击掌）表现出舒适感、语气柔和宜人、表现出提出探究性问题的能力，或 提供诚实的答案等。最重要的是，一个好的引导者必须具备谦逊的品质。

5. Be approachable - *Many group members will be fearful to approach the facilitator for any number of reasons related to personality or insecurity. There will also be others who will actively seek out the facilitator to control your time and attention. As a facilitator, you must be approachable. A good facilitator will actively engage with the participants during activities, during breaks, or before and after meetings. This is extremely valuable time for you to connect with those you are working with. Being approachable involves having good social skills such as: making eye contact, wearing an inviting smile, demonstrating the ability to listen, showing a comfort level with appropriate physical touch (handshake, hug, high-five), having a soft and welcoming tone of voice, showing the ability to ask probing questions or provide honest answers. Above all, a good facilitator must be humble.*

使用游戏和活动建立连接
Building a Connection Using Games & Activities

Image credit: Inc.com

建立团队（在课堂、在办公室、在教职员之间等）之间的联系对于最终取得成功至关重要。为此，你需要花费时间和精力进行仔细的计划和设计。作为建筑师，引导者必须对团队的最终目标有清晰的认识，以便制定有效的计划，提升成功的机率。不管有没有你的存在，团队的成长过程都会发生，但若要成功，引导者就需要明智地指导成长过程。

Building connection within your group (classroom, office, faculty, etc.) is imperative for ultimate success. To do so requires the intentional investment of your time and energy into careful planning and design. As the architect, the facilitator must have a clear vision of where the group should end up so that an effective plan can be created to increase the chances of success. The Group Growth Process will happen with or without you, but to be successful, the facilitator needs to wisely guide the growth process.

以下 10 项活动可用于补充你的引导技巧，并帮助你制定计划，以最佳方式指导团队的成长过程。如何使用它们以及何时使用它们取决于你的直觉、舒适度以及团队的期望方向。有些活动可以直接导致或支持你想要的设计，而另一些活动可能只是"打破常规"的活动，用于有趣的过渡或当你需要从内容中解放出来时。作为目标建筑师，你可以自行决定何时何地使用它们。可以对它们进行修改，以适应各种标准、团队目标或时间分配。冒险并尝试其中的一些吧！

The following 10 activities can be used to complement your facilitation skills and help you design plans for how to best direct the group growth process. How you use them, and when you use them, depends upon your instincts, comfort level, and desired direction for the group. Some activities can directly lead to, or support, your intended program design, while others may simply be "break the script" activities for when you just need a fun transition or brain relief from the content. As the intentional architect, you decide when and where to use them. Activities like these can be easily modified to accommodate various criteria, group objectives, or time allotted. Take a risk and try some of them out!

在进行每项活动时，你必须考虑自己的个性，引导力量以及每个团队的动态感觉。你可能会觉得有必要进行修改，这些修改对于你的团队目标、过程或团队的方向性成长很重要或很恰当。任何活动，想要产生影响，关键都在于引导者。练习你的引导技巧，以便发扬你的长处，而你的弱点也不至于阻碍整个团队的成长过程。

With each activity, you must consider your personality, facilitation strengths, and the perceived dynamics of each group. You may feel the need to create modifications you see as important or appropriate to the group objectives, process, or directional growth of the group. Feel free to do so. They serve as a guide to use, not a script to follow. The key to any impactful activity rests predominantly with the facilitator. Practice your facilitation skills so that your strengths develop and so your weaknesses do not hinder the overall group growth process.

1. 名字游戏——大家围成一圈，参加者花时间思考他们名字的首字母。我们的任务是想一个正面的形容词（不要用自我贬低的形容词），

225

该形容词与其名字的首字母相同；这可能还会使其他人洞悉与他们的性格有关的特征或他们希望别人如何看待他们。

例如，"嗨，我叫爵士简，因为我喜欢演奏爵士乐。"或者，"嗨，我叫谨慎卡尔，因为我通常在新的社交环境中表现得比较害羞。"

1. **NAME GAME** - With each person sitting in a circle, the participants to take a moment to think about the first letter of their first name. The task is to think of a positive-sounding (no self-putdowns) adjective that begins with the same letter of their first name; one that might also give others insight into characteristics related to their personality or how they want others to perceive them.

For example, "Hi my name is Jazzy Jane because I like to play Jazz music." Or, "Hi, my name is Cautious Carl because I am usually shy in new social situations.

2. 沟通队列——首先，让参与者排成两条平行的队列，这样每个人对面都有一个伙伴，两个队列距离约为一米。目的是"强迫"对话并营造一种氛围，让参与者可以感受并处理他们的脆弱性。主持人通过提供"交流话题"来指导活动，双方可以在给定的时间内讨论和分享。交流主题可以从惬意的幽默环境到有关主题数据、内容、感觉或公司的使命和价值观的问题等。可能性是无止境的。

例如，"与你的伙伴讨论你小时候做过的梦？"或"与你的伙伴分享你想共进晚餐的名人，以及原因。"或者，如果你希望它与主题内容或数据有关，请说出这个问题，以便学生互相讨论自己学到的知识。活动的目标可以进行改变，以满足你的需求。

你可以决定让大家保留相同的伙伴，也可以在每个问题后让其中一个队列向前移动一个位置。

2. LINES OF COMMUNICATION - Begin by having participants form two parallel lines so each person is facing a partner with about one meter of space separating the lines. The object is to "force" conversation and create an atmosphere where vulnerability is felt and dealt with by the participants. The facilitator guides the activity by offering "communication topics" which both individuals can discuss and share for a given length of time. Communication topics can vary from random humorous circumstances to questions about subject data, content, feelings, or the mission and values of a company. The possibilities are endless.

For example, "Discuss with your partner a popular dream you had as a child?" or, "Share with your partner the name of a famous person you would love to have dinner with and why?" Or, if you want it to be about subject content or data, phrase the questions so students are discussing what they have learned with one another. The objective for the activity can change to meet your needs.

You can decide to keep the same partners or have 1 line move down 1 space after each question.

3. 思考 / 配对 / 分享——这是一种简单但有效的团队活动，可用于分享想法、感觉、情感，甚至评估学习或发现学习内容的差距。首先是结对。一种简单的方法是让团队成员找到在身高上最接近他们的伙伴（或使用你想要的任何配对条件）。目标是快速有效地为活动创建配对，并避免朋友或熟人为了舒适而结成对。然而，事实上，这些结成的对子将随着每个主题而变化，因此在整个活动中，人们最终都将转移到一个新的伙伴上。

配对后，引导者可以向整个班级介绍讨论的话题（与内容有关或与内容无关）。鼓励两人轮流分享和回应。一个人发言时，另一人应记下他所讲的内容。演讲者说完他们关心的所有内容后，听众就会"重述"前者所说的内容，保证其清晰度和含义。切换角色。 完成所有人的工作后，想出一种创新的方式来切换伙伴。

3. THINK/PAIR/SHARE - This is a simple but effective group activity that can be used to share ideas, feelings, emotions, or even assess learning or reveal gaps in content learned. Begin by creating partner pairs. One simple way is to ask group members to find a partner who is closest to them in height (or use any matching criteria you want). The goal is to quickly and effectively create pairs for the activity and to possibly avoid friends or acquaintances pairing up for comfort sake. However, the truth is, these pairs will change with each topic, so they will end up moving to a new partner quite a bit throughout this activity.

Once pairs are made, the facilitator can present the entire class with the discussion topic (content or non-content related). Encourage the pair to take turns sharing and responding. While one is speaking, the other should take notes on what is said. Once the speaker has said all they care to, the listener "restates" what was said to ensure clarity and meaning. Switch roles. Once everyone is done, come up with a creative way to switch partners.

4. 汽车站——该活动是一种揭示性的冒险活动。要求参与者用椅子排成两个单独的队列。（如果你的团队人数为 15 人或更少，则排成一列。如果人数超过 15，可排成两列，以便所有人都能听到你的指令）。排成列后，要求每个人坐下。说明他们都在汽车上并且汽车将沿着路线在不同站点停靠。至于下车，只需根据他们想给的答案站在他们的椅子的左边或右边即可。

每个公交"停靠站"都是引导者给出的一对词语。聆听然后对给出的单词做出反应将确定它们站到队列的哪一侧。如果坐车的人识别或喜欢第一个单词，他们可以站在椅子的"右"侧"离开公共汽车"。如果他们认同或偏爱第二个单词，他们可以站在椅子的"左"侧"离开公共汽车"。如果他们一个词都不喜欢或没有意见，则可以继续坐在公共汽车上。

可以考虑从简单的选择开始。 根据你何时进行此活动，建议从一些非常基本的概念配对开始，例如：早餐或晚餐。如果他们喜欢早餐，他们会"下车"并站在椅子的右侧。如果晚餐是优选的选择，那么它们会站起来并站到左侧。 如果他们没有偏好，则可以继续坐在车上。

该活动可以塑造为你的团队目标，包括主题内容，术语和定义，数学问题的答案或揭示对环境的情感反应。单词配对也可以用来建立社群和娱乐。以下是可能的例子：炎热或寒冷的天气；水果或糖果，咖啡或茶，面食或大米，冰淇淋或糖果，跑步或散步，自行车或摩托车。

4. BUS STOP - This activity is a revealing, risk-taking activity. Ask participants to form one or two single file lines using their chairs. (If you have a group of 15 or fewer, 1 line is preferred. If you have more than 15, form 2 lines so all can hear your instructions). Once the line is formed, ask each person to be seated. Explain the scenario that they are all on the BUS and the bus is going to stop at different stops along the route. Getting off the bus is accomplished by simply standing to the LEFT or RIGHT of their chair, depending on the answer they want to give.

Each bus "stop" is a pair of words given by the facilitator. Listening and then reacting to the words given will determine which side of the bus they exit on. If the rider identifies with or prefers the first word, they "exit the bus" by standing on the "RIGHT" side of their chair. If they identify with or prefer the second word, they "exit the bus" by standing on the "LEFT" side of their chair. If they do not prefer either word or have no opinion, they may remain seated on the bus.

Consider starting with simple choices. Depending on when you present this activity, it may be advisable to start with a few very basic concept pairings such as: BREAKFAST or DINNER. If they prefer Breakfast they would "exit" and stand on the RIGHT side of their chair. If dinner is the preferred choice, they rise and stand on the LEFT side. If they have no preference, they can remain on the bus.

The activity can be molded to your group objective, including subject content, terms and definitions, answers to math problems, or to reveal emotional responses to circumstances. Word pairings can also be used to build community and fun. Examples might include: HOT or COLD weather; FRUIT or CANDY, COFFEE or TEA, NOODLE or RICE, ICE CREAM or CANDY, RUNNING or WALKING, or BICYCLE or MOTORCYCLE.

5. 快速曲奇饼——快速曲奇是一项有趣的活动，其中2个团队在主题内容范围内或仅为娱乐而选择的主题上互相竞争。首先创建两条平行的参与者队列，相互之间的距离为5英尺（主持人可以沿着这些线的中间走动）。目的是在5秒钟内对已宣布的主题给出正确的（且不重复的）答案。如果回答正确，则转至另一队，后者有机会提供新的，正确的和未给出的答案。如果一个团队犯了错误（重复已经说过的答案、给出错误答案或根本没有给出答案），则另一个团队将获得一分，并有权选择一个新类别。游戏从另一个类别继续进行。

例如，给定的主题类别是：水果。第一个排队的第一人必须提供准确的答案，才能"传递"给另一个团队。他们大声说："苹果。"现在轮到另一支队伍，第一个人说"梨"；答题的尝试继续在团队之间来回移动，直到有人给出错误或重复的答案（或5秒钟内给不出答案）为止。这是一项轻松的活动，其中可包含主题内容信息。

5. FAST COOKIE - Fast cookie is a fun activity where 2 teams compete against each other in subject content areas or topics selected just for fun. Begin by creating two parallel lines of participants separated by 5 feet (enough for the facilitator to walk down the middle of the lines). The object is to give the correct (AND UNREPEATED) answers within 5 seconds to the announced topic. If answered correctly, the turn moves to the other team who is given the chance to provide a new, correct and UNREPEATED answer. If a team makes a mistake (by repeating an already stated answer, answering incorrectly, or not having an answer at all) a point shall be awarded to the other team and a new category is chosen. The game continues from where it left off with another category.

For example, the topic category given is: FRUITS. The first person in line one must provide an accurate answer in order to "pass" the attempt to the other team. They loudly say, "Apple." The turn now moves to the other team and their first person says, "PEAR." The answer attempt continues moving back and forth between the teams and down the line until such time as an incorrect or repeated answer is given (or no answer at all after 5 seconds). This is an easy activity in which to include subject content data.

6. 互动之轮——对于这项活动，你需要足够的空间来围成一个大圆圈，并在外部圆圈的内部形成一个较小的圆圈。让一半的参与者形成一个内圈，并排站立，但面对外圈。其余所有参与者将面对"内圈"的一个人。（拥有相等的数字很重要，因此每个人都必须与圈子中的另一个人配对。如果参与者的数量为奇数，则你可以考虑加入，以形成偶数。

告诉团队，你将给他们一个单独的话题。他们将与面对的伙伴一起轮流进行响应。根据你的目标，建议每个人的响应时间限制为 60-90 秒。彼此分享后，请伙伴们继续前进之前提出一些离开的手势（击掌，握手，握拳）。让他们知道，在你执行"旋转"命令时，轮子的外圆将向左移动一个位置（如果你想的话，也可以向右移动）。轮子的内圈不旋转。它保持不动。当大家有了"新"伙伴时，他们应该进行简单的自我介绍，并询问对方的名字、生日和最喜欢的电影（或发起对话的内容），以增进彼此的了解。他们这样做之后，请在与以前相同的时限内提供一个新的讨论主题。重复此过程，以便他们与团队中的 5 个或更多的人进行有关选定主题的互动对话。

6. WHEEL OF INTERACTION - For this activity, you need enough room space to form a large circle with a smaller circle inside of the outer one. Ask half of the participants to form an inner circle, standing shoulder to shoulder but facing toward what will become the outer circle. All remaining participants will stand facing ONE person on the "inner circle." (It is important to have equal numbers, so each person is paired up opposite another person on the circle. If the number of participants is odd, you might consider joining in to even the numbers.

Instruct that you will be giving the entire group a single topic of conversation. Together, with the partner they are facing, they will take turns responding to the topic prompt. Depending on your objectives, it may be advised to say each person will be limited to a 60-90 second response time. After both have shared with one another, ask the partners to come up with some sort of departing gestures (high five, handshake, fist pump) before moving on. Let them know that on your command to "ROTATE," the outer circle of the wheel will move one space to the LEFT (or right if you prefer). The inner circle of the wheel does NOT rotate. It remains fixed. When they have their "new" partner, they should conduct a simple personal introduction and greeting of name, birth month, and favorite movie (or something to initiate the conversation) to help get to know one another. Once they have done so, provide a new topic for discussion with the same time limits as before. Repeat the process so they get to experience engaged conversation on selected topics with 5 or more people in the group.

7. 排队——组成 2 组参与者，每组人数相同。 告诉他们这是一个合作团队活动，第一个正确完成任务的团队将成为获胜者。提醒他们必须正确完成任务，并要根据你可能对小组施加的任何条件（例如不讲话）完成任务。

引导者将调出命令"按姓氏开头字母顺序排列"。第一个这样做的人便"赢得"了这一点。你可以决定添加一些条件，例如"不允许任何人讲话"或"某些人（可能是最大声的人）不许讲话"。更改条件或限制可以帮助创建有趣的团队动态。

排队的点子：

- 根据的出生月份和日期排列。
- 按姓氏的字母顺序排列。
- 按名字的字母顺序排列。

- 按出生那个月的日期（1 号至 31 号）排队
- 根据鞋子的尺寸排列。
- 按年龄排列-从大到小
- 按高中毕业年份排队。
- 按出生体重排队

活动问题可以进行调整，以满足许多团队的成长目标。

7. LINE UP - Form 2 groups of participants with the same numbers in each group. Reveal that this is a cooperative group activity, and the first group to finish the task correctly will be declared the winner. Remind them that the task must be done correctly and according to any conditions you may put on the group (such as no speaking).

The facilitator will call out the command, "Line up in alphabetical order according to last name." The first group to do so "wins" the point. You may decide to add conditions, such as "no one is permitted to speak" or "certain people (those who may be the loudest) are not permitted to speak." Changing the conditions or restrictions can help create interesting group dynamics.

Line Up Ideas:
- Line up according to your birth month and day.
- Line up in alphabetical order by last name.
- Line up in alphabetical order by first name.
- Line up by the day of the month you were born (1st - 31st)
- Line up by shoe size.
- Line up by age - oldest to youngest
- Line up by high school graduation year.
- Line up by birth weight

Activity questions can be adapted to meet many group growth objectives.

8. 骄傲起立——当试图了解一个团队时，这是一个很好的初始活动。你发现的内容可以导致更深入的对话、联系和理解。对于此活动，不需要进行特殊设置。无论房间的设置或设计如何，都可以提问。主持人只是问一些问题，"如果"适用，参与者只需要站起来。

例如：如果你曾经去过美国，请骄傲地站起来

如果你很容易尴尬，请骄傲地站起来

如果你曾经获得过一等奖，请骄傲地站起来

如果你喜欢面条，请骄傲地站起来

如果你喜欢篮球，请骄傲地站起来

如果你在学校没有通过考试，请骄傲地站起来

如果你触犯法律并被抓住，请骄傲地站起来

8. STAND UP PROUD - This is a good initial activity when trying to get to know a group. What you discover can lead to deeper conversations, connections, and understanding. For this activity there is no special set up needed. Questions can be asked regardless of the room set up or design. The facilitator simply asks questions and, "if" the question applies, the participants simply stand to their feet.

For example: Stand proud if you have ever travelled to the United States?

Stand proud if you embarrass easily?

Stand proud if you have ever won a first-place award?

Stand proud if you love noodles?

Stand proud if you love basketball?

Stand proud if you ever flunked a test in school?

Stand proud if you ever broke the law…and got caught.

9. 八种握手——这是一项很好的活动，可以帮助参与者安顿下来并建立彼此之间的联系。首先要求参与者排成两条平行队列（相距约 3 英尺），以便每个人都有一个伙伴。在每条平行线后的 5-6 英尺处创建一

条"清晰的线"。（清晰的线只是为了下一次握手之前返回与各自的伙伴见面的地方）。

参与者将创造 8 个特殊的握手方式，当所有握手方式放在一起时，将成为一组独一无二的握手方式，只有他们两个人自己知道。鼓励创造力，使他们的创造力与其他人有所不同。

一次创建一个"握手"方式。 在创建、练习和掌握了握手的每个部分之后，每个伙伴将转身并退回到在其后 5-6 英尺处创建的那条线。每个参与者只需回到自己的"空白线"，然后回到面对对方的原始位置。当合作伙伴聚集在一起时，他们将进行已建立的握手的所有部分，然后再添加下一个部分。重复这个过程，直到每对都集齐 8 个独特的握手部分并向团队进行展示。

9. 8-PART HANDSHAKE - This is a good activity to help participants settle in and forge connections with each other. Begin by asking participants to form two parallel lines (about 3 feet apart) so each person has a partner. Create a "clear line" 5-6 feet behind each of the parallel lines. (The clear line is simply a place to go before returning to meet your partner when adding the next handshake).

Participants will be creating 8 special HANDSHAKES that, when all put together, will be a UNIQUE set of handshakes that only the 2 of them will know. Encourage creativity so theirs is different from what others may come up with.

Each handshake "segment" is created one at a time. After each segment of the handshake is created, practiced and mastered, each partner will turn and retreat to the line that was created 5-6 feet behind them. Each participant simply touches their "clear line" before returning to their original spot facing their partner. When the partners come together, they do any and all segments of the handshake already established before adding the next segment. This process is repeated until each pair has 8 unique handshake parts to show to the group.

10. 向下看 / 向上看——这是一个有趣且简单的"打破常规"游戏。形成小圈子的参与者（每 6-8 人为一组，站在一起）。每个小组都将玩同一个游戏，但是当某个人"离开"时，他们将离开该小组并加入另一个小组。告诉参与者，尽管小组中没有领导者，但仍需要有人负责进行口头指示。

该活动从站立在圆圈上的成员之一发出的简单口头命令开始："向下看，（暂停）向上看！"在"向下看"命令上，所有人的头和眼睛都低头看着地板。当发出"向上看"的指令时，所有参与者都将抬起头，看着圈子中其他人的眼睛。如果两个人碰巧彼此直接看向对方，那么他们两个都"出局"，离开小组并加入另外的圈子。（大家不可以移开视线，改变正在看的人）。

根据你有多少个圈子，一个圈子可能会减少到只有 2 个人。 他们可以选择玩游戏，或者只是等待邀请其他圈子中的人加入他们的行列。

10. LOOK DOWN/LOOK UP - This is a fun and simple "break the script" activity game. Form small circles of participants (6-8 standing in each group). Each group will be playing the same game, but when someone is "out" they will leave that group and join one of the others. Instruct participants that although there is no leader in the groups, someone will need to take charge to give the verbal directions.

The activity begins with simple verbal commands given by one of the members standing on the circle, "**Look down, (pause) Look up!**" On the "Look down" command, all heads and eyes look down at the floor. When the command, "Look up" is given, all participants will raise their heads and look at the eyes of someone else on the circle. If two individuals happen to be looking directly at one another, they are both "out" and they leave and go join different circles. (You may not look away or change the person you are looking at).

Depending how many circles you have, it is possible for a circle to get down to 2 people. They can choose to play or simply wait to invite someone who gets out in another circle to join them.

额外活动
Bonus Activities

额外活动 #1 把他们整合起来——这是一个非常有趣的活动，可在团队第一次聚在一起时使用。（你要确保自己有足够的身体空间供团队移动，因此请确保没有椅子、书桌或其他可能妨碍安全移动的障碍物。）

告诉团队，作为引导者，你会拍手，你拍手的次数等于他们必须尽快形成的小组人数。例如，如果你拍手四次，参与者要迅速组成四人小组，彼此牵手抱成一团。

被"排除在外"的参加者被视为"出局"。但是，他们有机会在下一次拍手时加入。

（注意：停下来并指出人类行为是很有趣的，当他们意识到多出了一个或两个成员时，当他们"推挤"一个成员时，或者当他们意识到自己缺了1个或2个人而从另一个群体"窃取"成员时，都十分有趣。）

Bonus #1 GROUP 'EM - This is a fun activity to be used the very first time a group is together. (You will want to ensure you have enough physical space for the group to move about, so make sure there are no chairs, desks, tables or other obstacles that could prevent safe movement.)

Instruct the group that, as facilitator, you will be clapping your hands. The number of claps you do is equal to the size of the group they must form as quickly as possible. For example, clap 4 times and participants quickly form groups of 4 people huddled and holding on to one another.

Participants who are "left out" of a group are considered "out." However, they have a chance to get back in on the next clapping number.

(*Note: It is quite funny to stop and point out the human behavior you will see as groups "push out" a member when they realize they have 1 or 2 too many, or when they "steal" from another group when they realize they are short 1 or 2.*)

额外活动 #2 如果你曾...就跟我动起来吧——这是一项有趣的活动，可以帮助发现有关团队成员的一些有趣事实，或者通过查找团队成员的共同点来建立更牢固的联系。这项活动需要足够的空间，让团队站立成一个大的圆圈，每个人与两侧的人大概保持一条手臂的距离。每个参与者还需要某种位置标记，例如可以在圆圈上站立的橡胶"点"。如果在室内，并且你空间不多，请使用胶带或甚至是纸盘（不会轻易移动的东西）在圆圈上确定每个人的地点。

首先（一旦形成了圈子，并且每个人都有一个清晰的点位），引导者站在圈子的中间，告诉大家到他们在圈子上没有额外的点位，但是他们都希望确保得到一个 。如果点位被引导者成功抢走，别的人可能最终将站在中间。中间的人都是以相同的话语开头："如果你曾……就跟我动起来吧"。中间的人用一些他们认为可能适用于多个成员的词来完成该语句，并使他们离开圆圈点位。你可以规定中间的人必须完成或不执行他／她说的话，具体取决于你如何运作该活动。如果说的内容确实适用于圆圈中的任何人的话，那么所应用的对象必须离开他们的位置并移至圈子中的另一个空点位。同时，在中心的人要试图占据一个空点位，迫使某人失去点位。在圆圈上没有抢到点位的人将去到中心位置。

例如，"如果你曾经乘飞机，就跟我动起来吧！"无论谁乘过飞机，都需要离开他们的位置去占据新的位置。你不能去占领紧邻你左边或右边的空位。你与原点位之间的距离至少应隔开一个位置。

Bonus #2 MOVE WITH ME...IF YOU EVER - This is a fun activity that can help uncover some interesting facts about members of the group or create stronger connections as a result of finding what group members have in common. This activity requires enough space for the group to stand in one large circle with about 1 arm length separating them from the person on either side of them. Each participant will also need some sort of place marker, like a rubber "poly-spot" on which to stand on the circle. If indoors, and you don't have poly-spots, use masking tape or even a paper plate (something that won't move too easily) to establish each person's spot on the circle.

To begin, (once the circle is formed and each person has a clear spot marked) the facilitator stands in the middle of the circle noting to the group that they do NOT have a spot on the circle, but that they would like to get one. If successful, someone else will end up standing in the middle. Whoever is in the middle is the person who starts with the same phrase: "Move with me if you ever..." The person in the middle completes the phrase with something that they think might apply to multiple members and get them moving off their spot on the circle. You can stipulate that the person in the middle has to have done what he/she says, or not, depending on how you want to run the activity. If what is said does apply to anyone on the circle, those to whom it applies must leave their spot and move to another open spot on the circle. At the same time, the person who was in the center is trying to occupy an open spot, forcing someone to be without a spot. Whoever is left without a place on the circle, takes over the center spot.

For example, "Move with me if you ever have flown on an airplane!" Whoever has flown on a plane is obligated to leave their spot to occupy a new spot. YOU MAY NOT TAKE A SPOT THAT OPENS UP ON YOUR IMMEDIATE RIGHT OR LEFT. THERE MUST BE AT LEAST 1 SPOT BETWEEN YOU AND THE PLACE FROM WHICH YOU ORIGINATED.

额外活动 #3 ZIP，ZAP，ZOOM——对于这个游戏，团队成员围成 6-8 个参与者组成的小圈子。（较大的团队也可以用，但效果不佳。）

该游戏类似于"往下看，往上看"，没有"领导者"，但需要一个人来启动游戏并保持下去。

该游戏有一个模式，它总是以相同的 Zip－Zap－Zoom 模式进行 。

该模式中的每个单词都伴随着手势：

——"ZIP"是将左手或右手抬到额头处敬礼。ZIP（敬礼）手指指向的方向决定了圆圈中的谁必须用下一个手势做出响应。

——"ZAP"要求将手抬至胸部敬礼（不是在额头处）。同样，这是

239

用右手或左手完成的。手指指向的方向确定了该模式的第三个单词也是最后一个单词的响应对象。

——"ZOOM"是将双手的手掌放在一起，手臂伸直，向前并指向圆圈中的其他人的响应。指向谁，谁就使用 ZIP（敬礼）重新开始该模式。

当某人按顺序犯任何错误时，他们"出局"，离开圈子。去参加正在进行的另一场比赛。

更改单词：如果不用 Zip，Zap，Zoom，可以改用：滴，答，砰，或你好，再见，我爱你。

Bonus #3 ZIP, ZAP, ZOOM - For this game, group members stand in small circles of 6-8 participants. (Larger groups can work, but not as effectively.)

This game, similar to "Look down, Look up", has no "leader" but needs a person to start the game and keep it going.

This game has a PATTERN and it always goes in the same pattern of Zip – Zap - Zoom.

There are hand motions that accompany each word in the pattern:

- "ZIP" is a salute with either the right hand or the left hand up to forehead. The direction that the ZIP (salute) fingers are pointing determines who in the circle must respond with the next hand gesture.

- "ZAP" requires a hand motion that is a chest high salute (not at the forehead). Again, this is done with the right or left hand. The direction the fingers point determines who is next to respond for the third and final word of the pattern.

- "ZOOM" is a response in which the palms of both hands are placed together, with the arms stretched out, forward, and pointing to someone else on the circle. Whoever is being pointed at starts the pattern over again, with ZIP (and the salute).

When someone makes a mistake, of any kind, in the sequence, they are "out", and they leave the circle. They must go and join another game in progress.

Change the words: Instead of Zip, Zap, Zoom, insert: Tick, Tock, Bang, or: Hello, Good-bye, I Love You.

关于作者
About the Author

　　史蒂夫.海恩斯是一名教育家、引导师、营地设计师兼指导员，在领导和引导学生和成人的团队成长过程方面拥有 25 年以上的经验。25 年时间教授中学历史、卫生和体育课程，以及设计和指导儿童夏令营项目。这些丰富的经验帮助他发展和提高了他作为团队引导者和培训负责人的技能。通过他的引导经历，他注意到所有团队都会经历团队成长的过程。"我曾经与之合作的每一组学生，夏令营工作人员或领导团队都经历了类似的成长过程。有时候，这种成长会朝着预期的方向发展，但是有时候它会达到我没有想象或不一定希望的地方。"史蒂夫认为，团队成长的过程尽管每个团队各不相同，但应以引导者的有意设计为指导。史蒂夫并没有让团队的成长成为"偶发事件"，而是向他的研讨会参与者介绍了成为过程中有意识地"建筑师"的重要性。他认为，这是通过创造性的设计和理解人群在团队环境中的行为方式和参与方式来实现的。

　　Steve Haines is an educator, facilitator, camp designer and director with more than 25 years of experience leading and facilitating the Group Growth Process with both students and adults. He spent 25 years teaching middle school History, Health, and Physical Education, as well as designing and directing summer camp programs for children. These varied experiences helped develop and sharpen his skills as a group facilitator and training leader. Through his facilitation experience, he noticed that all groups go through a group growth process. *"Each class of students, summer camp staff, or leadership team I have ever worked with goes through a similar growth process. Sometimes that growth goes in the intended direction, but occasionally, it goes to a place where I did not imagine or necessarily desire."* Steve believes that the group growth process, although uniquely different with each group, should be guided by the intentional design of the facilitator. Instead of letting the group growth just "happen," Steve educates his workshop participants about the importance of being the intentional "architect" of the process. He believes that this is accomplished through creative design and by understanding how groups of people behave and engage when in a group setting.

本手册旨在通过为引导者配备一些简单的游戏和活动来增强他们的能力，他们可以利用这些游戏和活动来指导他们的团队成长过程，以达到预期的目标。这些活动可能并不总是能将团队带到期望的目的地，但是它们总是可以帮助将团队带向期望的方向。

This booklet is designed to empower facilitators by equipping them with some simple games and activities, which they can utilize to guide their group growth process toward their intended destination. The activities may not always take the group to the desired destination, but they can always help lead the group in the desired direction.

史蒂夫.海恩斯是 Camp Concepts 和 Advantage-USA 的总裁兼首席执行官。Camp Concepts 在宾夕法尼亚州亚德利地区设计并指导多个夏日日间营。Advantage-USA 则开展国际业务，包括国际教育咨询，以帮助国际高中生和大学生在美国找到"合适的"学校。海恩斯先生就其工作的许多方面进行演讲和培训，特别是与领导力、营地管理、游戏和活动以及引导技能有关的主题。

Steve Haines is the President & CEO of Camp Concepts and Advantage-USA. Camp Concepts designs and directs multiple summer day camps in Yardley, Pennsylvania. Advantage-USA handles his international initiatives, including international education consulting, which helps international high school and university students find the "right fit" schools in the United States. Mr. Haines does speeches and trainings on many aspects of his work, particularly on topics related to leadership, camp management, games & activities, and facilitation skills.

Advantage-USA

咨询，演说或培训联络
Contact for Consulting, Speaking, or Training

有关教育咨询、团队、老师、员工或领导力培训，请通过以下联系方式与史蒂夫联系：

For educational consulting, team, teacher, staff, or leadership training, please contact Steve through the following contact methods:

www.CampConcepts.org
www.Advantage-USA.org
www.ImmeriveEducationAssociates.com
email: CampConcepts@comcast.net
email: Advantage-USA@comcast.net
email: info@immersiveeducationassociates.com

附加值奖励：耐心计划
Added Bonus: The Patience Plan

Image credit: Flickr

本部分针对希望在课堂内学习更多有关冲突解决管理的老师。其中一些很容易运用于工作场所，但它是从教育者的角度编写的。

This section is specifically for the teacher who wants to learn more about conflict resolution management inside the classroom. Some of it could easily be adapted to the workplace, but it is written from an educator perspective.

本部分主要是为经验不足的老师设计的，经验更丰富的资深老师也可能在这里找到一些新想法，或者能重温以前已经理解的概念，从而获益。如果你具有完善的课堂规则和稳定的课堂文化，则可跳过此部分。如果你是一位新手老师，那么你可能想更仔细地阅读这个部分。要认识到这并不是一个可以简单照搬的模板。这是一个计划的想法，可以根据你的个性、学生年级水平和领导风格进行修改或调整。

This section is primarily designed for less experienced teachers, though even more seasoned, veteran teachers may find some new ideas herein, or at least benefit from revisiting previously understood concepts. If you have

246

well-established classroom rules and an established classroom culture, you may want to skip this section. If you are a new teacher, then you may want to read it a bit more closely. Recognize that it is not a template to simply put in place. It is a plan idea that can be modified or adjusted to fit your personality, student grade level and your leadership style.

"耐心计划"旨在使你成为一名教师领导者，表现出强大的情商，并始终控制住自己的情绪，即使在面对叛逆和不听话的学生时也是如此。即使对于最有经验的老师来说，具有挑战性行为的学生也可能让你在课程或职业中耗尽精力和激情。了解如何建立教师主导的课堂并为其奠定基调，可能会帮助你管理课程并保持耐心和理智。

A "Patience Plan" is designed to empower you as a teacher leader to exemplify strong EQ and remain in control of your emotions at all times, even amid disruptive and disobedient students. Even for the most experienced teacher, behaviorally challenging students can drain the energy and passion from your lesson or your career. Understanding how to establish, and set the tone for, a teacher led classroom may help you manage your class and keep your patience and sanity.

"耐心计划"与教师的管理纪律无关，而与教师如何通过让学生参与设计并同意明确的行为期望有关，进而使学生能够采取适当的行动。告诉学生做什么和什么时候做是一回事，但你能让他们做是另一回事，因为他们认为这是履行他们作为你的课堂参与者所做出的承诺。我相信，"耐心计划"消除了许多情况下的主观性，并将纪律负担从教师转移到学生身上。毕竟，这是他们表示了同意的事情。

A "Patience Plan" is less about the teacher administering discipline and more about how the teacher can empower students to act appropriately by engaging them in the process of designing and agreeing to clear and desired behavioral expectations. It is one thing to tell a student what to do and when to do it, but it is a different level of influence when you can get them to do it because they see it as fulfilling an agreement to which they contributed as a participant in your class. I believe the "Patience Plan" takes much of the subjectivity out of many situations and transfers the discipline burden from the teacher to the student. After all, they agreed to it.

　　我在教书的时候就开始了"耐心计划"。 我没有用这个名字来称呼它，但是多年以来，我逐渐了解了我所使用的过程，并且自此以后就为我的全球教师培训创造了这个术语。我发现，无论我在哪里旅行，总会出现一个普遍的问题："如何控制学生的行为？"实施起来很容易，但是是否需要强大的教师引导技能来让学生"认可"？请与你的个性和引导技巧相结合，使用、调整和更改这些想法。希望它们可以成为你的工具，并使你保持耐心。好了，请允许我向你介绍"耐心计划"。

　　I started the "Patience Plan" back when I was teaching. I did not call it by that name, but over the years, I have come to understand the process I was using and have since coined this phrase for purposes of my global teacher trainings. I find that no matter where I travel, one universal question always arises, "How do I control student behavior?" Implementation is easy, but does take strong teacher facilitation skills to set the appropriate tone for student "buy-in". Feel free to use, modify and alter these ideas to blend in with your personality and facilitation skills. I hope they can be tools that equip you, as well as preserve your patience. Let me introduce you to the "Patience Plan".

设定成功的基调
Setting the Tone for Success

　　我相信大多数学生都希望在学校学习并感受到成功。 尽管学生可能在第一天就以积极的态度和新鲜的状态走进你的教室，许多新老师从陈述学生的学业和行为要求开始，于是，那些寄予厚望的学生突然陷入低谷。许多学生很难理解每个老师的教学风格不一样。在不同的老师 那里，授课方式、学业期望和个性都有所不同。中小学生经常认为，所有教师都是从同一个老师的模范中复刻出来的，因此，他们的举止都是一样的。直到高中，学生才开始意识到教育的一部分正是弄清每位老师的风格，以便他们学会如何适应，以满足每位老师的具体要求。

I believe most students want to enjoy and feel successful in school. Whereas students may enter your classroom on day 1 with a positive attitude and a fresh "clean slate", many new teachers begin by stating the academic and behavioral demands of the students, and, with that, those high hopes suddenly sink to low depths. It is difficult for many students to understand that every teacher has a different style of teaching. Delivery methods, academic expectations, and personalities all vary within different teachers. Primary and middle school students often think that all teachers are cut from the same teacher mold and, therefore, all act the same. It is not until high school that students begin to comprehend that part of the education game is trying to figure out each teacher's style, so they can learn how to adapt their work to meet the specific requirements of each teacher.

我认为重要的是要尽早确定教师与学生相处的方式。为此，老师可以选择分享一些个人的故事，例如有关老师的家庭、爱好或经历的信息。这很容易让你决定为了什么而授课、你的教学理念以及你将容忍哪些行为以及你无法容忍哪些行为。你的初期课程应精心设计，以展现你作为老师和作为个人的身份。这样做可以将猜测排除在学生的脑海之外，从而为你和学生之间的成功定下基调。这很可能决定着他们是否将你作为教育者而接受你。

I think it is important to set an early tone regarding how personable the teacher intends to be with the students. To do this, the teacher may choose to share something personal such as information about the teacher's family, hobbies, or experiences. This can easily lead into an explanation of why you decided to teach, your teaching philosophy, and which behaviors you will tolerate and which you will not. Your initial class should be carefully crafted to reveal YOU as a teacher and as a person. Doing so can keep the guess work out of the student mind and, in turn, set the tone for your success, and that of your students. From this, they will likely form an opinion as to whether or not you may be a teacher they will embrace as an educator.

我更喜欢以轻松有趣的方式开始我的第一堂课，因为那是我的一个面，我希望我的学生早点知道这一点。我喜欢大笑，我希望他们会发现我的课堂是一个有趣的学习场所。现在，我认识到，并不是每个班级都能让人热闹和愉快。毫无疑问，必然有一些课程是缓慢而又不那么令人兴奋的，有些必须要教授和学习的知识，学生可能会发现它们跟以前的方法一样乏味。这是在所难免的。但是，我发现，由于许多课程都很有趣并且包含笑声，因此大家对无趣的课程的容忍度更高，它们的频率也更低。使用幽默可以帮助我在学生为不那么有趣或没有那么具有启发性的课程建立"储备耐心"库。

I prefer to start my first class with something fun and light, because that is a side of me that I want my students to learn early. I love to laugh, and my hope is that they will find my classroom experience to be a fun place in which to learn. Now, I recognize that not every class can be hilarious and enjoyable. There will undoubtedly be those slow, less-than-exciting classes where information must be taught and learned, where the students may find the methodology used to be tedious. It will inevitably happen. However, I find that because many classes are fun and include moments of laughter, the uninteresting classes are far more tolerable and less frequent. Using humor helps me to build a reservoir of "reserve patience" in the students for the times that I may not be funny or quite so inspirational.

以一些有趣的事情开始之后，我喜欢分享我为什么决定做老师。我的故事是学业失败、运动和社会成就的其中一样。我与学生一样，也经历过挫折，当我没有兴趣、无法专注时，我经历了挫折，无法通过数学和科学课程的学习。但是，在篮球场、足球场、棒球场或体育教学区（体育馆）里，我便是一位表现卓越的学生。如果不是一个有爱心和有联系的老师建立我的自信和自我价值的话，我不知道我的人生会走上什么道路。是他让我知道，我未来的职业计划可能不会涉及高级数学或科学计算。我也得以看到，我在那些核心学科领域的劣势可能会使我将来不去涉及这种思维方法的工作和研究领域。但是，这位老师建议我专注于我的领导才能。他帮助我相信，我在体育方面的领导才能以及与人之间的牢固社交关系成为我关注的重点。我带着那宝贵的礼物，攻读了大学学位。我最终获得了硕士学位，并开始了 25 年的教学生涯。有趣的是，我教体育、卫生、历史，并执教过篮球、足球和网球，这与我的导师完全一样！老师即是领导者。 影响的能力可以改变人生轨迹。我就是活生生的证明！（多谢你，唐. 马丁代尔。）

After starting with something fun, I like to share my philosophy of why I decided to become a teacher. My story is one of academic failure, and athletic and social success. I share the frustration I experienced as a student having to try, but failing miserably, to get through Math and Science concepts when my mind was anything but interested and focused. However, on the basketball court, soccer field, baseball field or in Physical Education (gymnasium), I was a high achieving student. Had it not been for a caring and connecting teacher who made it his mission to build my self-confidence and self-worth, I do not know what path my life may have taken. He let me know that my future vocational plans probably would not involve careers requiring high level Math or Scientific computations. I, too, could see that my weaknesses in those core subject areas would likely keep me from future fields of work and study that involved such methods of thinking. However, this teacher suggested that I focus on my leadership skills instead. He helped me believe that my leadership skills in sports, along with my strong social connections, should be where I focus more attention. I took that precious gift of hope and pursued a college degree in teaching. I eventually earned my master's degree and embarked on a 25-year teaching career. Ironically, I taught Physical Education, Health, History and coached Basketball, Soccer and Tennis – the exact same job that my mentor teacher had! A teacher is a leader. The ability to influence can change the trajectory of a life. I am living proof! (Thank you, Don Martindale.)

　　我讲我的学业挣扎故事是因为我知道它可以使我在学生免前更像个普通人。对于某些老师来说，这种故事分享似乎是不合适的，因为他们认为老师应该成为学术上的卓越表现的代表。对于另一些人来说，这显然并不是他们的背景故事，因此，分享它没有意义。我的意思不是你要**分享的具体内容**，而是你**要分享**。我相信，由于我与学生之间的个人联系，我的教学得到了加强。我希望他们了解我当初的挣扎。我认为这可能会使那些不安全的学生放心，从而对他们起到帮助。我希望他们看到自己在学业上的挣扎只是他们也可以克服的整体人生旅程的一部分。

　　I tell my story of academic struggle because I know it helps humanize me to my students. For some teachers, that reveal seems inappropriate because they think that the teacher should exemplify academic excellence. For others, that clearly isn't their background story and, therefore, sharing it doesn't make sense. My point is not so much WHAT YOU SHARE as much as it is THAT YOU SHARE. I believe my teaching was strengthened because of my personal connection with students. I wanted them to know my struggles. I think it might have helped those insecure students by putting them at ease. My hope was that they saw their own academic struggles to be just a part of their overall journey that they too could overcome.

　　我认为，作为一名教育工作者，我取得的成功很大程度上与我的智商无关，而与我的高情商更有关。如果我的高中老师给我进行情商测验，我相信我会在这方面取得很高的分数。不幸的是，学校似乎并不在乎我的情商，而只在乎我的智商。我希望我那些高情商的学生感受到希望，也希望我那些高智商的学生知道，情商对整个人生是至关重要的。实际上，我相信情商将占未来人生成功的 75-80％。因此，尝试同时提高情商和智商是很有价值的，但是通常其中一个会盖过另一个。随着年龄的增长，我一直在努力学习更多并了解自己的情商（EQ）。我认为，对教师进行教育和培训以更好地了解情商的重要性和价值是非常重要的。

I think that much of my success as an educator has not been about my IQ, as much as it has been about my high EQ. Had my high school teachers given me an EQ test, I am confident I would have scored very highly on it. Unfortunately, schools did not seem to care about my EQ, just my IQ. I wanted my high EQ students to feel hope and I wanted my high IQ students to know that EQ matters in the overall preparation for life. In fact, I believe EQ will account for 75-80% of future success in life. Therefore, it is valuable to try to sharpen both EQ and IQ, but typically one will dominate over the other. As I have gotten older, I have worked hard to learn more and understand my own emotional intelligence (EQ). I believe it is important for teachers to educate and train their students to better understand the importance and value of EQ.

分享过去的失败经历之后，我还将与他们分享成功的故事。教育是关于过程的，而不是仅仅关注结果。太多的学生发现自己的自我价值仅体现在他们取得的成绩上。他们开始将自己与他们可能会或可能不会擅长的每个主题的成功（或失败）区分开来。大脑的发展和学习都不相同。老师们谈论教育全面发展的孩子，但常常忘记教育每个孩子。如此一来，教师们开始忽略每个孩子学习时经历的微妙过程。

Once I share my past failures, I also share with them stories of success. Education is about the process, not just the outcome. Too many students find their self-worth wrapped up only in the grades they achieve.

They begin to compartmentalize their success (or failure) in each subject that they may or may not do well in. Each brain develops and learns differently. Teachers talk about teaching the whole child, but often forget to teach every child. In doing so, teachers begin to ignore the delicate process that each child goes through when learning.

至少可以说，我的学业智商学习之路是艰难的。我有很多老师让我认识到我的挣扎是有效的和有价值的，而其他老师则使我感到自己的职业前景暗淡无光。由于大脑的皮质区域发展较晚，对于许多人而言，直到20世纪20年代后期，人们很可能在学习早期都经历了学业挣扎，但这只是一种延迟，而不是永久的无能。我是一个后进的学习者。由于学习延迟，我称自己为愚蠢和无能的人。现在我已经长大了，我已经重新学习了曾经学过的许多概念，而且其中的许多似乎已经不再那么难了。小学、初中甚至是高中的学业失败并不意味着你不会学习，学业成就也不能保证未来的业务或社会成功。教师必须具有积极而强大的影响力，并且在这样做的过程中，请确保不要在学生的学习过程中压倒他们作为人的精神。它很脆弱！

My academic IQ road was rocky to say the least. I had many teachers who made me recognize that my struggle was valid and valuable, while others made me feel that it would lead me to a bleak vocational future. Because the cortical region of the brain develops late, for many, not until the late 20's, it is quite possible that the academic struggle people experience early in their education is simply a delay, not a permanent disability. I was a late blooming learner. Because of my delayed learning, I labeled myself as stupid and incapable. Now that I am older, I have relearned many of the concepts once taught, and many do not seem so hard anymore. Elementary school, Middle School, or even High School academic failure does not mean you can't learn, nor does academic achievement guarantee future business or social success. Teachers need to be a positive and powerful influence and, in so doing, be sure not to squash the human spirit in their students' learning process. It is fragile!

在学年之初，你要为成为某种类型的老师定下基调。这将帮助学生认识你，并希望你对作为个人和老师的身份感到满意。它的好处大于缺点。让学生了解你将帮你创造有用的影响力，这将帮助你更有效地领导和影响你的学生。

At the start of the year, it is important for you to set the tone as to what type of teacher you will be. This will help students get to know you and hopefully feel comfortable with who you are as a person and as a teacher. The benefits outweigh the negatives. Allowing the students to know you will create useful leverage, which will help you to more effectively lead and influence your students.

建立行为期望
Establishing Behavioral Expectations

在分享对学生的期望之前，我先分享我的个人故事。我展示出我的人性，因此可以请求他们合作。如果你只是从对学生的期望入手，那么我认为你避开了与他们建立有价值的初始联系点，而这可能会建立关系影响力。人类是自主的生物。他们天生渴望好玩、有力量、有爱心以及自由。作为老师，我们必须培养人性的这一面，同时，向我们的学生表明，课堂上大家也必须达成一致的社会和行为秩序。对于教师而言，这并不是一个很难理解的概念（尽管有时会曲解这一概念的含义！）我们要意识到规范我们社会行为规矩的存在。我们可能不喜欢被抓住并面对后果，但在内部，我们了解违反这些既定规则的后果。我相信学生想知道这条线在哪里，如果弄清楚了这条线以及可能的后果，那么他们就可以更好地处理可能出现的结果。这是建立师生关系的价值所在。

I share my personal story before ever sharing my expectations for students. I reveal my humanity, so I can then ask for their human cooperation.

If you simply start with the student expectations, then I think you avoid establishing a valuable initial connection point with them that could potentially build relationship leverage. Humans are autonomous beings. They have an innate desire to be playful, powerful, loving, and free. As teachers, we have to nurture that aspect of human nature, while at the same time, make clear to our students that there must also be an agreed upon social and behavioral order to the classroom. This is not a concept that is difficult to understand for teachers (though sometimes miss the mark on this notion!) We realize there are laws that govern our social behavior. We may not like getting caught and facing the consequence, but inside, we understand the consequences for breaking these established rules. I believe students want to know where the line is and, if it is made clear, along with the possible range of consequences, then they can much better handle the result that may follow. This is the value of relationship building between teacher and student.

我将"耐心计划"设计成一种"社会契约",而不是一系列规则。也许我想掩饰这一点,但是我认为这是一种成功的方法,可以把未来的后果从你手中移走,转化为学生的选择,并将良好行为的责任重新置于他们自己做出的选择上。

I craft my "Patience Plan" as more of a "social contract" than a list of rules. Maybe I am trying to disguise it, but I think this is a successful way to take the future consequences of the students' choices out of your hands and place the responsibility for good behavior right back on the choices that they make.

通常,我首先要为一类学生陈述对他们的目标。听起来可能是这样。"我受雇教你[插入主题]。以这种方式为你服务是我的荣幸。我热衷于与你分享我对这一主题的知识和热爱。希望你能像我一样爱它。我持续进行的一件事是学习。我认为自己是终生学习者,我对我所知道的、认为自己知道的或想知道的事情充满源源不断的好奇。*由于有更多关于该主题的知识，我希望我的好奇心不会消失。我认识到你们中的一些人对此主题有先入为主的感觉。你们中的许多人可能会喜欢它，而其他人则可能受不了它。尽管我无法让你喜欢它，但我的建议是寻求对该主题某些领域的更深层次的好奇心，因为如果你发现一件令人好奇的事情，那么它可能会帮助你激发对我们正在学习的内容的深入研究。它可以帮助你拥抱它，而不是作为你不喜欢的东西而拒绝它。我希望你永远保持对所有事物的好奇心，因为那些有好奇的人将是终身学习者。"* 我觉得这样的话语会让学生放心，并与他们分享我关于教育价值以及我的学习方法的信息。

I typically start by stating my goals for them as a class of students. It might sound like this. *"I have been hired to teach you [insert subject]. It is my pleasure to serve you in this way. I am passionate about sharing my knowledge and love of this subject with you. I hope you learn to love it as much as I do. One thing I continue to do is learn. I consider myself a life-long learner, who is continually curious about things I know, think I know or want to know. Because there is so much more to learn about this subject, I hope my curiosity never fades. I recognize some of you here have a pre-conceived feeling about this subject. Many of you may love it, and others perhaps cannot stand it. Whereas I cannot make you love it, my advice would be to seek deeper curiosity into some area of the subject, because if you can find one thing to be curious about, it may help inspire you to dig a little deeper into what we are learning. It may help you embrace it, rather than reject it as a subject you don't like. I hope you never stop being curious in all things because those who are curious will always be life-long learners."* I feel a statement such as this puts learners at ease and shares my message about the value of education, as well as my philosophical approach to learning.

然后，我朝着实现他们的成功的目标迈进。我可以这样说：*"你的*

学业成绩对我很重要，但这并没有掩盖我更深层的愿望，即确保你不仅为下一阶段的学业做好准备，而且也为人生做好准备。你可能会忘记在这堂课中学到的知识，但好奇心可能会再次出现，并挑战你继续追求进一步的知识。我们都应认识到，教师必须评估你的学习，并在评估中附加一个等级来代表你的学习水平。我将对你进行评估，但我还将尝试提供许多不同类型的评估，以确保教育不同风格的学习者，而不仅仅是成绩优异的学习者。如果你有成长型心态，并且意识到自己的态度决定了自己的高度，那么每个人都可以确定自己的潜力和成功。你的得分可能低于预期，但是你的努力只能由自己决定的。最终，你将与你自己而不是周围的人竞争。如果我们所有人都拥有相同的才能，才华和能力，并且数值相同，那么就将与周围的人竞争。在本课程中，请专注于与自己的竞争。设定可以实现的目标，将自己推出舒适区。如何定义成功将决定你是否达到了目标。我想帮助你取得长期成功，而不仅仅是暂时的好成绩。 这对你的人生而言更加重要。"

I then move to my goals for their success. I may say something like this: *"Your academic success is important to me, but it does not overshadow my deeper desire to make sure you are prepared for not only the next academic level but also prepared for life. You may forget the knowledge learned in this class, yet piqued curiosity may come back and challenge you to pursue further knowledge down the road. We all recognize that teachers must assess your learning and, in doing so, attach a grade to represent the level of your learning. I will assess you, but I will also try to provide many different types of assessment to ensure that I teach to all styles of learners, not just those who memorize well. Each of you can determine your own potential and success if you have a growth mindset and realize that your attitude determines your altitude. You may not score as well as you may want to, but your effort can only be determined by you. Ultimately, you compete against yourself and not those sitting around you. If we all had the same gifts, talents, and abilities, and all in the same amounts, then competition would be with the individuals around you. In this class, focus on your competition with yourself. Set attainable goals and goals that will push you beyond your comfort zone. How you define success will determine whether or not you meet your goals. I want to help you achieve long-term success, not just temporary good grades. This is better for your life."*

现在，我已经概述了个人目标的重要性，并要求他们定义个人成功对他们而言是什么，我现在准备进入行为标准领域了。同样，我的目标是避免出现正面和负面行为的典型列表。相反，我恳请他们采纳用这些"标准"，作为所有学习者实现其目标和潜力所必需的内容。这将帮助我们通过团队"认可"来塑造课堂文化。

Now that I have outlined the importance of personal goals and asked them to define what personal success is to them, I am now prepared to move into the areas of behavioral standards. Again, my goal is to avoid a typical list of positive and negative behaviors. Rather, I will implore them to adopt these "standards" as necessary for all learners to reach their goals and potential. This will help us shape the classroom culture by getting group "buy-in".

班级的每个成员都是学习社群的成员。作为老师，我只是社群的一部分。这样，为了使这个社群（老师和学生）能够有效地共同运作，它必须专注于自我改善，以实现提升。所有伟大的社会都有支配成员行为的法律。这些法律阐明了社群的权利和特权，以便让大家都清楚社群对他们行为的期望。我们的学习社群还将采用一些准则，这些准则将有助于我们保持班级文化，增强我们的社群，并促进每个成员的发展，也进一步促进整个社群的发展。这为学生奠定了基调，使他们意识到他们是挂毯中至关重要的纱线，并且个人和社群都有责任互相帮助，以使整个团队获得成功。

Each member of the class is a member of a learning community. As the teacher, I am also only one part of what makes up the community. As such, for this community to function effectively together (teacher and students), the community must be focused only on bettering itself in order to strengthen the community. All great societies have laws that governed behavior. These laws spell out the rights and privileges of the community, so all know what is expected. Our learning community will also adopt guidelines that will help us preserve our class culture, strengthen our community, and seek to further not only each individual member, but the community as a whole. This sets the tone for the students to realize that they are vital threads in the tapestry, and that there is an individual and community responsibility to help each other, in order for the whole group to be successful.

尊重
R-E-S-P-E-C-T

我强调，我们的社群将坚持一个简单而又复杂的概念——尊重。作为一个社群，我们将使用尊重这个标准来反映行为到底恰不恰当。我们都遵守和保护如下四个方面：

I stress that our community will adhere to 1 simple, yet complex concept - **RESPECT**. As a community, we will use RESPECT as our lens for what is or is not appropriate. There are 4 key areas of respect we all observe and protect:

1.**尊重老师**——尽管我认为自己是终身学习社群的一员，但我被公认为领导者，因为这是我被聘用从事的工作。因此，社群中的每个成员都必须尊重老师。学生必须认识到老师在以清晰而令人难忘的方式传授必要的知识。学生将始终获得老师所能提供的最好的帮助，而老师又期望学生尽最大的努力来回报自己。教师寻求真诚的学习努力，而不仅仅是为获得考试或科目的成绩所需的努力。

1. **RESPECT THE TEACHER** - Although I consider myself a

260

member of the life-long learning community, I am recognized as the leader because it is the job I have been hired to do. As such, it is necessary for each member of the community to respect the teacher. The students must recognize that the teacher is there to present necessary knowledge in a clear and memorable way. Students will always get the best a teacher has to offer, and in turn, the teacher expects the students to give their best effort in return. Teachers seek sincere effort in learning, not just the effort necessary to earn a grade for the exam or subject.

在以下情况下，教师感觉不受尊重：

- 学生未按时完成布置的作业。
- 学生以粗鲁或不适当的方式和老师讲话。
- 当老师在讲话、教学的时候，或者在其他不恰当的时候，学生大声说话或打扰他人。

Teachers do not feel respected when:

- Students do not complete their assigned work on time.
- Students speak to the teacher in a manner that is rude or inappropriate.
- Students speak out or disrupt others when the teacher is speaking, teaching or at other inappropriate times.

2. 尊重自己——每个学生都是学习过程中至关重要的部分。 该过程涉及成功和失败。通过强烈的成长心态，学生的自我价值可以远远超过获得的分数或成绩。学生必须足够尊重自己，以了解自己的优点和缺点。我非常赞同这句格言：“热爱自己，好事自来。”我们并不会以相同的步调或时间走向成熟。尽管表现会令人失望，但学会爱自己却带来了未来人生中所需要的韧性。

2. RESPECT YOURSELF - Each student is a crucial part of the learning process. The process involves success and failure. By having a strong growth mindset, a student's self-worth can be seen as far greater than just an earned score or grade. Students must respect themselves enough to know their strengths and weaknesses. I often espouse the adage, "Love yourself and good things will follow." We do not all mature at the same pace or at the same time. Learning to love oneself, despite a disappointing performance, reveals the resiliency needed for life in the future.

为了尊重自己，学生们应该：

- 尝试可以扩展和发展其经验的新事物。 保持好奇。
- 有效地计划他们的时间，以便按时完成作业，并能反映其预期的工作质量。
- 提高他们的努力水平，以准确反映他们的职业道德和学习承诺。
- 着眼于发展自己的成长型心态，使他们能做到的事情超出自己的想象。

To respect themselves, students should:

- Commit to trying new things that stretch and develop their experience. Always be curious.
- Efficiently budget their time so that they can complete work on time and of a quality that is reflective of their intended effort.
- Allow their level of effort to accurately reflect their work ethic and commitment to learning.
- Focus on developing their growth mindset so that they can do more than they imagine possible.

    3. 尊重他人——教导学生尊重和拥抱他人的多样性将是你课堂文化的重要组成部分。如果你在以结果为导向的教育体系中任教，这是最困难的事情之一，因为该体系会促进学生与学生之间的竞争。当学生专注于与同学竞争时，他们对建立社群并没有兴趣。我竭尽所能表明，我们将共同努力构建一个学习社群，每个学习者都有自己的长处和短处。因为我们都各不相同，所以我们意识到优点和缺点在每个人中可能都会有不同表现。作为一个社群，我们必须尊重我们的诸多差异，并庆祝我们彼此之间的不同。每个人都有独特的天赋，把我们塑造成我们自己的样子。每个社群成员的大脑也都处于不同的发展阶段。 目前，有些人具有较高的复杂推理能力，而另一些人则具有较强的创造力，社交能力甚至语言习得能力。我们对这种多样性以及大家当前的发展阶段表示欢迎，而不是试图迫使每个学生进入相同的学业或社会模式。

3. **RESPECT OTHERS** - Teaching students to respect and embrace the diversity in others will be an important component of building the culture in your classroom. It is one of the most difficult things to accomplish if you teach in a results-driven education system because this promotes student-to-student competition. When students focus on competing against their fellow classmates, they are not interested in building community with them. I state as passionately as I can that, together, we seek to be a community of learners, each of whom has individual strengths and weaknesses. Because we are all different, we realize strengths and weaknesses may reveal themselves differently in each person. As a community, we must respect our many differences and celebrate that we are not all alike. Each personality has a unique set of gifts that help shape who we are becoming. Each community member's brain is at different stages of development. At this moment, some have higher complex reasoning skills, while others have stronger creativity, social skills, or even language acquisition skills. We celebrate this diversity, along with the current stage of development, and do not seek to force each student into the same academic or social mold.

我们应该重视每个人都有与生俱来的天性，需要与其他人建立联系，并渴望成为社群的一份子。有时，这些关系会经历紧张和人际冲突。这是不可避免的。 我们将在产生这些意见分歧时进行投入，因为我们相信冲突带来的技能将使我们更好地掌握必要的人生技能。如果我们作为社群成员能够学会更好地管理自己的情绪，那么我们将能够在需要时协助和帮助他人管理自己的情绪。

We should value that each human has an innate need to be connected to other humans and a yearning to be a part of a community. At times, these relationships will experience strain and interpersonal conflict. It is inevitable. We will invest in these times of disagreement because we believe the skills learned as a result of conflict better equip us with necessary life skills. If we, as community members, can learn to better manage our own emotions, then we will be able to assist and help others manage their emotions when needed.

为了尊重他人，我们必须同意：

- 给别人怀疑的权利。不要急着假设或判断他人。
- 允许犯错、自私和伤害的机会。当别人做错事时要保持优雅。
- 在有必要时以诚实和尊重的态度与他人面对面认真解决冲突。
- 只与自己竞争。记住，总会有人比我们更有才华。如果我们所做的只是与他人竞争，一旦更有才华的人出现，我们就会感到不满。

To Respect others, we must agree to:

- Give others the benefit of the doubt. Be slow to assume or judge others.
- Extend the opportunity to be wrong, selfish, and hurtful. Be graceful when others are wrong.
- Honestly and respectfully confront others when the need arises. Respectfully work out conflicts.
- Compete only against ourselves. Remember, there will always be those who are far more talented than we are. If all we do is compete with others, we only feel satisfied until someone more talented comes along.

4. 尊重学习——尊重学习的概念意味着每个人都可以选择如何对学习过程做出反应。有些人出于担心成绩差而做出反应，因此最终选择了糟糕的高中或大学。其他人则担心成绩差将使他们家族蒙羞。获得分数并不总是能说明每个学生的真实学习状况或完整的理解水平。实际上，成绩可能无法准确反映出你对知识的掌握程度。高分只能显示出参加或通过考试的卓越能力。同样，低分可能会显示考试能力缺乏或仅仅是不善于这种评估。其他影响测试结果的因素可能包括评估方式、测试复杂性、成功或不成功的猜测，甚至是可能一直在"指导测试"的老师的重视程度。个人学习更多是一个人追求自我完善的过程。你作为学习者的成熟程度取决于你自己的步调，并且该步调可能与你周围的步调不同。对学习的真正尊重意味着对数据、概念、相关性和应用所学材料的欣赏和理解，这可以通过学生的成绩进行证明。我知道许多人可以"解决"该问题，但却对"何时或如何"应用该问题缺乏了解。这个想法是知识定义的重要组成部分。

RESPECT LEARNING - Respecting the concept of learning means that each person has a choice in how to respond to the learning process. Some respond and react out of the fear of earning poor grades and, therefore, ending up with poor high school or university options. Others fear poor grades that will bring disrespect on their family name. Earned grades do not always tell the full or complete story about each individual student's true learning or understanding. In fact, grades may not be an accurate reflection of one's mastery of the information. A high grade could simply reveal a superior ability to take or pass a test. Likewise, a low grade may reveal test taking weakness or simply a struggle in that type of assessment. Other factors contributing to testing results may include the assessment style, test complexity, successful or unsuccessful guessing, or even the emphasis of the teacher who may have been "teaching to the test". Personal learning is more about one's quest for self-improvement. Your maturation as a learner is at your pace and that pace may be different than that of those around you. A true respect for learning suggests an appreciation and understanding of the data, the concepts, the relevance and the application of learned material as demonstrated by student achievement. I know many who can "do" the problem, but lack the understanding of "when or how" to apply it. This idea is an important part of the definition of knowledge.

关于尊重学习的信息包括一些供学生考虑的关键点。在这方面的目标包括帮助学生：

My message about having a respect for learning includes some key points for student consideration. My goals in this area include helping students:

1. 认识到学习的过程不按学业主题或学年划分。我们经常谈论要成为"终身学习者"。这明确地意味着，随着年龄的增长，我们将继续寻找新知识，但是我们也必须重新思考以前学习的知识。很多时候，我重新研究我以前学过的东西，却发现首先要对这个主题有更多的了解。我的（心怀好意的）老师只给了我一小部分知识，因为在那时，我可能无法吸收全部的复杂性或概念。根据你从评估中获得的成绩就认为你已经知道某个主题的全部知识的话，这是一个错误。你的分数永远不能代表你所学学科的全部真实性或全部知识。总会有更多的东西要学习。

1. Recognize that the learning process must not be compartmentalized into 1 academic subject or school year. We talk a lot about being a "life-long learner." This accurately implies that as we grow older, we continue to seek out new knowledge, but we must also reconsider previously learned knowledge, as well. Many times, I have gone back to re-study something I thought I had previously learned, only to find that there was much more to understanding about the subject in the first place. My teacher (well-meaning) only gave me a small piece of the story because, at that level or at that time in my process, I may not have been able to absorb the full complexity or concept. Thinking that you know everything there is to know about a topic, based on what you earn on the assessment, is a mistake. Your score can never represent the full truth or the full knowledge of a subject you study. There is always

more to learn.

2. 认识并欣赏学习过程中的挣扎。我的高中教练会告诉我，"失败是成功之母。"我很难理解，因为在那个阶段，我认为赢得比赛意味着我的团队表现优于其他团队。但是，经验表明，有时我们的执行情况很好，但是却输给了技术水平较高的团队。当我们回过头来分析我们的比赛时，我们可以看到比赛中的成功和失败之处，这成为了新的改进练习计划的基础。我在数学和科学课程方面苦苦挣扎。有时候，我觉得自己的努力应该会获得更高的成绩。个人的挣扎包括额外的学习、与老师一起度过的时间，或被数学学科爱好者所辅导的过程。额外的学习并不一定总能帮你取得更高的成绩，但这是我整个学习过程不可或缺的一部分。最重要的是，它教会了我勤奋工作的价值。

2. <u>Recognize and appreciate the struggles involved in the process of learning.</u> My high school coach would tell me that, "Losing is the backdoor to success." I had a hard time understanding that because, at that stage, I thought winning the game meant that my team executed better than the other team. However, experience revealed that sometimes we executed very well, but lost to a superiorly skilled team. When we would go back and analyze our play, we could see success and failures in our play, which became the basis of a new practice plan for improvement. I struggled badly in Math and Science. There were times I felt as if my effort should have resulted in a much higher grade earned. That personal struggle included a process of additional work and time spent with the teacher or being tutored by my more math-minded friends. The extra work did not always result in higher grades, but it was very much an integral part of my full learning process. Most importantly, it taught me the value of hard work.

3. 尊重其他同学的挣扎可能与你有所不同，并且是可以接受的。在许多学校中，学生之间的竞争非常激烈。我曾在中国的教室里，学生们能记住前 30 至 40 位学生的排名！对更高排名的追求激发了许多人花费更长的时间学习和准备，以提高他们的等级。如果个人对改进的追求不会引起对"对手"的轻视，那么我认为外部动机或决心水平就没有问题。当发生对他人的鄙视时，对他人的尊重规则就会失效。我曾看到许多学生在看到"水平高于他们的学生"考差了、排在他们后面而感到高兴不已。在别人的失败中取乐并不代表尊重。

3. Respect that your classmates' struggle may be different from yours and be OK with that. In many schools, the competition between students is fierce. I have been in classrooms in China where students know the ranking of students through the first 30-40 spots! The quest for a higher class rank inspires many to spend longer hours studying and preparing in order to elevate their class rank. I have no problem with that external motivation or level of determination, if the personal quest for improvement does not breed a disdain for the "opponent." When disdain for others occurs, the RESPECT RULE FOR OTHERS is broken. I have seen many students gleam with joy when those "above them" score poorly and therefore elevate the rank of others. Taking joy in someone else's defeat does not model respect.

4. 认识到每个学生都在控制自己的努力程度。努力是无法量化的。努力始于一种心态，而努力的效率有许多促成因素。我在大学里有一个朋友，他似乎有照片记忆（过目不忘）。他甚至承认："由于我的大脑吸收信息的方式，我不必在这方面付出努力。"我觉得我表现出的真正努力比他要重要得多，但对我们的考试结果进行比较并没有得出相同的结论。我不得不意识到我的努力是我的努力。我是唯一知道我是否尝试某件事以及如何努力的人。有些事情对我来说很容易（历史、体育、卫生……还有午餐！）。在其他科目上，我很难做出同样的努力。有一些老师说我需要付出更多的努力。有时我可以诚实地表示同意，但是有时候，我觉得我当时已经付出了最大的努力。

4. Recognize that each student controls his/her own effort. Effort is

not quantifiable. Effort starts with a mindset, and the efficiency of your effort has many contributing factors. I had a friend in college who seemed to have a photographic memory. He would even admit, "I don't have to try that hard because of the way my mind absorbs information." I felt I displayed true effort far more significantly than he did, but a comparison of our results did not tell the same story. I had to come to realize that my effort is MY EFFORT. I am the only person who knows if and how hard I tried at something. Some things came easily to me (History, PE, Health...and lunch!). In other subjects it was much harder for me to put forth the same effort. I had some teachers say I needed to apply more effort. Sometimes I could honestly agree and yet, other times, I felt as if the effort given at the time was my best.

我希望我的学生尊重**他们的**学习过程；无论是苦苦挣扎还是收获成功。最终，这就是学习者的故事。成绩不会定义他们未来的成功或人生。他们表现出的勇气、努力、毅力和决心将对他们前进有很大的帮助。每个学习者的学习过程都不同。 学习者必须确定并欣赏将为自己的学习故事做出什么样的努力。 拥抱并拥有它。

I want my students to respect THEIR learning process; both the struggle and the success. Ultimately, this is what makes up their story as a learner. Grades will not define their future success or life. It is the grit, effort, perseverance and determination they put forth that will serve them well as they move forward. The learning process is different for each learner. Learners must identify and appreciate what kind of effort will contribute to their story. Embrace it and own it.

要尊重学习，学生们应该同意：
- 庆祝努力的过程，而不仅仅是获得的成绩。
- 承认只有每个人自己才知道自己所付出的努力水平。
- 将其注意力集中在个人的学习过程上，而不是与他人的竞争上。

- 对那些与自己相似或不同的人表示同情。了解大多数学生不想得低分。他们的学习过程可能与你不同。要表现出仁慈、关怀和理解，而不是在他们的苦苦挣扎中获得快乐。

To respect learning, students should agree to:

- Celebrate the effort, not just the earned grade outcome.
- Acknowledge that only the individual can know the level of effort given.
- Focus their attention on the individual learning process and not on the competition with others.
- Show empathy for those who struggle similarly or differently than they. Understand that most students do not want to score poorly. Their learning process may be different from yours. Show kindness, consideration, and understanding, as opposed to finding joy in their struggle.

　　教授尊重的四个方面需要时间。我通常会在每学年年初给学生重新提及。作为老师，我必须不断回顾并指出尊重何时被打破，并庆祝那些美好的模范时刻。因为尊重这四个方面是班级文化的核心，所以我会花时间和精力来教学生学会尊重，让大家都听清楚，并且知道它将被严格执行。建立班级文化不是一蹴而就的事情。就像学习一样，随着老师对学生的了解，这是一个必须逐步发展的过程。当然，我们可能会建议和讨论许多其他准则，但我会再将其保存下来。我希望保留有关学生行为的讨论，以及个人学习过程是如何与尊重这样简单（但很复杂）的哲学道理相联系的。

　　Teaching the four areas of respect takes time. I typically revisit it often in the early part of the year. As the teacher, I must keep coming back and pointing out when respect has been broken and celebrate clearly when it has been modeled beautifully. Because the 4 areas of respect are at the core of my class culture, I devote time and attention to teaching it, so it is clearly heard and students know that it will be strictly enforced. Building class culture does not happen overnight. Like learning, it is a process that has to develop gradually, as the teacher gets to know the students. Of course, there are many other guidelines that we might suggest and discuss, but I'll save those for another time. I like to keep the main discussion about student behavior, and how the individual learning process is connected to the simple (yet complex) philosophy of RESPECT.

我发现以这种方式开始会奠定积极的班级基调和文化共性，从而影响每个人在我的课堂内的行为和互动方式。它使许多学生感到放心，因为可以实现尊重的文化，并且创造了心理上安全的学习场所。我传达的信息并不是要求他们获得最好的成绩，而是我们讨论尊重自我和学习时的内在要求。我希望他们努力奋斗、成功、失败并超越他们好奇心的界限。当他们这样做的时候，我可以将他们塑造成终身学习者，让他们时刻寻求学习和重新学习所学的知识。

I have found that starting out this way creates a positive tone and commonality of culture that influences how each person will act and interact inside my classroom. It is reassuring to many students because the culture of respect feels possible to achieve and it creates a psychologically safe place to learn. My message contains no demands for them to get the best grades, but that is built in when we discuss respect of self and of learning. I want them to struggle, succeed, fail, and push the limits of their curiosity. When they do this, I can shape them as life-long learners who always seek to learn and re-learn what is taught.

尽量让规则保持简单明了。书面规则有助于确保它们保持固定性和强制执行。我相信学生真的很想知道这条线在哪里。如果规则似乎仅适用于某些人，而不是适用于所有人，则有可能削弱学生对公正性以及最终对教师权威的信心。简明扼要、措辞谨慎、合理执行应成为你的班规。

Try to keep the rules simple and clear. Rules in writing help to ensure that they remain fixed and enforced. I believe students really want to know where the line is. If rules seem to only apply to certain individuals, and not to all individuals, that can erode student confidence in the impartiality and, ultimately, the authority of the teacher. Simply written, carefully worded, and fairly enforced should be the criteria for your class rules.

解决冲突的哲学
Philosophy of Conflict Resolution

耐心计划的第二个同样重要的方面涉及冲突发生时你如何回应学生。建立班级文化后，你将如何应对在学校环境中难免出现的冲突？我将继续使用"冲突解决"一词。在我参加过培训课程的几乎每所学校中，我都被问到一个与教师管理学生行为有关的问题。往往是年轻的老师在管理和"控制"学生方面苦苦挣扎，但是我遇到的资深教学工作者，他们仍然没有掌握真正的课堂管理技能。你计划的这一部分将需要一种清晰而深思熟虑的哲学，即你将如何与学生互动以及如何期望他们彼此互动，尤其是在发生冲突的时候。如果没有解决冲突的计划，冲突将支配你和你所教的学生并使他们感到沮丧。对于某些人来说，这部分的专业准备决定你整个学年的成败，并且也可能严重影响学生的学习。它可以是激发灵感的最佳方式，也可以从教室中把活力带走。

The second, and equally crucial aspect of your Patience Plan involves how you respond to the students when conflicts arise. Once you have established your class culture, how do you deal with the conflicts that inevitably arise in a school setting? I will use the term "conflict resolution" moving forward. In almost every school in which I have ever done a training session, I get asked a question related to teacher control of student behavior. It is often young teachers who struggle with managing and "controlling" their students, but I have met veterans to teaching who still have not grasped true classroom control techniques. This part of your plan will require a clear and well-conceived philosophy of how you will interact with students and how you expect them to interact with one another, especially when the conflicts arise. Go in without a plan for conflict resolution and it will dominate and frustrate you and the students you teach. For some, this area of your professional preparation will either make or break your school year, and it can seriously affect the learning of your students, as well. It can be the single best energizer of inspiration or it can suck the life right out of your classroom.

当我开始我的教学生涯时，我"深思熟虑"的计划是我想成为一个很酷的老师，让学生感到开心。我相信，如果学生们认为我很酷，他们会更轻松地听课，而且我也不必对他们进行严格的管教。但是，我认为的"计划"根本不是计划！相反，是一个年轻而幼稚的老师把自己丢进了狮子坑里。我就像落入水中，而鲨鱼盘旋而动，毫不留情地夺人性命。我知道经验没有捷径，但是我希望我有一个"耐心计划"，以便在实施的过程中至少在获得支持以完善我的经验。与经验丰富的老师交谈（那些能与学生融洽相处，并得到学生的相互尊重的老师），并了解他们如何将其融入课堂。我并不是说你需要的是"耐心计划"，而是根据我的个性和引导技巧，我发现它对我来说非常有效。

When I began my teacher career, my "well-conceived" plan was that I wanted to be the cool teacher with whom the students had fun. I believed that if the students thought I was cool, they would more easily listen, and I wouldn't have to discipline them very much. However, what I thought was a "plan" was not a plan at all! Instead, it was the ill-conceived notion of a young, naïve teacher who was throwing himself into a pit of lions. I was like "chum" in the water, and the sharks circled and moved in for the kill quickly and without mercy. I know there is no shortcut for experience, but I wish I had a "Patience Plan" to at least implement for support as I gained the experience necessary to perfect it. Talk to veteran teachers (who you see has a rapport with, and mutual respect from the students) and find out how they built that into their classroom. I am not suggesting my "Patience Plan" is all you need, but based on my personality and facilitation skills, I found that it worked very well for me.

我的理念是在多年的夏令营教学、工作和管理中形成的。我对自己学到的东西不会感到理所当然，因为我是在别人的指导、讨论和观察中做到的，他们都做得比我好。我自己对学习的尊重以及对我提高领导才能的能力的部分原因是，我认识到了自己可以从他人的智慧和经验中学到很多东西。找到你尊重的人。"解读"他们，与他们谈话并征求他们的意见，以帮助塑造你自己的理念和计划。

My philosophy was shaped over many years of teaching, working, and administrating my summer camps. I do not take credit for what I learned because I did it with the guidance, discussion, and observations of others who did it better than I did. Part of my own respect for learning and for my ability to grow my leadership skills stems from the recognition that there is much to be learned from the wisdom and experience of others. Find those you respect. "Read" them, interview them and seek their advice, to help shape your philosophy and your plan.

根本上说，我的理念始于考虑人需求的同时了解人所处的状况。将二者融合在一起后，它为我提供了人类意识的基础，而这正是我借以进行观察的视角。

At the core, my philosophy begins with understanding the human condition while considering human needs. When blended, it provides me with a basis of human awareness, which becomes the lens I look through.

从本质上，我认为人是自私的，在大多数情况下，我们寻求获得即刻满足。大多数人在需要时，都想要他们想要的东西，并为了获得它而做出重大妥协。对许多人来说，这些妥协的价值观之一就是说出真相……全部真相。多年来，我评断过无数营员和学生之间的冲突。我认为我已经非常擅长找出真相，这些真相经常揭示出欺骗的方面或至少已经发生的其他情况。最初总是以"他做了某事，或者她说了某句话"开始，通常是由最初被认为是受过冤屈的人发起控诉的。通过许多这样的经历，我的询问技巧、对人类反应的理解虽然不是100%准确，但是却得到了提高。经验没有捷径，我会保持学习。人际冲突的许多根源来自自私和"我们想要"时的"渴望"。其他冲突源于口头、误会或曲解的伤害性话语。

I think humans are basically and intrinsically selfish, and we seek immediate gratification in most instances. Most humans want what they want, when they want it and make significant compromises in their values to get it. One of those compromised values for many is telling the truth...the whole truth. I have listened to countless camper and student conflicts over the years. I think I have become pretty good at pulling out the nuggets of truth which often reveal aspects of deception or at least alternative circumstances that have taken place. What starts out as a "he did, or she said" usually turns out to have been initiated by the one initially thought to have been wronged. My interrogation skills, understanding of human responses and reactions, though not 100% accurate, have been sharpened through many such experiences. There is no shortcut for experience, and I continually learn as I go. Many sources of interpersonal conflict arise from selfishness and having "wants" when "we want." Other conflicts arise out of hurtful words, either spoken, misunderstood or misinterpreted.

学生或营员发生冲突时，我觉得自己应该用自己的经验帮他们解决。但是，我认为有很多情况可以通过使用对等调解来处理。我鼓励发展学生领导。尽管并不总是那么完美，但我发现那些愿意参与此过程的学生将其视为宝贵的、赋权的领导学习经验。我认为，花时间在年轻人中发展他们的技能，使他们能够创建和运行学生解决会议，对于老师来说是值得的投资。像其他任何事情一样，初期投资需要时间，但是如果管理和调整得当，这对你的学生领导和（作为老师的）你都是有益的。

There are student or camper conflicts that arise that I feel deserve my experience and that I am best equipped to manage. However, there are many cases that arise which I think could be first handled and dealt with by using a peer mediator. I encourage the development of student leadership opportunities. Whereas not always perfect, I find that those students willing to partake in the process find it as a valuable and empowering leadership learning experience. I think that taking the time to develop the skills in young people that would allow them to create and run Student Solution Sessions would be a worthwhile investment for a teacher. Like anything, the initial investment takes time, but if managed and shaped properly, it can be good for your student leaders and for you as the teacher.

人际冲突过程
Interpersonal Conflict Process

最好以书面形式进行，口头解释也行。当"法律"以书面形式出现时，人们对真理和后果的理解程度往往会有所不同。当一个学生觉得自己与另一个学生发生冲突时，立即参考"尊重他人"指南，并提出一些问题将大有帮助：

It is good to have this in writing, as well as explained verbally. There tends to be a different level of understood truth and consequences when the "law" is in writing. When a student comes in feeling they conflict with another student, it is helpful to immediately refer to the RESPECT FOR OTHERS guideline by asking a few simple questions:

(1) 你在不尊重这个人的情况下做了什么？

(2) 你是否尝试过亲自与他其交谈以向对方解释你的感受？

（3）你是否尝试过将怀疑的好处给到他们，并告诉自己他们的言行不是有意的？

(1) Have you done anything in the situation that has not shown respect to this individual?

(2) Have you tried to speak to this individual personally to explain your feelings?

(3) Have you tried giving them the benefit of the doubt and telling yourself that is not what they intended by their words or actions?

根据上述问题的回应，我们再决定下一步如何进行最好。作为老师，学生是信任你的，因此你要对他们表达的感情表示同情。你还希望这对他们个人来说是一次有价值的情商提升体验，因此你的最初反应很重要。根据双方所讲的故事，如果你认为与你谈话的人有明显的过失，那么请你告诉他们，听起来他们本来对该问题能有更大的贡献，并鼓励他们回头去与对方直接交谈以制定双方都满意的解决方案。向学生建议，讨论，必须包括道歉，并且必须以重建的态度进行道歉，以便这个信息可以被对方听进去。学生对你的建议的回应决定了下一步该怎么做。

Based on their responses, we decide how best to proceed. As the teacher, they came to you in trust, so you want to show empathy to their expressed feelings. You also want this to be a valuable EQ sharpening experience for them personally, so your initial response is significant. If, based on the story told, you sense that clear fault rests with the individual you are speaking with, you tell them that it sounds like their contribution to the matter could have been handled better and encourage them to return to the individual with a focus on talking directly to the individual to work out a solution with which they are both satisfied. Suggest to the student that part of the discussion must include an apology and that it has to be given with an attitude of rebuilding so the message can be heard. The student's response to your suggestion determines the next step of the process.

当学生尝试我的建议，或者若他们告诉我，他们认为这样的面对面对他们而言在心理不安全是，我会使用"学生解决方案"会议给予他们另一条可行的途径。学生解决方案会议是与学生解决方案委员会的成员一起经过预先批准和训练有素的学生召开的会议。当学生向该委员会提请关注时，该学生的同龄人将审理该个案。委员会根据学生的培训和对问题的理解，讨论情况并为学生提供解决方案。关于学生解决方案会议委员会的说明——你可以选择并确定接受该委员会的标准，但请务必选择受人高度重视并具有出色情商的学生。你的学生委员会成员必须是那些受到普遍尊重的成员，他们将保持公平、公正并具有较强的社交技巧。绩点和高智商倒不一定会在委员会成员的选择中起很大的作用。对于那些在学术上苦苦挣扎但表现出始终如一的高情商技能的人来说，这个委员会的成立可能是他们理想的领导场所。你可以草拟一套简单的标准，以选择该委员会的成员，还可以使用学生提名或征求意见的方式，说明为什么有人应该或不应该加入委员会。最终，教师应根据一组规定的标准做出最终选择。这是领导职务，理应这样对待。选择错误的学生，该过程就可能会遭遇失败。选择正确的解决方案，它就将为健康的冲突解决提供潜在的变革机会以及强大的情商提升机会。

When students have tried my suggestion, or if they tell me that they do not feel such an encounter is psychologically safe for them, I empower them with another plausible path using a STUDENT SOLUTION SESSION. A student solution session is a peer session with pre-approved, and trained classmates who are part of a Student Solution Committee. When a student brings a concern to this committee, the student's peers hear the case. The committee discusses the situation and offers solutions to the student, based on their training and understanding of the problem. A note about the student solution session committee - The criteria for acceptance on to this committee can be selective and determined by you, but be sure to pick students who are highly regarded and have exemplified strong EQ skills. Your Student Session Committee members must be among those generally respected and who will be impartial, fair, and possess strong social skills. Grade point average and high IQ should not necessarily weigh heavily into committee selection. This committee formation may be the perfect leadership place for someone who is struggling academically, but who demonstrates consistently high EQ skills. You can draft a simple set of criteria to use in selecting members of this committee and you can also use student nominations or solicited opinions as to why someone should or should NOT be on the committee. Ultimately, the teacher should make the final choice based on a prescribed set of criteria. This is a leadership position and should be treated as such. Select the wrong student and the process may fail. Pick the right ones and it will provide a potentially transformational opportunity for change as well as a powerful EQ sharpening opportunity in a healthy conflict resolution process.

以下是关于学生解决方案会议工作方式的详细信息：感到自己面临人际冲突的学生可以请求召开学生解决方案会议。该学生将填写"学生解决方案会议"申请表，并提交给委员会考虑。该委员会（我建议 5-7 名成员，取决于班级人数）开会审议情况。 委员会可以批准所请求的会议，或者可以建议先召开会议向委员会进行澄清。

Here are the details about how a STUDENT SOLUTION SESSION works: A student who feels they are struggling with an interpersonal conflict can request a Student Solution Session. That student will fill out the STUDENT SOLUTION SESSION request form and present it to the committee for consideration. The committee (I suggest 5-7 members depending on the class size) meets to consider the situation. The committee may grant the requested session or may suggest a clarification meeting with the committee first.

如果请求被批准，委员会成员将与该学生会面，并告知他／她需要召开会议。在会议开始前，两名委员会成员可以与被要求尝试达成共同协议的学生会面，或者如果不可行的话，他们可以决定开始澄清情况的细节，并记录下来。他们应该知道此时并没有假设谁有错、谁清白。他们的首要任务是表示对解决人与人之间的冲突的尊重，并维护所有人的利益。届时，邀请学生和提出要求的学生都将被邀请参加学生解决方案会议。会话应安排在双方都同意的时间，但必须在提交请求后的 36 小时内进行。（延迟时间超过 36 小时可能意味着无视提出要求的学生，并且还可能冒着事件改变或问题进一步升级的风险。）因为你将这一过程融入了课堂文化中，所以被邀请参加冲突会议的学生无法拒绝该会议。请记住，既不假设谁有错也不假定谁清白。会议目的是提高所有人的情商，并使人们更好地理解大家的感受和环境。判谁有错可能是最终的结果，可能还会有相应的后果，但寻求真相并尊重流程是至关重要的。

If the request is granted, a committee member will meet with the student and inform him/her that a session may need to take place. Prior to the session, 2 committee members may meet with the student about whom the request was made to try to come to a mutual agreement, or, if that is not possible, they may decide to begin getting the thoughts and details of the situation clarified and documented. They should know that there is no guilt or innocence assumed. Their first priority is to show a respect for resolving an interpersonal conflict for the betterment of all involved. At that point, both the requesting student and the student about whom the request was made are invited to a STUDENT SOLUTION SESSION. The session should be scheduled at a time agreeable to both, but it needs to happen within 36 hours of the request submission. (Delays longer than 36 hours may imply disregard for the requesting student and may also risk the possibility of the story changing, or the problem escalating even further.) Because you build this process into your class culture, a student who is invited to a conflict session cannot refuse the session. Remember, neither guilt nor innocence is assumed. The purpose is to sharpen the EQ of all and to arrive at a better place of human understanding of feelings and circumstances. Guilt may be the eventual result, and consequences may also be included, but seeking the truth and respecting the process is crucial.

学生解决方案会议不应由老师参加，而应由两名受过训练的学生委员会成员进行调解。在此计划中，你作为老师的最大时间投入必须是对学生委员会成员的培训。如果你没有充分培训领导者，则会议过程将遭遇失败。他们都必须保持公正，在所有事实都被阐明之前，他们不得妄下判断。成员应始终寻求问题的清晰阐述，并对各方分享和表达的感受表示同情。在这些会议中分享的任何内容都必须保持隐私，如果成员在委员会之外共享相关信息，则立即将其除名。同样，调解员应避免在会议期间做出任何判断或表达自己的感受。这些会议的目的是在委员会成员的情感支持下（希望所有学生都参与提名或选举），为参与会议的各方创造一个安全的地方，以相互尊重和诚实地分享各自的看法。理想的情况下，要求参加会议的人与被邀请参加会议的人一样安全。

A STUDENT SOLUTION SESSION should not be attended by the teacher, but should be mediated by 2 trained student committee members. In this program, your biggest time investment as the teacher has to be in the training of the student committee members. If you do not adequately train your leaders, the session process will fail. They all must be impartial, and they cannot pass judgment until all the facts have been illuminated. Members should always seek clarity and show empathy for all feelings shared and expressed. Anything shared in these sessions must be regarded as private, and members would be immediately removed if they shared any of the details outside of the committee. Likewise, peer mediators should refrain from giving any judgments or expressing their feelings during the session. The sessions are to be about creating a safe place for those involved to share respectfully and honestly in front of one another with the emotional support of committee members (that hopefully all students have had a part in nominating or electing). Ideally, the individual requesting the session feels as safe as the person invited to the session.

会话中的过程无法真正编写脚本，但应强调某些原则。

1. 所有参与者将致力于表现出对自我、他人以及在整个过程中可能发生的学习的尊重。

2. 双方将有机会与有关各方或彼此之间诚实坦率地分享自己的看法。会议请求者将被赋予首先发言的权利。在请求者说完他／她的所有内容之前，不允许受邀者讲话。

The process in the session cannot really be scripted, but certain principles should be stressed.

1. All involved will commit to demonstrating respect for self, others, and the learning that can happen through the process.

2. Both sides will have the opportunity to share honestly and directly with or between those involved. The session requester will be given the privilege to speak first. The one invited will not be permitted to speak until the requester has said all he/she needs to say.

由于"感觉"可能已经受到伤害，因此必须建立基本规则。以下是一些基本规则的建议：

Because "feelings" may already be hurt, establishing ground rules is necessary. Here are some suggested ground rules:

1. 会话请求者将被授予第一个发言的机会。

1. The session requester will be granted the first opportunity to speak.

2. "受邀者"应在给予回应之前先倾听。

2. The "invited guest" shall listen before being given the opportunity to respond.

3.各方都会鼓励和期望尊重的话语和"我"的语言（我感觉，我注意到，我希望，我感觉，我意识到）。不以这种方式参与进来则会破坏整个过程，并可能损害学生解决冲突的能力。

3. Respectful discourse and "I" language (I feel, I noticed, I hope, I sense, I perceived) will be encouraged and expected from all parties involved. Failure to engage in this manner will damage the process and may compromise the ability of the students to resolve the conflict.

4.我们强调同情的定义——无论内心是否同意他们的感受，能够感受他人的感受的能力。 他们表达的感情构成了**他们的事实**，但那不一定是**事实本身**。

4. We stress the definition of empathy - the ability to feel what the other person may feel, regardless of whether you agree or disagree. Their expressed feelings make up THEIR reality, not necessarily THE reality.

5.在给每个参与者公平的分享时间之后，委员会成员将提出澄清的问题。（重要的是，委员会成员的问题不得打断或干扰双方的分享。委员会成员在聆听时应写下问题，并在分享停止后向他们发问。

5. Committee members will ask clarifying questions after each participant has been given fair time to share. (It is important that committee member questions do not interrupt or interfere with the sharing. Committee members should write down questions while they are listening and ask them after the sharing has stopped.

6.控制会话请求者和受邀者的情绪是必不可少的，但并不总是那么容易做到。 通常，情绪可能以哭泣或愤怒的形式表现出来。委员会应设法避免和管理任何极端的情绪表现。眼泪并不总是表明另一方做错了事，因此，认为哭泣的人承受了别人对他们造成的"伤害"是不正确的。许多学生可以用眼泪获得同情，或出于其他许多原因而这样做。愤怒、对后果的恐惧和其他情绪都很容易使双方不堪重负。 委员会成员必须使会议保持信息和细节的清晰，而不是指责是谁的过错。

6. Controlling the emotions of both the session requester and the one invited is essential, but not always easy. Frequently, emotions may pour out in the form of tears or even anger. The committee should try to avoid and manage any extreme displays of emotions. Tears do not always indicate a wrong has been done and, therefore, it would be incorrect to assume that the person crying is so distraught over the "harm" done to them. Many students can turn on and off the flow of tears to gain sympathy, or for a host of other reasons. Anger, fear of consequences, and other emotions can easily overwhelm both parties. Committee members must keep the session about clarity of information and details, and not about assigning fault or blame.

7. 一旦会议请求者和受邀者同意不再发言，会议应以委员会一名成员的闭幕词结束。结束语听起来大致是： *"我们谨代表学生解决方案委员会感谢你们每个人今天同意来到这里。我们相信，有机会聚在一起表达和分享感受，交流互动是健康的事情，并且有助于个人成长和我们团队（班级）的成功。重要的是，这次会议应作为最后的场所，以便对相关情况进行考虑和决定。本委员会的目标是，请求者和受邀者都认为他们的声音和经历很重要。我们将作为委员会开会讨论双方分享的事实和感受，然后在36小时内（如果时间和计划允许的话）与双方重新开会。我们认为至关重要的是，两者之间的任何互动和个人交流都应积极而有益。如果随后的个人互动是报复性的，或试图让对方感到尴尬或暴露对方，则委员会可以决定在此问题上采取其他相关步骤。应积极维护学生解决方案会议，以保持不满情绪处于安全范围，以期达到个人理解和双方关系的恢复。与此相反的任何互动将不利于和解的达成和问题的解决。当我们所有人都离开这个地方时，让我们同意不与别人分享此次会议的内容或情感，除非我们彼此之间直接互相分享。任何其他做法都将被视为对流程及其预期结果的违反。"*

7. Once the session requestor and the invited person agree that they have no more to say, the session should conclude with a closing statement by one of the committee members. The closing statement should sound something like: *"On behalf of the Student Solution Committee we want to thank each of you for agreeing to be here today. We believe the opportunity to come together to express and share feelings, and exchange mediated interaction is healthy and helpful to the personal growth and the success of our group (class). It is important that this meeting serve as a final place to allow the situation to be considered and decided upon. It is the goal of this committee that both the requestor and the invited guest feel that their voice and experience matters. We will meet as a committee and discuss the facts and feelings shared, then reconvene with both of you within 36 hours (if timing and schedule permits). We believe it is crucial that any interaction and personal exchange between both be positive and helpful to the cause. Should subsequent personal interaction be vindictive or seek to embarrass or expose the other amongst peers, the committee may decide to take additional steps in the matter. The Student Solution Session shall be actively preserved as a safe place to air grievances and feelings, in hopes of reaching personal understanding and the restoring of relationships. Any interaction to the contrary will be detrimental to the cause of reconciliation and resolve. As we all leave from this place, let us agree to not share the content or emotions expressed unless we do so directly with one another. Anything else will be considered a breach of respect for the process and its intended result."*

8. 说完之后，会议可以休会，直到另行通知。

With that, the meeting can be adjourned until further notice.

9. 然后，委员会将在**老师在场**的情况下召集会议，讨论调查结果和双方表达的信息。委员会不得与非委员会成员讨论任何会议的任何细节。

9. The Committee will then convene <u>in the presence of the teacher</u> to discuss the findings and information expressed. The committee may not discuss any details of any meeting with non-committee members.

10. 委员会将决定他们如何应对请求者和受邀者，以帮助解决人际冲突。陈述的事实必须经过仔细考虑。当务之急是会议请求者发现他／她的声音和感受得到了证实和仔细考虑。同样，受邀学生也必须感到被认可和倾听，这样他们才能认为该过程是公平的。

10. The committee will decide how they will respond to both the requestor and the invited person with the intent of helping to heal the personal conflict. Careful consideration must be given to the facts as they were presented. It is imperative that the session requestor finds that his/her voice and feelings were validated and carefully considered. Likewise, the student invited to the session also must feel validated and heard for the process to be considered fair.

11. 对结果的判断应在下次会议上提出。听起来大致是这样的：*"学生解决方案委员会的成员要感谢每个人为解决人际矛盾所做的贡献表现出的兴趣。成立该委员会的目的是让我们所有人都学会如何更好地处理和尝试解决人际冲突。私下处理个人之间的分歧也是可以的，但有时候当这类分歧被带到委员会时，可以达到更好的清晰度。委员会在此为所有学生提供服务，通过这种做法，我们大家都将学习并从中受益。我们为请求者和受邀者提供服务。我们对调查结果的决定对我们拥有的任何个人友谊都是公正的，在本次会议中每个人都应对此保持尊重。本委员会的目的仅仅是为了促进在这种情况下的公正判断，从而使两个人都能实现个人关系的恢复。我们并不是要寻求错误或清白的判决，而是要在这种情况下寻求澄清事件。因为通过澄清，我们便获得了同理心、知识以及对他人感受和感知的尊重。在听完双方意见，并仔细考虑和讨论了所陈述的所有事实之后，学生解决方案委员会希望对我们在这种情况下*

发生的事情进行评估。（领导委员会成员根据与会人员给出和听取的事实清楚地陈述调查结果）。我们认为可以在以下过程中实现解决和恢复。” （"以下过程"是一个措词正面的和解声明，其中每个人的感受都得到了证实和表述，但同时又以尊重的方式清楚而小心地澄清了谁"有错"。如果做出了相应后果的建议，请在此处一并说明。）

A judgment of findings shall be presented in the next meeting. It may sound something like this: *"The members of the Student Solution Committee want to thank each individual for his/her contribution and interest in resolving the personal conflict. The committee is established with the intent that we all learn how to better handle and try to resolve inevitable interpersonal conflicts. Handling such disagreements privately between individuals is ideal, but sometimes better clarity can be achieved when brought before the committee. The Committee is here to serve all students and, in doing so, we all can learn and benefit. We serve both the requestor and the invited. Our decision on the findings is impartial to any personal friendships we have and should be respected by each person in this meeting. The intent of this committee is simply to facilitate impartial judgment in the situation so that both individuals can achieve personal restoration of the relationship as a result. It is not that we seek to find guilt or innocence, as much as it is for us to find clarity in the circumstances. For through clarity, we gain empathy, knowledge, and the respect for the feelings and perceptions of others. After having listened to both individuals, and after careful consideration and discussion of all facts as they were presented, the Student Solution Committee would like to give our assessment of what we think happened in the situation. (A lead committee member states the findings clearly, based on the facts as they were given and heard by those in attendance). We think resolution and restoration can be achieved in the following process."* (The "following process" is a positively worded reconciliation statement where each person's feelings are validated and re-stated, but also where aspects of "guilt" are clearly and delicately stated in a respectful manner. If consequences are recommended, they are delineated here, and at this time, as well.)

12. 积极和解——该声明应大声朗读（并以书面形式提供给每个相关人员）。*"生活中充满了分歧和冲突。它是人类社会不可避免的一部分。人类受到情感的影响，情感即是我们的情绪。它们可以控制我们的生活和应对方式。因为我们感受到，所以我们在意。因为我们在意，所以我们的分歧可以被深刻地感受到，因此必须谨慎并以尊重的态度加以处理。情况就是这样。一个人深受他/她的情绪影响，并寻求解决人际冲突的方法。双方都在意自己的感受，因为他们在意，所以他们寻求解决冲突的帮助。这是令人钦佩的并且可取的做法。在人为事件中，如果有分歧的人找不到健康的方法来解决问题，他们就可能会转向不利的方法，从而破坏人际关系并导致进一步的冲突。*

12. POSITIVE RECONCILLIATION - This statement should be read aloud (and given in writing) to each person involved. *"Life is full of disagreements and conflicts. It is an inevitable part of human society. Humans are affected by feelings and feelings are our emotions. They can control our lives and responses. Because we feel, we care. Because we care, our disagreements can be felt deeply and therefore must be carefully and respectfully managed. That was the case here. One individual was deeply affected by his/her emotions and sought resolution for the interpersonal conflict. Both parties cared about their feelings and because they cared they sought assistance in solving the conflict. This is admirable and desirable. In the course of human events, if people who disagree cannot find healthy ways to resolve problems, they may turn to less favorable methods, which destroy relationships and lead to further conflict.*

当然，大多数人不喜欢冲突解决会议。但是，参与其中是发展一项必要且有价值的生活技能。我们希望该解决过程摆脱任何先入为主的想

法，并提供对关系和人类尊重的简单恢复。进行的过程使每个人的感受都得到倾听和考虑，并根据其所分享的事实做出决定。两个人都向其提交了自己的陈述，因此，每个人都应该尊重所执行的过程。现在，我们要求成熟和宽恕，以便进行实现疗愈和恢复的目的。

Granted, most people do not enjoy conflict resolution sessions. However, participation in them is a necessary and valuable life skill to develop. We wanted this resolution process to be free from preconceived ideas and to provide simple restoration of the relationship and human respect. The process undertaken allowed each person's feelings to be heard and considered, and a determination was made based on the facts shared. Both individuals submitted to it and, as a result, each should respect the process that was carried out. We now ask for maturity and forgiveness to allow healing and restoration to take place.

我们不要求你们奇迹般地成为最好的朋友，而只是要求你们尊重各自所表达的感受和在恢复关系的过程中进行投资的愿望。恢复的很大一部分是回到一个相互理解和相互尊重的位置。为了向前迈进，冲突中的个人感到被倾听、重视和理解是很重要的。理想情况下，感到"冤枉"的一方现在可以感受到宽容，并本着宽恕的精神向前迈进。同样的，受邀者可以承担一些冲突责任，更好地理解请求者的感受，并向前迈进。"

We do not ask that you magically become best friends, but that you simply respect the feelings expressed and the desire to invest in the process of relationship restoration. A big part of restoration is getting back to a place of understanding and mutual respect. It is important that, in order to move forward, individuals in conflict feel heard, valued, and understood. Ideally, he/she who felt "wronged" can now feel validated and move forward in the spirit of forgiveness. In the same way, the person who was invited into the resolution session can accept some responsibility for the conflict, better understand the feelings expressed by the requester and move forward as well."

接下来的步骤： "我们大家希望尊重现在所进行的过程。我们希望每个人都可以从中学到东西，并在学习如何更好地应对未来的人际冲突中提高自己的情感成熟度。希望所有参与者都同意不诋毁或贬低参与该解决会议的任何其他人员。不得将解决方案的内容向朋友或其他人分享。会议应保持私密性，其唯一目的是恢复人际关系。如果学生解决方案委员会得知某人将讨论的内容与他人进行了分享，则可以对该人采取进一步的纪律处分。分享此处所说的话只会阻碍关系的恢复，并损害那些将来需要此类帮助的人。维护本委员会的诚信和声誉对我们来说至关重要，因此，参与其中的每个人也应如此。"

Next steps: *"It is our desire that the process undertaken be respected. We hope that everyone can learn from it and grow in their emotional maturity, having learned how to better deal with future personal conflicts. It is expected that all participants agree to not slander or disparage any other person involved this resolution session. The details of what was said or decided will not be shared with friends or others. The sessions should remain private and for the sole purpose of restoring personal relationships. If the Student Solutions Committee were to hear one person sharing about what was discussed, then further discipline action could be taken against that individual. To share what was said would only serve to hinder any relationship restoration and damage this process for those who need such help in the future. Preserving the integrity and the reputation of this committee is of the utmost importance to us and so it should also be to everyone who has been part of it."*

继续前行
Moving Forward

学生解决方案委员会是"耐心计划"的一部分。作为领导者，你正在尝试创建和培育一种社群内部相互尊重的文化。这种尊重有助于训练他们的情商，并为他们提供实用的构建基础。建立个人尊重的文化并不能消除人际冲突，但确实为解决出现的问题提供了一个明智而有价值的过程。这也是学习过程的一部分。 进行构建需要时间和投资，但是正确完成构建会为个人和整个班级带来巨大的好处。

The Student Solutions Committee is part of the Patience Plan. As the leader, you are trying to create and foster a culture of community respect for one another. This respect helps train their EQ and gives them practical building blocks for the future. Building a culture of individual respect does not eliminate personal conflict, but it does provide a sensible and worthwhile process for resolving issues that arise. This, too, is part of the learning process. It takes time and investment to build, but there are great individual and class-wide benefits when it is done correctly.

我发现，当我精心构建期望的社会模型，清晰地传达、执行和公开讨论时，违纪情况和人际冲突会大大减少。如果一切顺利，学生解决方案委员会就不需经常开会，因为尊重的文化已经牢固地植根于你的课堂。

I find that when I carefully construct the social model of expectations, clearly communicate it, enforce it, and openly discuss it, discipline situations and interpersonal conflicts are significantly reduced. If all goes well, the Student Solutions Committee doesn't meet that often, because the culture of respect is firmly rooted in your classroom.

这种类型的课堂文化并不是奇迹般发生的，但是当它完全根植于你的身份以及你作为老师的领导方式时，它看起来就很神奇。最终，班级的学生会在已经了解你的课堂文化和声誉的情况下开始。随着时间的流逝，你需要做的越来越少，因为学生会谈论并传播有关你作为领导者所传达的信息。即将开设的新班级已经听说过你领导的文化和过程。它确实需要大量的早期投资，但是一旦奠定了基础，你的管理就将变得越来越容易。

This type of classroom culture does not happen magically, but when it is fully entrenched in the fabric of who you are and how you lead as a teacher, it is magical to observe. Eventually, you will have students starting in your class already knowing your classroom culture and reputation. With each year that passes, you will do less and less because students will talk and spread the word about you as a leader. New classes coming in will already have heard about the culture and process of your leadership. It does require heavy early investment, but when the foundation is set, it becomes easier and easier for you to manage.

经验没有捷径。经验就像是教育——你可以汲取经验教训，并将其应用于你所面临的各种情况。作为一名教师和领导者，你将评估你正在建立和投资的文化过程，以便在遇到新情况时，可以利用自己的经验来解决新问题。"耐心计划"是一个有用的工具，不仅可以用于管理你的课堂，还可以指导你的学生发展更高的情商，并以更好的尊重和理解来解决难以避免的人际冲突。

There is no shortcut for experience. Experience is a lot like education - you draw upon lessons learned and apply them to situations faced. As a teacher leader, you will evaluate the culture process you are establishing and investing in, so that as new situations are encountered, you will draw on your experience to solve new problems. A Patience Plan is a helpful tool, used not only to manage your classroom, but also to mentor your students into developing a stronger EQ and certainly a greater respect for, and understanding of, the resolution process for those inevitable times of interpersonal conflict.